THE LAWBOOK EXCHANGE, LTD.
FOUNDATIONS OF THE LAWS OF WAR

GENERAL EDITOR: JOSEPH PERKOVICH

A TREATISE ON THE LAW OF WAR

Foundations of the Laws of War Series

General Editor Joseph Perkovich

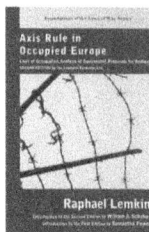

Axis Rule in Occupied Europe
Analysis of Government, Proposals for Redress (1944)

Raphael Lemkin

xxiii (new introduction), xxxviii, 674 pp.

With a New Introduction by
SAMANTHA POWER
*Author of "A Problem from Hell": America and the Age of Genocide,
winner of the 2003 Pulitzer Prize*
Introduction to the Second Edition by Lawbook Exchange by
WILLIAM A. SCHABAS
National University of Ireland

In this pathbreaking study Polish emigre Raphael Lemkin [1900-1959] coined the term "genocide" and defined it as a subject of international law. While the term has come to mean the extermination of a people, Lemkin used it to describe all programs that sought to increase "Aryan" birthrate while working to exterminate the social, cultural and economic independence of non-Germanic peoples.

Hardcover (2nd ed. 2008)
ISBN 978-1-58477-576-8
$69.95

2008 Paperback
ISBN 978-1-58477-901-8
$59.95

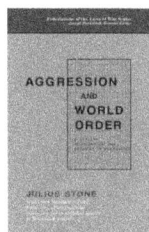

Aggression and World Order
A Critique of United Nations Theories of Aggression (1958)

Julius Stone

xxvii (new introduction), xiv, 226 pp.

With a New Introductory Essay "Paradoxes of a Sharp Legal Mind: Professor Julius Stone and International Aggression" by BENJAMIN FERENCZ
Pace University, Chief Prosecutor for the United States at the Nuremberg War Crimes Trial

Efforts to enforce world peace during the twentieth century through international organizations created a demand for a legal definition of aggression. A U.N. committee attempted to provide one in a 1956 report. Stone rejected it for two reasons. Citing a broad array of examples, he shows that the concept of aggression eludes definition. More important, he argues controversially that a definition is not necessary for the goals of international peace-enforcement.

Hardcover 2010
ISBN 978-1-58477-601-7
$49.95

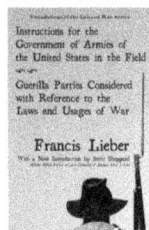

Instructions for the Government of Armies
of the United States in the Field (1898)

Francis Lieber

x (new introduction), 51 pp.

[With]
Guerilla Parties Considered with Reference
to the Laws and Usages of War (1862)

Francis Lieber

22 pp.

With a New Introduction by
STEVE SHEPPARD
University of Arkansas School of Law

Known officially as General Orders No. 100, Lieber's code (1863) was the first of its kind. The foundation of the modern international law of war, it served as the model for several European military codes and was an important source for the second and fourth Hague Conventions (1899, 1907). It was an authority during the Nuremberg and Tokyo war crime trials. Its use by the framers of the 1998 Rome Treaty, which established the International Criminal Court, demonstrates its lasting value in our time. Indeed, with only a handful of modifications it is used by the U.S. Military today.

Hardcover 2005
ISBN 978-1-58477-526-3
$29.95

Paperback 2011
ISBN 978-1-61619-152-8
$9.95

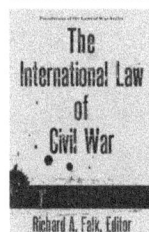

The International Law of Civil War (1971)

Richard A. Falk, Editor

xix, 452 pp.

Explores the complex relationship between international law and civil war through 6 case studies: *The American Civil War, 1861-65* by Quincy Wright, *International Legal Aspects of the Civil War in Spain, 1936-39* by Ann Van Wynen Thomas and A. J. Thomas, Jr., *The Algerian Revolution as a Case Study in International Law* by Arnold Fraleigh, *The Postindependence War in the Congo* by Donald W. McNemar, *The Relevance of International Law to the Internal War in Yemen* by Kathryn Boals and *The Vietnam Struggle and International Law* by P. E. Corbett. *Summary and Interpretation* by Edwin B. Firmage.

Hardcover 2010
ISBN 978-1-58477-721-2
$49.95

Prices subject to change.

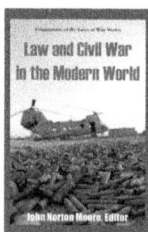

Law and Civil War in the Modern World [1974]

John Norton Moore, Editor

xii (new introduction), xxv, 648 pp.

With a New Introduction for this Edition
by JOHN NORTON MOORE
University of Virginia School of Law

Hardcover 2010
ISBN 978-1-58477-722-9
$49.95

"[This volume] is a major contribution to the literature of the international aspects of civil war."
Robert Gilpin, *Foreign Affairs* 53 (1974-1975) 777

A Manual of the Law of Maritime Warfare (1854)

William Hazlitt and Henry Philip Roche

XXVI (new introduction), xvi, 457 pp.

With a New Introduction by
WILLIAM E. BUTLER
Pennsylvania State University Dickinson School of Law

Hardcover 2009
ISBN 978-1-58477-660-4
$35.

Beyond its utility as a guide to maritime warfare as interpreted by an agent of the leading naval power of the 19th century, this is historically significant as the first English treatise to draw on American court decisions and the writings of James Kent and Henry Wheaton.

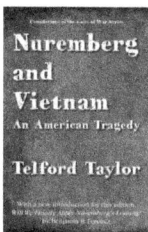

Nuremberg and Vietnam
An American Tragedy [1970]

Telford Taylor

xxiii (new introduction), 224 pp.

With a New Introductory Essay
"Will We Finally Apply Nuremberg's Lessons?"
by BENJAMIN FERENCZ
Pace University, Chief Prosecutor for the United States at the Nuremberg War Crimes Trial

Framed in reference to the Nuremberg Trials, Taylor gives a sober account of the Vietnam conflict from the perspective of international law.

Hardcover 2010
ISBN 978-1-58477-999-5
$36.95

Paperback 2010
ISBN 978-1-61619-033-0
$29.95

A Treatise on the Law of War
Being the First Book of His Quaestiones Juris Publici
Translated From the Original Latin (1810)
by Peter Stephen du Ponceau (1810)

Cornelius van Bynkershoek

xlvi (new introduction), xxxiv, 218 pp.

With a New Introduction by
WILLIAM E. BUTLER
Pennsylvania State University Dickinson School of Law

Addresses the customs of land and sea warfare. A notably humane work, it condemns actions against civilians and advocates the fair treatment of prisoners of war. Du Ponceau's able translation includes a biography of the author, a table of cases and an annotated bibliography.

Hardcover 2019
ISBN 978-1-58477-566-9
$28.95

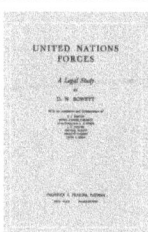

United Nations Forces
A Legal Study of United Nations Practice [1964]
Foreword by Lord McNair, QC

D.W. Bowett

xiii (new introduction), xxiv, 579 pp.

With a New Preface by
H.E. JUDGE ROSALYN HIGGINS
President, International Court of Justice

"This is a most impressive work based on considerable research as well as on the author's first-hand experience in the United Nations, and marked with a rare insight into the problems currently facing the international community."
B.K. Spitz, *South African Law Journal* 82 (1965) 270

Hardcover 2008
ISBN 978-1-58477-715-1
$49.95

A

TREATISE

ON

THE LAW OF WAR.

Translated from the original Latin of
CORNELIUS VAN BYNKERSHOEK.

BEING

THE FIRST BOOK

OF HIS

QUÆSTIONES JURIS PUBLICI.

WITH NOTES,

BY PETER STEPHEN DU PONCEAU,
Counsellor at Law in the Supreme Court of the United States
of America.

—— Ne fortior omnia possit.—OVID.

THE LAWBOOK EXCHANGE, LTD.
Clark, New Jersey

ISBN 978-1-58477-566-9

Lawbook Exchange edition 2008, 2019

The quality of this reprint is equivalent to the quality of the original work.

THE LAWBOOK EXCHANGE, LTD.
33 Terminal Avenue
Clark, New Jersey 07066-1321

*Please see our website for a selection of our other publications
and fine facsimile reprints of classic works of legal history:*
www.lawbookexchange.com

Library of Congress Cataloging-in-Publication Data

Bijnkershoek, Cornelis van, 1673-1743.
  [De rebus bellicis. English]
  A treatise on the law of war : being the first book of his
  quaestiones juris publici / by Cornelius van Bynkershoek ;
  translated from the original Latin with notes by Peter Stephen
  du Ponceau ; with a new introduction by William E. Butler,
  John Edward Fowler.
      p. cm. -- (Foundations of the Laws of War)
  Originally published. Philadelphia : Farrand & Nicholas, 1810.
  Includes bibliographical references and index.
  ISBN-13: 978-1-58477-566-9 (cloth : alk. paper)
  ISBN-10: 1-58477-566-1 (cloth : alk. paper)
  1. War (International law) I. Du Ponceau, Peter Stephen,
1760-1844. II. Title.
  KZ2243.A3Q8413 2007
  341.6--dc22   2007038876

Printed in the United States of America on acid-free paper

Peter Stephen Du Ponceau and the Development of International Law in America

William E. Butler

John Edward Fowler Distinguished Professor of Law
Dickinson Law, Pennsylvania State University

T he history of international law may be traced from several vantage points. One of those is the life history of individuals who made substantial contributions to international law. In the instance of the United States of America, that is one of the vantage points least explored. Many individuals contributed to the development of views in America relating to international law and to the formal positions adopted by the Government of the United States in relations with other powers. They did so, as a rule, without special training in the law of nations; indeed, given the absence of law schools in post-revolutionary America, they did so without formal legal training at all. Nonetheless, issues of the law of nations figured significantly, sometimes prominently, in the political writings of eighteenth century America, and evidence was given of a wide acquaintanceship with the leading European works in the field.

One means of making European works not published in England available to an American audience was legal translation. Peter du Ponceau played a pre-eminent role in this respect, making the leading work by Bynkershoek on neutrality and the law of warfare at sea available to an American audience in a version universally acknowledged to be superior to one issued in London many decades before. He left translations of other works in manuscript.

The first quarter century in the history of the newly-formed United States of America was, so far as the seas and oceans were concerned, turbulent and uncertain. Whether a country was technically at war or not mattered little; its neutral vessels and cargoes were suspect in the eyes of belligerents elsewhere. The Law of Prize flourished in sufficient measure to provide a comfortable source of revenue for many lawyers in ports around the world, not least the City of Philadelphia. The threat of armed conflict hovered as a dark cloud on the horizon, whether in the form of engagement in European conflicts as part of the Napoleonic wars or relatively minor campaigns against Tripoli. For the legal practitioner the manual published some seventy-five or so years previously on the law of war by an eminent Dutch judge and legal scholar served as an authoritative statement of the relevant legal rules to be used in matters as different as foreign policy formulation and the resolution of individual cases in court or arbitration.

The book was known to the English-speaking world, as the American translator, Peter S. du Ponceau acknowledges in his Preface. A London barrister, Richard Lee, produced a version entitled *A Treatise of Captures in War*, whose insufficiency " ... to supply the place of our author's text is everywhere admitted".[1] Both versions, by Lee and Du Ponceau, were however widely read and quoted in their day and throughout the nineteenth century. Du Ponceau did produce the superior version with useful commentary that has deservedly become a landmark in the history of international law.

---

[1] Preface, p. vii. Du Ponceau refers to Richard Lee, *A Treatise of Captures in War* (London, Printed for W. Sandby, 1759). viii, 264 p.; a second edition appeared in London, Printed for W. Clarke & Sons, 1803, with enlargements. In Du Ponceau's view, the Lee version was "incorrect and incomplete".

Bynkershoek

Du Ponceau gives his own account below of the Life and Writings of Cornelius (sometimes: Cornelis) Bynkershoek that has stood the test of time very satisfactorily. Our version will stress certain information not available to du Ponceau with relatively minor overlap.

Cornelius van Bynkershoek (also spelled: Bijnkershoek) was born into a well-to-do sailmaking family at Middelburg, in the seafaring province of Zeeland, on 29 May 1673 (Du Ponceau, Phillipson, J. B. Scott) or 19 August 1673 (de Louter).[2] He distinguished himself at the local Latin school, where he acquired a sound grounding in the classics and in mathematics. A life in the church was originally contemplated for him, so he also studied Hebrew. At the Frisian University (Franeker) from 1689, he pursued interests initially in theology, the humanities

---

[2] This account of Bynkershoek is based collectively on the following: J. S. de Louter (1847-1932), "Introduction", in C. van Bynkershoek, *On Questions of Public Law. Two Books of which the First is On War the Second on Miscellaneous Subjects* (1930), pp. ix-xlvi; A. Nussbaum, *A Concise History of the Law of Nations* (1947), pp. 142-148; C. Phillipson, "Cornelius van Bynkershoek", in J. MacDonell and E. Manson (eds.), *Great Jurists of the World* (1914), pp. 390-416 (with portrait), having first appeared in the *Journal of the Society of Comparative Legislation*, IX (1908), 27-49; Bynkershoek's place in the history of international law has been reassessed, but without biographical data of consequence, in K. Akashi, *Cornelius van Bynkershoek: His Role in the History of International Law* (1998). By common consent the leading account of Bynkershoek's life is Oncko Wichen Star Numan (b. 1840), *Cornelis van Bynkershoek, zijn leven en zijne geschriften* (Leiden, J. Hazenberg, 1869), which deserves an English translation. For Bynkershoek's writings, see L. G. Arias, "Cornelio van Bynkershoek, su vida y sus obras", *Boletin de la Universidad de Santiago de Compostela*, nos. 49-50 (1947). De Louter offers a superb précis of this book in his Introduction, cited above. Also see: "Bynkershoek, Cornelis van", in D. M. Walker, *The Oxford Companion to Law* (1980), pp. 163-164.

generally, and then changed to Roman, Dutch, and public law. There he attracted the attention of the eminent Professor Ulrich Huber (1636-1694), who extolled his virtues and promise. He was awarded the *doctor juris utriusque* for a triple dissertation *De pactis juris stricti contractibus in continenti adjectis* in May 1694.

Bynkershoek became an advocate in The Hague upon completing his university studies and developed a successful practice. Until the authorities became annoyed with it, he published anonymously a journal, *The New Hague Mercury* (1699), full of satire, observations, and criticism. He continued his interests in the Roman law and in Dutch law, producing several dissertations on subjects of Roman law and a substantial treatise, *Corpus juris Hollandici et Zelandici* (never published, at his request). He took to pamphleteering in 1701 to refute criticisms of some of his theses by a professor at the Groningen University in *Contentio literaria*. In 1703 the first of his three principal works on the law of nations appeared,[3] published together with *De lege Rhodia de jactu liber singularis*.

Shortly after publishing his work on dominion over the seas, he was appointed a judge of the Supreme Court of Holland, Zeeland, and West Friesland, becoming in 1724 the President of that Court. He married Esther van Buytenhem (d. 1726), who gave birth to thirteen children, two of them sons (of the chil-

---

[3] Bynkershoek, *De dominio maris dissertatio* (Hague Batavorum, apud Joannem Verbessel, 1703). There is a copy at the Harvard Law School Library which bears this date. Many authorities (Du Ponceau, Henry Wheaton, Phillipson, J. B. Scott, and others) give the date of this work as 1702, but no example has been discovered of this date. Akashi and Numan both concur with the 1703 date. See Akashi, note 2 above, pp. 7-8, who viewed the copy at the Royal Dutch Library in The Hague. The confusion may originate in the Dedicatory letter that appears in the work, the letter being dated 20 September 1702.

dren, only six daughters survived their father).[4] Based in The Hague, he had ample opportunity to see statecraft in action and consider the law of the sea against the numerous cases which found their way to his court for judgment. Rumour has it that in 1704 he resisted the blandishments of Tsar Peter the Great to take up service in Russia. He returned to Roman law with the first part of an extensive study, *Observationum juris Romani libri quatuor* (1710). In 1721 he published *De foro legatorum in causa civili, quam criminali, liber singularis*,[5] addressing the rights and duties of ambassadors with particular reference to immunities in civil and criminal cases (the Act of Anne (1709) in England had reduced some of these to statutory form, being followed a few years later by analogous enactments in Russia). Just as those legislative acts, Bynkershoek's monograph was stimulated by an actual incident, in his case at The Hague. By far his most substantial work appeared in two volumes: *Quaestionum juris publici libri duo, quorum primus est de rebus bellicis, secundus de rebus varii argumenti* (1737), which contained in volume one the *De rebus bellicis* – the work published herein in the Du Ponceau translation.[6]

Lesser works also touch upon the law of nations, but mostly in passing and not in ways that are central to understanding Bynkershoek's thought.[7] An uncompleted work, *Quaestiones*

------

[4] After the death of his first wife, Bynkershoek married Gererdina Cloot, a widow with one son; her marriage to Bynkershoek was childless.

[5] A second edition appeared in 1744, the year following his death.

[6] All three of Bynkershoek's works were freshly translated for the Carnegie Endowment "Classics of International Law" series, reprinted several times and also available in digital format.

[7] For example, *Observationes Tumultuariae*, ed. E. M. Meyers, A. S. de Blécourt, et al. (Haarlem, 1926-62), continued by Willem Pauw (1712-1787) as *Observationes tumultuariae novae*, containing decisions of the Hooge Raad 1743-87 (1964-67).

juris privati libri quatuor (1744), appeared after his death, which occurred on 16 April 1743.

Professor Béat Philippe Vicat (1715-1770), who held the Chair of Jurisprudence at the University of Lausanne, prepared a collected edition of Bynkershoek's published writings in folio format (Geneva, 1761); these were published again with greater editorial care by Luchtmans in 1767 at Leiden; Du Ponceau evidently worked from the 1761 edition, as a copy of this version was sold from his Library at auction in 1844. There also was an Italian edition published at Naples in 1766 in large quarto.

Bynkershoek's place in the history of international legal doctrine is undergoing reassessment. His place of eminence is undoubted and handsomely acknowledged by his contemporaries and followers. Being a figure of the judiciary rather than an academic theorist, his works amounted not to a comprehensive treatment of the system of international law in the tradition of Grotius, Pufendorf, or Vattel, but rather a jurisconsult's appraisal of the practical issues embedded in causes as they presented themselves in litigation. Respect for his works was enhanced by his willingness even while holding high judicial office to advance positions and arguments not necessarily consistent with Dutch maritime practice at the time nor with Dutch interests. He had a thorough command of the literature and an abundance of common sense. Whether, however, he should be grouped among the positivists or the natural lawyers remains the lively subject of debate, and readers may well conclude that he ultimately was a natural lawyer with a positivist bent.

In his writings on maritime law Bynkershoek is celebrated for advancing the cannon-shot rule as determinative of the breadth of the marginal territorial sea of a coastal State, which in those days was equated with the distance of three nautical miles (although whether he had introduced a flexible standard that moved with improvements in weaponry was much debated). As for diplomatic and consular law, Bynkershoek championed the cause of all public ministers, irrespective of title or rank, to enjoy equal protection of the law together with their families, servants, and suite. Many of the principles which he advocated were subsequently incorporated into the law of nations.

The work translated herein has been extolled for the attempt to resolve solutions to urgent problems of the law of war at sea:

> It is not too much to say that his treatment of commer-
> cial and maritime questions, and especially the relationships
> between neutrals and belligerents, is more thorough, more
> searching, more related to actual practice, more pervaded
> with sound sense, with legal and statesmanlike skill, than that
> of any other work on the subject before his time.[8]

It was these qualities that no doubt commended the book to Du Ponceau for translation and to the United States Supreme Court, among others, for its helpfulness in determining the true state of the law applicable to causes coming before that tribunal.

The Translator

The translator of Bynkershoek is of no less interest than the learned Dutch jurist himself. Peter Stephen du Ponceau was born at St-Martins, Isle of Ré, an island off the port of La Pallice in the southwestern part of France, on 3 June 1760, the son of a

---

[8] Phillipson, note 2 above, p. 404. Akashi likewise was impressed by the "practicality" that permeates Bynkershoek's works, accepts that Bynkershoek was a "realist" who demonstrates modern legal thinking, was not a "pure positivist"; his real contribution to the law of nations was "his practical approach in resolving the questions of *jus gentium*, rather than his cosmetic positivist tendency". Akashi, note 2 above, pp. 178-179.

French army officer.[9] By the age of five he had memorized a Latin and French vocabulary. He began formal studies at a grammar school and was instructed at home by private tutors. Latin he studied with Father Raymond, later chaplain of the hospital La Charité, and a military officer, Mallorme. At a neighbor's home one day, he accidentally found an English

---

[9] Du Ponceau deserves a thorough biography that gives full due to his achievements as a jurist and a specialist in languages. For this study I have consulted printed sources: "Duponceau, Peter S., LL.D.", in J. L. Blake (ed.), *A Biographical Dictionary: Comprising a Summary Account of the Lives of the Most Distinguished Persons of All Ages, Nations, and Professions: Including More than Two Thousand Articles of American Biography* (1856), p. 391; "Duponceau, Peter Stephen", in J. G. Wilson and J. Fiske (eds.), *Appletons' Encyclopedia of American Biography* (1888), II, p. 263; "Duponceau, Peter Stephen", in *The Biographical Encyclopedia of Pennsylvania of the Nineteenth Century* (1874), p. 194; G. W. Gawalt, "Du Ponceau, Pierre Etienne", in J. A. Garraty and M. C. Carnes, *American National Biography* (1999), VII, pp. 112-113; J. Mooney, "Peter Stephen Duponceau", *The Catholic Encyclopedia*, V (1909), p. 205; K. H. Nadelmann, "Peter Stephen du Ponceau", *Pennsylvania Bar Association Quarterly*, XXIV (April 1953), pp. 248-256; John Pickering, "Peter S. Du Poneacu, LL.D.", *Journal of the American Oriental Society*, I, no. 2 (1844), p. 167; "Ponceau, Pierre Etienne du", in M. le Hoefer (ed.), *Nouvelle Biographie générale depuis les temps les plus reculés jusqu'a nos jours* (1862), XL, cols. 733-735, W. A. Tieck, "In Search of Peter Stephen Du Ponceau", *Pennsylvania Magazine of History and Biography*, LXXXIX (1965), pp. 52-78; R. F. Weigley (ed.), *Philadelphia: A 300-Year History* (1982); T. I. Wharton, "Peter S. Duponceau", in H. Simpson, *The Lives of Eminent Philadelphians, Now Deceased Collected from Original and Authentic Sources* (1859), pp. 329-333; James L. Whitehead (ed.), "Autobiography of Peter Stephen Du Ponceau", *Pennsylvania Magazine of History and Biography*, LXIII (1939), 189-227, 311-343, 432-461; (1940), LXIV, pp. 97-120; 243-269. Among manuscript sources, see the relevant holdings of the American Philosophical Society and of the Historical Society of Philadelphia, both of which enjoyed Du Ponceau's services as President at some point. Also see W. E. Butler, *Peter Stephen du Ponceau: Legal Bibliophile* (2010); Butler, "Peter Stephen du Ponceau: Pennsylvania Lawyer Extraordinaire", *Pennsylvania Bar Association Quarterly*, LXXXIX (2018), pp. 156-165.

grammar and proceeded to undertake self-study of that language, testing his skills with English, Irish, and Welsh families quartered in the town. Soon he was devouring Milton, Thomson, Young, Pope, and Shakespeare.[10] As a student he shared a room with a young Irishman, Edmund Stack, and they "spoke English together to our hearts' content".[11] Then it was the turn of the Italian language, which he acquired in the same manner and tested his skills with an Italian regiment quartered locally. Tutoring in other disciplines – mathematics, geography, history, and military science – he received from various recruits who volunteered their services to his father. Hopes for a military career were dashed by extreme nearsightedness.

Greek he acquired a bit, partly through self-study and partly through informal classes which he arranged with like-minded colleagues. Ultimately, however, he was sanctioned for this and never worked seriously with the language. As for Russian, this too he acquired, as he related in his Autobiography:

> While I was employed as Secretary to the learned Count de Gébelin at Paris, I became acquainted with a Russian nobleman, who was then on his travels through Europe. His name was M. Pisaroff, and he told me he was a nephew to Admiral Count Gleboff. He lived in great style, and was attended by several of his serfs.
>
> My acquaintance with him began in this manner. I was in a bookseller's shop, where I went to lounge almost every day, and where I found a grammar of the Russian language. I amused myself with copying a few Russian sentences in the proper character. M. Pisaroff, who was also in the habit of visiting the same shop, saw the paper which I had written,

---

[10] Recounted in R. Dunglison, "Biographical Sketch of Peter S. Du Ponceau", *American Law Magazine*, no. 9 (April 1845), pp. 53.

[11] See P. S. du Ponceau, "Autobiography", ed. J. L. Whitehead, note 9 above, LXIV, pp. 99-100, 102, 110.

and was so pleased with it, that he desired the bookseller to introduce me to him, which he soon afterwards did. My Russian nobleman took a great fancy to me, and during five or six weeks that he remained in Paris, gave me lessons in his language in which I began to make some progress, and in return I gave him English lessons. He told me that he was going to Italy to finish his tour, and that if on his return he should find me in Paris, and I was willing to accompany him, he would take me with him to St. Petersberg and there obtain for me the place of teacher of the English language in the Imperial College of Cadets ...[12]

His next formal education at age thirteen he received at a Benedictine college, St. Jean Angely, where he excelled in philosophy and continued his studies of English. He left after eighteen months, at age fifteen, upon his father's death. Under a combination of maternal and clerical pressure agreed to enter a seminary ("took the tonsure", as he put it, and became monsieur l'abbé) on condition that he not be expected to enter the priesthood. Through the intervention of the Bishop of Rochelle, Augustin Roch de Menou de Charnisal (1681-1767), a friend of the family, the young abbé was appointed a regent in his episcopal college at Bressiure, in Poitou, where he instruct-

------

[12] Ibid., LXIII, pp. 443-444. This episode may help date the manuscript "Sea Terms" which du Ponceau later presented to the APS. There are Cyrillic jottings, mostly the word "Louis" in Russian, rendered as "Ludwig" transcribed. No Russian materials dating from du Ponceau's Paris period were included in his bequest of books to the APS. Pickering records that "in early life he had studied the Russian, which at that period was a terra incognita to scholars in general; and on his arrival in this country he kept his journal in the French language, written in the Russian character". Pickering, note 9 above, p. 168. In his will he left to the APS his Russian grammar and dictionary: Johann von Heym (17﹣-1821), *Dictionnaire portative ... francois-russe-allemand* (Riga, Hartmann, 1805); *Russische sprachlehre* (new ed., enl.; Riga, Hartmann, 1804).

ed a much older class of students in the elements of the Latin language (for his period there he was credited with having received his bachelor's degree, having passed the examinations with distinction).[13] Bullying by the other regents and, at their instigation, students there persuaded him to leave, and on 25 December 1775 he repaired to Paris to seek subsistence. Eventually he found freelance work by translating English works on a per sheet basis for other professed translators who sold on his work as their own; he also translated commercial letters for merchants and tutored in the English and French languages. For several months he acted as secretary to the protestant minister, Antoine Court de Gébelin (1719-1784), a celebrated philologist.[14]

He then found employment as secretary-interpreter with Baron Friedrich Wilhelm Augustus von Steuben (1730-1794)[15] and sailed with him from Marseilles to America, landing at Portsmouth, New Hampshire on 1 December 1777.[16] As von Steuben spoke no English whatsoever, du Ponceau found himself obliged to cope with American English at once. After a few days in Portsmouth, von Steuben repaired to Boston, where

---

[13] Du Ponceau relates the examinations with relish in his autobiography. See Whitehead, note 9 above.

[14] Dates of birth differ: 1719, 1724, 1728. The Count was a fervent supporter of American independence.

[15] See F. Kapp, *Life of Friedrich William von Steuben* (2d ed.; 1858), pp. 192-199.

[16] Of this period there survives a little journal and notebook containing a variety of incidental materials, including scribblings, some poetry, small maps, and an account of the journey from Portsmouth to Yorktown. Although the text is mostly in French, du Ponceau often has recourse to Russian, suggesting that he was resorting to code and also was studying some Russian on his own. This item is held by the Historical Society of Delaware. He did own a copy of John Locke (1760) in Russian, which he later gave to the APS; his notebook on "Sea Terms" also contained some Russian words.

du Ponceau, by now a stern republican, met John Hancock (1737-1793) and Samuel Adams (1722-1803). He then accompanied Baron von Steuben to Yorktown, where they met General Horatio Gates (1727-1806) and, upon von Steuben's request, du Ponceau was appointed captain, by brevet, in the United States Army.[17] On 19 February 1778 he and von Steuben went to Valley Forge, where on 24 February du Ponceau was presented to General George Washington (1732-1799). It was at Valley Forge that du Ponceau met his first American Indian. In time the Baron was appointed a major-general and inspector-general of the armies of the United States, in consequence of which du Ponceau, as secretary to the Baron, also became aide-de-camp and, by courtesy, the rank of major. During his Valley Forge days, du Ponceau also came to befriend General Marie-Joseph Paul Yves Roch Gilbert du Motier, Marquis de Lafayette (1757-1834), a relationship that endured until the latter's death.

For four years he served von Steuben[18] with the rank of captain until ill health (consumption) obliged him to resign. His doctors believed him to be incurable, a judgment which alienated him from the medical profession for the remainder of his life. He settled in Philadelphia and became, on 25 July 1781, a citizen of the Commonwealth of Pennsylvania by oath. Seeking employment, he was recommended to Robert R. Livingston (1746-

---

[17] In due course du Ponceau received a revolutionary war pension as a captain of infantry of the line until his death.

[18] Among his tasks of international legal interest was to translate, see through press, and arrange the distribution of von Steuben's *Regulations for the Order and Discipline of the Troops of the United States* (Philadelphia, 1779). A draft entitled "L'Exercise des Troupes" survives in the New York Historical Society. This, the first manual of discipline for the United States Army, was reprinted numerous times and amended from time to time. For his labors on the manual du Ponceau was rewarded by Congress with the sum of $400 in addition to his pay.

1813), sometime chancellor of the State of New York who had been appointed secretary for foreign affairs. Judge Richard Peters (1744-1828) wrote of du Ponceau to Livingston on 19 October 1781:

> ... He has an exceeding industrious turn, and has a most remarkable facility of acquiring languages. French is his native tongue. English he has acquired perfectly, and he understands German, Italian, and Spanish. He can translate Danish and low Dutch with the help of a dictionary, but a little application will make him master of these. He is also a good Latin scholar ...[19]

On 22 October 1781 du Ponceau took up his duties as secretary to Livingston at a salary of $750 per annum payable in French crowns or *louis d'or* (the currency of the day). The house that Livingston occupied until his retirement from office became the house in which du Ponceau resided from 1801 until his death in 1844, at Sixth and Chestnut Streets in Philadelphia.[20]

When the War ended, du Ponceau decided to enter the legal profession and studied law with William Lewis (1751-1819), whom he regarded as "the most celebrated lawyer in Philadelphia, and perhaps in the United States".[21] On 24 January 1785, upon the motion of Mr. Lewis, du Ponceau was admitted as an

---

[19] Note 10 above, p. 16.

[20] The house was diagonally opposite the State House. Du Ponceau purchased the house at a sheriff's sale, also acquiring at the same time the adjoining property to the rear along Sixth Street, described as a three-story brick tenement where Livingston had accommodated the foreign affairs office. Between the mansion and the tenement was a small low cottage that du Ponceau used as his law office. Du Ponceau later rented out space to a bookseller who proved to be delinquent in his rent. See Tieck, note 9 above, pp. 59-60.

[21] Note 10 above., p. 17.

attorney of the court of common pleas and, on the favorable
report of the examiners, he was received. He had previously
been appointed by the executive council as notary public; in
1791 he was made sworn interpreter of foreign languages.
Success as a lawyer came rapidly; by September 1785 the court
docket showed that he was counsel in twenty-one actions
either for plaintiff or defendant.[22] In 1786, once more upon the
motion of William Lewis, du Ponceau was admitted as attorney
of the Supreme Court of Pennsylvania. He promptly found
himself traveling to Washington to argue cases before the
United States Supreme Court,[23] together with other leading
members of the Philadelphia Bar, as many cases ended up
there. Joseph Story (1779-1845), who enjoyed observing the
United States Supreme Court in 1808 and when disengaged
would dine and sup with the judges, heard du Ponceau argue
and described him as follows:

> Duponceau is a Frenchman by birth, and a very ingen-
> ious counselor at Philadelphia. He has the reputation of great

---

[22] There is some evidence to suggest that he may have formed a partnership
with Maurice Desdevens. In September 1816 du Ponceau presented a book
to the American Philosophical Society which bore the inscription: "The
Partenership of Peter Stephen Duponceau and Maurice Desdevens 8th
September 1785". The book was *Case of Peter du Calvet, esq. of Montreal in the
Province of Quebeck, containing (amongst other things worth notice) an account
of the long and severe imprisonment he suffered in the said Province by the order of
General Haldimand, the present governeur of the same, without the least offence,
or other lawful cause whatever* ... (London, 1784).

[23] See, among others, 1 Dallas 366 (C.P. Phila. 1788), 1 Dallas 436, 449 (Sup.
Ct. Pa. 1789); 2 Dallas 111, 144, 234, 270 (Sup. Ct. Pa. 1792-97); 3 Dallas 6,
121, 133, 285, 297, 302, 321, 336, 384 (U.S. 1794-98); 4 Cranch 209, 241
(U.S. 1808). Du Ponceau is mentioned in passing in Warren, *The Supreme
Court in United States History* (rev. ed.; 1937), I, pp. 55, 106, 114, 116, 133,
150, 318, 320. Du Ponceau describes himself on the title page of our work as
"Counsellor at Law in the Supreme Court of the United States of America".

subtilty and acuteness, and is excessively minute in the display of his learning. His manner is animated but not impressive, and he betrays at every turn the impatience and the casuistry of his nation. His countenance is striking, his figure rather awkward. A small, sparkling, black eye, and a thin face, satisfy you that he is not without quickness of mind; yet he seemed to me to exhaust himself in petty distinctions, and in a perpetual recurrence to doubtful, if not to inclusive arguments. His reasoning was rather sprightly and plausible, than logical and coercive; in short, he is a French advocate.[24]

Although himself a democrat in matters of politics, he was well connected with republican merchants and often represented them in property transactions or litigation. His letterbooks for the period from 1792 to 1809 show that the majority of his clients were individuals of French-origin in the United States, West Indies, or France and that his "important suits" were concerned with issues of international, commercial, and maritime law.[25] For a number of years he enjoyed a retainer from the French Republic.

In 1792 he became a founder and secretary of the Democratic Society of Philadelphia.

His command of Roman and European legal concepts and of international law, together with his language abilities, made

---

[24] W. W. Story, *Life and Letters of Joseph Story* (1851), I, pp. 162-163. Joseph Story wrote to du Ponceau on 30 January 1841: "To you and to Chancellor Kent I mainly owe whatever attainments I have made in foreign jurisprudence and the civil law". Cited in R. H. Heindel, "Some Letters of Peter Stephen Du Ponceau", *Pennsylvania History* (1936), p. 199.

[25] His Letterbooks are held at the Historical Society of Philadelphia, this data being drawn from J. D. Henderson, "'A Blaze of Reputation and the Echo of a Name': The Legal Career of Peter Stephen du Ponceau in Post-Revolutionary Philadelphia" (unpublished M. A. Thesis, Florida State University, 2004), p. 27.

him a natural advisor for European merchants, commercial agents, and diplomatic and consular officials. John Pickering (1777-1846) wrote of his law practice:

> ... he was engaged in all the important causes, which then came before the courts of the State as well as of the United States. At that day the controversies which arose between France and the United States, and the position of the United States as a neutral power, while all Europe was at war, gave rise to questions of international law for which our lawyers, generally, were then quite unprepared; and his knowledge of the civil and continental law of Europe, which were easily accessible to him, by means of his native language – a language then studied, or read, by very few persons in this country – gave him many decided advantages at the bar in cases of the kind alluded to.[26]

Henry Hugh Brackenridge (1748-1816) extracted two notes by du Ponceau under the head of "allegiance" from the American edition of the *Edinburgh Encyclopedia*, commenting that " ... Mr. Duponceau, whom all will admit, I take it, possesses the greatest knowledge of general law of any, in the U. States, and may be said to be the greatest universal jurist".[27]

He never sought public office after he left the employ of Robert Livingston, devoting himself to private and professional business and scholarship and apparently quite comfortable financially.

President Jefferson offered du Ponceau the position of Chief Judge of the Territory of Orleans, having regard to his reputation as a jurist learned in French and Roman law. This was seriously considered but declined in light of his associations and

---

[26] See Pickering, note 9 above, p. 164.
[27] See H. H. Brackenridge, *Law Miscellanies* (1814; reprint 1972), p. 417.

prospects in Philadelphia. Apart from his practice of law and his legal translations, three learned societies engaged the attention of du Ponceau, as follows:

> *Law Academy of Philadelphia.* Despite its name, this was not a law school in the traditional American meaning of the word, but it was dedicated to legal education. In many respects it resembled an Inn of Court in England, which was perhaps no coincidence. The origins of the Law Academy are traced to 1783, when du Ponceau, Bushrod Washington (1762-1829) (later a Justice of the United States Supreme Court), and John Wilkes Kittera (1752-1801), recently admitted to the Bar, formed the Law Society of Philadelphia.[28] Records are few, but apparently the members met from time to time to hear lectures upon legal topics or to engage in mooting. Various officers served from time to time, and possibly the name of the society itself changed.[29] In 1811 du Ponceau was elected President of the Society, although by then he was 51 years of age.

In 1820 efforts were undertaken to create a permanent foundation for such an organization, and to this end the Society for the Promotion of Legal Knowledge and Forensic Eloquence was established by a group of judges and lawyers. The object of the Society, as articulated in the Preamble to its Constitution,

---

[28] See G. Sharswood, *The Origin, History, and Objects of the Law Academy of Philadelphia: An Address Delivered Before the Academy, March 13, 1883* (1883); W. MacLean, Jr., *The Law Academy and the Growth of Legal Education in Philadelphia* (1900); For du Ponceau's own recollections of its founding, see P. S. du Ponceau, *Address Delivered Before the Law Academy of Philadelphia on the Opening of the Session 1831-2* (1831).

[29] MacLean and Sharswood quote sources who can document the existence of law societies during the period 1785 to 1811. Du Ponceau himself said he had "heard no more of Law Societies in this city, although some might have existed without my knowing it". Du Ponceau, note 27 above, p. 6.

was to "connect with the mode of instruction at that time
exclusively pursued, a more scientific and academical system,
whereby not only a greater degree of jurisprudential knowledge
might be acquired, but the students might be exercised in the art
of public speaking, so as to unite the talent of the orator with the
science of the jurist". This group then invited an alliance with
the Law Society, of which du Ponceau was again the President,
and suggested that the Law Society become a Law Academy as
an appendage of the new Society and under its control. Du
Ponceau was elected first Provost of the Academy.

The Law Academy formally opened on 21 February 1821
with what must have been a monumental address by du Ponceau
in the room of the Supreme Court before the Trustees and
members of the Society for Legal Knowledge and Forensic
Eloquence. On this occasion du Ponceau referred to fledgling
and unsuccessful efforts to persuade the University of Pennsylvania to establish a law school, noted the formation of law
schools elsewhere, and strongly urged that a national law school
be created in Philadelphia.[30] The parent society soon came to an
end (for essentially procedural reasons), but the Law Academy
lived on well into the twentieth century (initially as an informal
association, but incorporated by act of the legislature framed 14
April 1835).

Mooting was one activity of the Academy, the students being organized into teams and judged by legal professionals who
actually produced a written opinion in judgment of the argu-

---

[30] The theme of a "national law school" comes up with some frequency at this
period, also being encouraged during the 1820s by John Reed (1786-1850),
who founded the Dickinson School of Law in Carlisle, Pennsylvania in 1833,
now part of Pennsylvania State University. A close reading of du Ponceau's
address suggests that he believed a national law school was being created by
the opening of the Law Academy.

ments presented.[31] Students also wrote dissertations on legal subjects, several of which the Law Academy deemed worthy of publication. One, by a student twenty years of age, Antony Laussat (1806-1833), achieved the approbation of John Marshall (1755-1835) and James Kent (1763-1847) and became a standard work on equity.[32] Over the years the Law Academy published a number of works, including a seminal work by du Ponceau himself on jurisdiction.[33] At some later stage the Law Academy established the Peter Stephen du Ponceau Prize for an essay upon a subject, either legal or connected with the law, selected and proposed to the Law Academy by its Faculty for worthy works submitted anonymously. This "Duponceau Medal" was awarded to the best essay as the medal highest in value; the medal next highest in value was the Laussat Medal.[34]

In 1834 du Ponceau published another substantial monograph under the auspices of the Law Academy, this entitled *A Brief View of the Constitution of the United States*. It enjoyed

---

[31] The Opinion Book, entitled "Opinions Delivered Before the Law Academy of Philadelphia by the Provost and Vice Provost", covering the years 1820 to 1822 and signed by du Ponceau is preserved in the Manuscript Division of the American Philosophical Society, having been presented in 1862 by Robley Dunglison (1798-1869). 340.7 L41.

[32] A. Laussat, *Essay on Equity in Pennsylvania* (1826).

[33] P. S. du Ponceau, *Dissertation on the Nature and Extent of the Jurisdiction of the Courts of the United States* (1824); this volume appends du Ponceau's opening Address to the Law Academy delivered in 1821. Cited in Seminole Tribe v. Fla., 517 U.S. 44 (U.S. 1996); Planters' Bank v. Neely, 8 Miss. 80 (Miss. 1843). Also cited in J. Kent, *Commentaries on American Law* (1826), I, p. 322. The book was reviewed in *North American Review*, XXI (1825), 104 (C. S. Davies); *Thémis ou Bibliothèque du Jurisconsulte*, VII (1825), 420 (Daligny).

[34] See Article XII, *Charter, Constitution and By-Laws of The Law Academy of Philadelphia* (1867), p. 23. The Prize for 1904 was awarded to George J. Edwards, Jr., of the Philadelphia Bar, for his work *The Grand Jury: An Essay* (1906; reprinted in the Gryphon Legal Classics Library, 2003).

considerable success and was widely cited[35] and translated into French.[36] His interests of matters of jurisdiction and evidence led him to seek legislative change when he deemed this to be desirable. On 27 March 1826 he wrote to Congressman William Morris Meredith at Harrisburg:

> ... [It was reported] in the *National Intelligencer* of last Friday that the House of Representatives on the motion of Mr. Livingston, of Louisiana, that the Committee of the Judiciary be instructed to enquire into the expediency of empowering the Consuls of the U. S. to take the acknowledgement or proof of Deeds & other writings, & also to take the affidavits and Answers in Chancery. Mr. Livingston is a Member of the Judiciary Committee, and I have no doubt that the Report will be favorable.
>
> Seeing that Congress are taking the lead in a measure which had been one Year before our Legislature, would it not be well, on the ground of an honorable State pride, that we should be before ... with them – the Act of Congress can only affect lands in the District of Columbia, and affidavits &c. in the federal Courts; it can have no operation on State laws; I therefore beg leave to bring this Subject again before you, & request that it may be attended to this Session, if possible.[37]

American Philosophical Society Du Ponceau's contributions to the study of languages, particular those of the American Indians but also including Chinese and the Mexican heritage, were pioneering and immense, generating a larger secondary

---

[35] See, for example, Welch v. Texas Dep't of Highways & Public Transp., 483 U.S. 468 (U.S. 1987).

[36] Du Ponceau, *Exposé sommaire de la Constitution des Etats-Unis,* transl. by d'Homergue (1837). An abridged version printed in New York for distribution in Cuba and Puerto Rico appeared posthumously: *Breve Resena de la Constitución de los Estados Unidos* (1848).

[37] Letter in the Manuscript Archive, American Philosophical Society.

literature on this aspect of his life than on his legal career.[38] They seem to have begun with his membership in the American Philosophical Society (APS),[39] where he became the secretary of and prime moving force behind the Society's Historical and Literary Committee founded in 1815 (having been originally suggested by du Ponceau in 1811). This was the seventh committee of the APS, adding the social sciences and humanities to what heretofore had been a purely natural science organization. The Committee was charged with, *inter alia*, quasi-legal interests, including the collecting of original documents, such as official and private letters, Indian treaties, ancient records ... ".

The impetus for the early expansion of the APS outstanding holdings of native American linguistic collections was generated by du Ponceau and a Philadelphia wine merchant and biblio-

---

[38] See R. E. Goodman and P. Swiggers, *The American Philosophical Society and the Study of Language in the Early Nineteenth Century* (1993); M. D. Smith, "Peter Stephen Du Ponceau and His Study of Languages: A Historical Account", *Proceedings of the American Philosophical Society*, CXXVII (June 1983), pp. 143-179; P. Swiggers, "Americanist Linguistics and the Origin of Linguistic Typology: Peter Stephen Du Ponceau's 'Comparative Science of Language'", *Proceedings of the American Philosophical Society*, CXLII (March 1998), pp. 18-46.

[39] Du Ponceau was elected to membership on 15 July 1791, serving on committees and acting as councilor, secretary, and vice-president before assuming the Presidency of the Society in 1827. Prior to joining he made a spectacular gift to the Society Library, reported on 6 March 1789, which included a Russian language version (1760) of John Locke's Essay on education. See John Locke, О воспитании детей [On the Education of Children] (Moscow, 1760). 2 pts. Translated from the French by Professor Nikolai Nikitich Popovskii (c. 1730-1760), a protégé of M. I. Lomonosov who became the Rector of the Moscow University Gymnasium and favored introducing university lectures in the Russian language in preference to Latin.

phile, John Vaughan (1756-1841).[40] During the first decade of
the nineteenth century, Thomas Jefferson (1743-1826) served
simultaneously as the President of the United States and
President of the APS, and in those dual capacities commissioned
Albert Gallatin (1761-1849), assisted by du Ponceau, to undertake a study of Indian vocabularies. Jefferson believed there were
relationships between the Indian tribes reflected in the similari-
ties and differences of their respective languages. Du Ponceau
and Gallatin determined that there was a correlation between
similarity of language and the duration of time that had elapsed
since the tribes had migrated to other regions of North America.
Du Ponceau recorded his own findings in a monograph on the
grammatical system of Indian languages,[41] which on 2 May 1835
was awarded the Comte de Volney Prize of *Linguistique* of the
Institut de France.[42]

----

[40] Vaughan had joined the APS on 16 January 1784 and was appointed
librarian on 18 March 1803, a post which he held until 1841. See R. E.
Goodman and P. Swiggers, "John Vaughan (1756-1841) and the Linguistic
Collection in the Library of the American Philosophical Society", *Proceedings
of the American Philosophical Society*, CXXXVIII (June 1994), pp. 251-272.
Apart from an astute acquisitions policy, Vaughan was generous to the APS
with gifts of his own, itemized in ibid., p. 253, fn. 10. The APS preserves a
printed version of its Library catalog from 1824 with interpolations of new
acquisitions in Vaughan's own hand.

[41] P. S. du Ponceau, *Mémoire sur le système grammatical des langues de quelques
nations Indiennes de l'Amérique du Nord* (1838). A later authority said that the
Volney Prize had for du Ponceau the effect of certifying him as "one of the
few great linguists of the world". See C. Wissler, "The American Indian and
the American Philosophical Society", *Proceedings of the American
Philosophical Society*, LXXXVI (1943), p. 193.

[42] Du Ponceau had competed for the Volney Prize in 1825, submitting an
*Essai de solution du problème philologique propose en l'année 1823 par la
Commission de l'Institut Royal de France chargée de la disposition du legs de M. le
Comte de Volney*, but was unsuccessful. The manuscript of the submission

He then expanded his studies of language to encompass the Chinese system of writing with his *A Dissertation on the Nature and Character of the Chinese System of Writing, in a Letter to John Vaughan, Esq. by Peter S. Du Ponceau, LL.D., President of the American Philosophical Society, of the Historical Society of Pennsylvania, and of the Athenaeum of Philadelphia, Corresponding Member of the Institute of France, &c. &c. to which are subjoined, A vocabulary of the Cochinchinese language, by Father Joseph Morrone, R. C. Missionary at Saigon, with references to plates, containing the characters belonging to each word, and with notes, showing the degree of affinity existing between the Chinese and Cochinchinese languages, and the use they respectively make of their common system of writing by M. de la Palun, Late Consul of France at Richmond, in Virginia; and A Cochinchinese and Latin dictionary, in use among the R. C. missions in Cochinchina* (1838).[43] The main text of the book comprises a letter to John Vaughan, followed by appendices.

In assembling his materials on the American Indian languages he corresponded with individuals around the world. His correspondence with William Shaler (1773-1833), "On the Language, Manners, and Customs of the Berbers of Africa" was published by the APS,[44] as were his letters to and from John Gottlieb Ernestus Heckewelder (1743-1823), a Moravian missionary in Ohio working with Indian tribes there.[45]

---

reposes in the Manuscript Division of the APS at 410. D921. See Swiggers, note 37 above, pp. 18-19, 43.

[43] The book appeared as volume 2 in the *Transactions of the Historical and Library Committee of the American Philosophical Society*; reviewed favorably in *The North American Review*, XLVIII (1839), pp. 271-310 (John Pickering (1777-1846)).

[44] *Transactions of the American Philosophical Society*, II (n.s.; 1824).

[45] Ibid., I (1819).

Contemporary scholars in retrospect believe du Ponceau "can rightly be hailed as 'the father of American philology'" and his *Mémoire* "a pioneer work in language typology".[46]

A passing enthusiasm was the silk industry, to which he devoted three years of his life and four thousand dollars in order to introduce the production and manufacture of silk into the United States. An Act of Congress was required, and an appropriate bill submitted but not enacted. In the end he abandoned the project, "defeated in my patriotic design", but wrote two works on the subject in 1831 and, recounting his experiences, in 1837.

In all du Ponceau was a member of forty-two learned societies, of which nineteen were abroad, including the three above-mentioned. The University of Pennsylvania conferred the degree of M.A. (Hon.) on him on 21 March 1782 at a ceremony attended by General George Washington, Baron von Steuben, and members of Congress, among others. Harvard University conferred the degree of LL.D. (Hon.) in 1820. He later became a trustee of the University of Pennsylvania. He was elected to the American Academy of Arts and Sciences and, in 1791, to the American Philosophical Society; served as Provost of the Law Academy of Philadelphia (1821-1844), president of the American Philosophical Society (1827 1844), president of the Historical Society of Pennsylvania (1837-1844), president of the Athenaeum of Philadelphia (est. 1814; 1844), and on 20 April 1827 a Corresponding Member of the Institut de France.

Among his other works were *English Phonology; or an Essay towards an analysis and description of the component sounds of*

---

[46] Swiggers, note 37 above, p. 41; V. V. Belyi, "P. S. Duponceau – the Father of American Philology", *Zeitschrift für Phonetik, Sprachwissenschaft und Kommunikationsforschung*, XXVIII (1975), pp. 41-49.

the English language (1817);[47] *A Discourse on the Early History of Pennsylvania* (1821); *Eulogium in Commemoration of the Honourable William Tilghman, LL.D.* (1827); *An Historical Review of the Rise, Progress, Present State and Prospects of the Silk Culture* (1831); *An Historical Discourse Delivered Before the Society for the Commemoration of the Landing of William Penn* (1832); *A Discourse on the Necessity and Means of Making our National Literature Independent of that of Great Britain* (1834); and *The History of the Silk Bill, in a Letter to D. B. Warden* (1837).[48]

A number of his legal writings which appeared as part of other works are among his most important. There is a certain poetic irony that his translation of passages from Huber should become available to the legal profession thanks to the United States Supreme Court, who in an otherwise brief opinion appended the extract that "was translated for, and read in, this cause".[49] His first major published contribution, entitled "A Summary View of the Law of France Concerning Bankruptcy", was inserted as an appendix to Thomas Cooper (1759-1839),

---

[47] Published in *Transactions of the American Philosophical Society*, I (n.s., 1817), pp. 228-264.

[48] "D. B. Warden" was David Baillie Warden (1772-1845), author of the first manual on consular law in the English language: *On the Origin, Nature, Progress and Influence of Consular Establishments* (Paris, 1814; reprinted Lawbook Exchange, 2011).

[49] Ulrich Huber was, as noted above, Bynkershoek's teacher. The passages concerned the conflict of laws and appear in Emory v. Grenough, 3 U.S. 369 (1797). The particular work of Huber is not cited, but undoubtedly was *Praelectiones juris civilis* (1687). Pickering confirms that the translation was by du Ponceau. See note 9 above, pp. 164-165. Alan Watson confirms that the translation is from the *Praelectiones* 2.1.3.5, but credits the translation to Alexander J. Dallas, the reporter of the United States Supreme Court. See Alan Watson, *Joseph Story and the Comity of Errors: A Case Study in the Conflict of Laws* (1992), pp. 49, 51.

in his treatise comparing American and English bankruptcy law.[50] Kurt Hans Nadelmann (1900-1984) described the Cooper/du Ponceau work as "the first comparative law book ever produced in the United States and also the first scholarly presentation in English of the bankruptcy law of France".[51] Du Ponceau also contributed notes to the American edition of Butler's *Horae Juridicae Subsecivae*.[52] Following the Bynkershoek quickly were du Ponceau's translations of the French Commercial Code of 1808 and then the French Criminal Code.[53] For the *Edinburgh Encyclopedia* (American edition) he contributed the articles on "Allegiance" and "American Law".[54] When Kent's *Commentaries on American Law* appeared, he published a review of volume one.[55]

His translations of works on language and travel include: T. Campanius Holm, *A Short Description of the Province of New Sweden. Now Called by the English Pennsylvania, in America*, translated from the Swedish by P. S. du Ponceau (1834); John Eliot, *A Grammar of the Massachusetts Indian Language. A New Edition with Notes and Observations by Peter S. Du Ponceau and an Introduction and Supplementary Observations by John Pickering* (1822); John Heckewelder, *Histoire, moeurs et coutumes des nations indiennes qui habitaient autrefois la Pennsylvanie et les états*

---

[50] T. Cooper, *Bankrupt Law of American Compared with the Bankrupt Law of England* (1801); Cooper wrote the book while serving a prison sentence for violation of the Sedition Act under the Adams administration. Du Ponceau also added a translation of the Ordinances of Bilbao concerned with insolvency in Spain.

[51] Nadelmann, note 9 above, p. 249.

[52] See Charles Butler, *Horae Juridicae Subsecivae* (Philadelphia, 1808).

[53] Both appeared as appendices in the *American Review of History and Politics* (July and October 1811).

[54] Reprinted in *Port Folio*, VII (4th ser.; 1819), p. 267. Du Ponceau also wrote for Lieber's *Encyclopedia Americana* (1829).

[55] *American Quarterly Review*, I (1827), 162.

voisins, transl. from the English by Chevalier du Ponceau (1822); D. Zeisberger, *A Grammar of the Language of the Lenni Lenape or Delaware Indians*, transl. from the German manuscript by Peter S. Du Ponceau (1830).

His work as a translator, however, goes far beyond the fields of law and linguistics. Many papers submitted to the APS for possible publication were in foreign languages and required to be translated either for publication or for review by the publications committee. The records of the APS disclose, for example, that he translated the thermometrical observations of Peter Legaux; Pierre Samuel Du Pont's theory of winds; the last three volumes of Hollandsche Maatschappij der Weten-schappen te Haarlem; Italian medical works; a Spanish paper on the analogy of Spanish and English; among others.

On 21 May 1788 he married Anne Perry (1768-1792), of Massachusetts, the eldest daughter among eleven children of the Presbyterian pastor, Rev. Joseph Perry.[56] After the death of her parents, she moved to Philadelphia, where she met du Ponceau. There were three children: two sons who died in early infancy and a daughter, Louisa Frances (1790-1825). Anne died shortly after the birth of their third child. On 12 September 1794 du Ponceau married Anne Latouche (1759-1817), of New York; there were no issue of this marriage.

His nearsightedness was legendary, and accompanied by and doubtless contributed to an habitual preoccupation which could amount to complete absent-mindedness: "He walked

---

[56] A manuscript ex-libris ("Anne du Ponceau") appears with his on "Sea Terms in Different Languages", a notebook apparently carried by him to record the meanings of marine terms, mostly in Italian, Portuguese, and Spanish, but with some Russian jottings and Danish. Bound in are pp. 561-570 of an unidentified French marine conversation book. Presented by Du Ponceau to the American Philosophical Society and held by them in the Manuscript Division: 359.03 D92. Which "Anne" signed is not apparent.

always in deep thought, and must needs be addressed or arrested to recognize a passing acquaintance".[57] He also was intensely American to a degree that goes far beyond the normal understanding of patriotism. Although he preserved a "tender attachment" for France, his country of origin, he took to the United States immediately upon arrival with a passion that intensified over the years. "My American Character", he wrote, "I prize above all things".[58] Al-though raised in the milieu of Catholicism, he formed an early attachment to the principles of the Reformation, notwithstanding having become "monsieur l'abbé". In Philadelphia he worshipped for more than half a century at the local Presbyterian Church.

Personal Library

There are few, if any, better indicators of the breadth and depth of intellectual interests than a personal library. Du Ponceau was a serious book collector in his own home and through acquisitions made by the Library of the American Philosophical Society under his guidance.[59] He presented hundreds of volumes to the APS over the years, including manuscripts of unpublished translations, and by bequest, Although apparently du Ponceau did not have his own book-

---

[57] Quoted in Tieck, note 9 above, pp. 74-75.

[58] Ibid., p. 76.

[59] As secretary of the Historical and Literary Committee of the APS, du Ponceau "provided much of the impetus for the early growth of the Society's Native American Indian linguistic collections ... and the development of the Society "... into one of the premier centers for the study of Native American Indian languages". Quoted from APS finding aids for the "DuPonceau Collection". He also sat on committees of the APS which made decisions about bidding for books at auctions of private libraries, among them the library of Thomas Jefferson.

plate, some of his books bear what appears to be a stenciled ex libris "P.S.DUPONCEAU."; the APS described this as a "book stamp" in its Association File. Only a few volumes are recorded with this mark of ownership. Gifts to the APS commonly bore his manuscript ex-libris in his own hand and from time to time a donative inscription.[60]

Upon his death there passed to the APS by bequest 353 volumes and uncounted pamphlets, the great majority comprising grammars, dictionaries, histories, encyclopedias, and journals.[61] It was a collection of staggering quality, probably unsurpassed anywhere in the world at the time. Legal materials figured in the gifts he made from 1816 to 1840, and less so in his bequest. Among important titles with respect to the law of nations were: a collection of Spanish treaties;[62] Rayneval's treatise on the freedom of the seas;[63] Madison's anonymous tract on neutral rights;[64] Selden's classic on the closed sea;[65] von Steuben's

---

[60] The APS maintains an "Association File" that records bookplates, manuscript ex-libris, donative inscriptions, and the like, together with dates when available of the presentation or acquisition of the item concerned.

[61] A list of the books pertaining to language and the study of language which du Ponceau presented to the APS in the course of a half century, but mostly by his bequest in 1844, is appended to Smith, note 37 above, pp. 173-177.

[62] *Coleccion de los tratados de pas, alianza, commercio &c. Madrid* (1796-1801). 3 v. Presented by du Ponceau on 15 November 1839.

[63] J. M. Gerard de Rayneval (1746-1812), *De la liberté des mers* (Paris, 1811). 2 vols. Presented by du Ponceau on 17 July 1840, together with his manuscript translation.

[64] [James Madison, (1751-1836)], *An Examination of the Conduct of Great Britain Respecting Neutrals* (Philadelpia, 1807). Presented by Bequest on 3 May 1844.

[65] John Selden (1585-1654), *Mare Clausum* (London, 1636). Presented by du Ponceau on 1 May 1840.

disciplinary regulations for the American armies;[66] and Zouche's early work of the seventeenth century.[67]

The quality of his library may be measured by the auction catalog published for the public sale of his books on 16 October 1844.[68] Comprising 66 pages in all, the first half of which are devoted solely to law books, this was a substantial dispersal of a private library by any standard. The importance of the collection for public and private international law may be measured by the presence of, *inter alia*, the following titles: *A View of the Admiralty Jurisdiction* (London, 1685); N. Atcheson, *Report of a Case Recent Argued and Determined in the Court of King's Bench on the Validity of a Sentence of Condemnation by an Enemy's Consul in a Neutral Port &c.* (London, 1800); D. A. Azuni, *Principes de Système Universel de Droit Maritime de l'Europe* (Paris, 1802); A. Browne, *A Compendious View of the Civil Law and of the Law of the Admiralty* (London, 1802); G. G. Burlamaqui, *Natural and Political Law* (Nugent transl.; Dublin, 1791); J. G. Büsch, *Über die durch den jetzigen Krieg veranlasste*

---

[66] Friedrich Wilhelm August Heinrich Ferdinand, Baron von Steuben (1730-1794), *Regulations for the Discipline of the Troops of the United States* (Philadelphia, Printed by Styner and Cist, 1779). Presented by du Ponceau in October 1824 and inscribed by him: "By Frederick William Baron de Steuben, Inspector General of the American Armies. Original Ed.". The Regulations contains passages which today we would recognize as part of international humanitarian law. There is no specific mention of the law of nations.

[67] Richard Zouche (1590-1661), *Juris et judicil fecialis ...* (The Hague, 1659). Presented by du Ponceau on 1 May 1840.

[68] *Catalogue of Valuable Law and Miscellaneous Books, from the Library of the Late Peter S. Du Ponceau, LL.D. To Be Sold by Order of Executors On Wednesday Evening, Oct. 16, 1844, at 6 ½ o'clock, at M. Thomas & Son's Auction Store, No. 93 Walnut Street.* (Philadelphia, E. G. Dorsey, 1844). The APS holds a copy of this title, as does the Library Company of Philadelphia. A full facsimile of the catalog is reproduced in Butler, note 9 above (2010).

Zerrütting des Seehandels (Hamburg, 1793); C. van Bynkershoek, *Opera omnia* (1761); J. Chitty, *Law of Nations* (Boston, 1812); *Code des Prises* (Paris, 1784); *Code Nouveau de Prises* (Paris, 1799); *Code des Prises Maritimes, et des Armemens en course* (Paris, 1797); *Collection de Decisions du Conseil des Prises de la Republique Francaise sous le Consulat de Napoleon Bonaparte* (Paris, 1800-04); G. F. Martens, *Cours diplomatique* (Berlin, 1801); L. B. de Wolff, *Institutions de droit de la nature et des gens* (Leiden, 1772); F. N. Dufriche-Foulaines, *Code des Prises et du Commerce de Terre et de Mer* (Paris, 1804); Galiani, *Recht der Neutralitat,* transl. from the Italian (Leipzig, 1790); Hugo Grotius, *De Jure Belli ac Pacis* (1773) and the French edition of 1724; Hubner, *De la Saisie des Batimens neuters* (Paris, 1759); M. Koch, *Abrégé de l'Histoire des Traités de Paix entre les Puissances de l'Europe depuis la paix de Westphalie* (Basle, 1796); Lampredi, *Über den Handel Neutraler Völker in Kriegszeiten* (Leipzig, 1792); Samuel Livermore, *Dissertations on the Contrariety of the Positive Laws of Different States and Nations; De Jure Maritimo et Navali, or a Treatise of Affairs Maritime and of Commerce* (London, 1707); J. Marquardus, *De Jure Mercatorium et Commerciorum* (1662); G. F. Martens, *Essai concernant Les Armateurs, les Prises, et surtout les Reprises* (Gottingen, 1795); De Steck, *Essais sur divers sujets relative à la Navigation et au Commerce pendant la Guerre;* G. F. Martens, *Summary of the Law of Nations* (Philadelphia, 1795); *Ordonnance de la Marine du Mois d'Aoust, 1681* (Paris, 1714) and numerous others of France; S. Pufendorf, *Law of Nature and Nations* (London, 1729); Chr. Robinson, *Collectanea Maritima* (London, 1801); *Roccus' Manual of Maritime Law* (Philadelphia, 1809); T. Rutherforth, *Institutes of Natural Law* (1779); J. Savary, *Le parfait Negociant* (Paris, 1777); J. F. W. Schlegel, *Neutral Rights* (Philadelphia, 1801); *Sea Laws, A Complete Body of, and a General Treatise on the Domination of the Sea* (3d ed.; London);

Stypman, Kunke, and Loccenius, *Jus Maritimum* (Halase, 1740);
A. Verwer, *See-Rechten, Nederlants* (Amsterdam, 1764); Robert
Ward, *Law of Nations in Europe* (London, 1795); D. B. Warden,
*On the Origin, Nature, Progress, and Influence of Consular Estab-
lishments* (Paris, 1813); H. Wheaton, *A Digest of the Law of
Maritime Captures and Prizes* (New York, 1821); Wheaton,
*Enquiry into the Validity of the British Claim to a Right of Visita-
tion and Search of American Vessels Suspected of Being Engaged in
the Slave Trade* (Philadelphia, 1842); Wicqueforth,
L'Ambassadeur et ses Functions (1724); and R. Zouche, *The
Jurisdiction of the Admiralty of England* (London, 1663).

He had two sets of Blackstone's *Commentaries* (Philadelphia, 1774; and Philadelphia 1825). Catherine II's celebrated
Nakaz was present in a French translation published at Amsterdam in 1775. The *Consolato del Mare*, excerpts of which he
translated, was present in French (1808), Italian and Dutch
(1794) versions. Vattel was represented by the first edition
(London, 1758) and a Dublin edition (1792); a massive collection of law reports from around the world, including Coke
(London, 1776) in seven volumes. Six single-spaced pages were
devoted in the auction catalog alone to reports.

For all of its strength in international law, however, the collection was even stronger in comparative law and must have had
few, if any, rivals in the United States at the time. Du Ponceau
purchased widely and wisely, scouring continental and English
book dealers for desired titles and using, sometimes imploring,
friends and colleagues to seek titles which he required. No less
impressive is the non-legal component, rich in choice editions of
belles-lettres in many languages, history, biography, travels,
classics, philosophy, and a modicum of theology. Measured by
the quality of his library alone, du Ponceau deserves to be
numbered among the leading American intellectuals of his
generation.

The Translation

Du Ponceau relates in the Preface to Bynkershoek his approach to the translation and the various emendations and excisions he made to the text. They require no repetition here. He does say, however, that he had commenced the translation several years earlier for his own private use. Although the manuscript of his labors is not known to have survived, he did apparently enjoy the arduous, demanding, and challenging task of translating. In a Note accompanying another as yet unpublished translation whose manuscript was presented to the American Philosophical Society on 17 July 1840 Du Ponceau wrote in his own hand: "Translating is one of my methods of Studying. It may serve those who do not understand the original".[69]

Du Ponceau does not indicate what edition of Bynkershoek he used for the translation. When his Library was sold at auction in Philadelphia on 16 October 1844, two lots were devoted to Bynkershoek. One was a copy of the present translation; the other was the 1761 edition of Bynkershoek's works which contained the present volume and would have been the version available to du Ponceau. He did not present any version of Bynkershoek to the American Philosophical Library except his own translation, and that Library does not hold any other edition of Bynkershoek that could be a candidate for having served as the source of du Ponceau's translation. Circumstantial

---

[69] See Gerard de Joseph Maistre de Rayneval, "On the Freedom of the Sea", translated from the French by Peter S. De Ponceau. 2 vols. in manuscript. He completed the Rayneval after the Bynkershoek, as he worked from the 1811 edition of Rayneval. For the Du Ponceau translation of Rayneval, see J.-M. Gerard de Rayneval, *On the Freedom of the Sea*, ed. with intro. W. E. Butler (2013).

evidence therefore points to the 1761 edition having served as the source.

The translation was well regarded by contemporaries. There is circumstantial evidence that James Madison may have seen an early version of du Ponceau's translation of Bynkershoek long before publication was being considered. Madison was in frequent touch with du Ponceau when preparing his celebrated *An Examination of the Conduct of the British Doctrine, Which Subjects to Capture a Legal Trade, Not Open in Time of Peace* (1806). Bynkershoek is relied upon extensively by Madison, whom "treats the subject of belligerent and neutral relations with more attention, and explains his ideas with more precision, than any of his predecessors".[70] Du Ponceau helped Madison with a passage from Bynkershoek, and when his translation was published sent a copy at once to Madison with an accompanying note:

---

[70] Madison's text is published in *Letters and Other Writings of James Madison* (1865), II, p. 243 and appeared anonymously under the title above. According to notes in the Library of Congress, the text was prepared in the Department of State in 1805. The work was twice reprinted in London from the American edition also in 1806. See Cohen 7490-7492; Sabin 43707. Madison's work is often confused with another tract published under the pseudonym "Juriscola", *An Examination of the Conduct of Great Britain, Respecting Neutrals* (Philadelphia, 1807; 2d ed., Boston, 1808), which some have attributed to Madison, although authorship now seems certainly to belong to Tench Coxe (1755-1824), who acted as an unofficial advisor to Madison. See P. Onuf and N. Onuf, *Federal Union, Modern World: The Law of Nations in an Age of Revolutions, 1776-1814* (1994), p. 201. Du Ponceau wrote to Madison on 8 July 1805 in his capacity as Secretary of State, assuring Madison of his "zeal in any thing that may be agreeable to you ..." and sending notes " ... on the history and motives of the British prohibition of the Trade of neutrals with the Colonies of her Enemies". The Letter is in the Library of Congress holdings of Madison papers.

I had the honor of mentioning to you when you was last in this City in 1805 that I had made, for my private use, a Translation of the first Book of Bynkershoek's Quaestiones Juris Public. I have since been induced to publish it & beg leave to present you with the first copy of it that has issued from the press. It is an homage due to the Statesman who has best understood and appreciated the merits of my author, & who has given to the world the most correct character of his writings.[71]

A copy sent to the President of the United States, James Madison, in December 1810 prompted the following response:

I am glad to find that in the midst of your professional occupations, you have completed a work which was so much wanted, and which required that accurate knowledge of both languages which you possess. The addition of your notes will contribute to recommend both the subject & the Author of that valuable Treatise, to the attention both of our Statesmen & Students.[72]

His friend and former employer, Robert R. Livingston, wrote upon receiving the book that "you appear to me to have done the amplest justice to your author, and rendered it much more interesting by your notes, as well as elucidated some passages which appeared obscure or contradictory in the original".[73]

William Pinkney (1765-1822), colleague and sometime adversary, wrote to du Ponceau on 3 July 1815 from Baltimore:

------

[71] Letter of 15 November 1810, cited in Henderson, note 25 above, p. 50.
[72] Letter of 8 December 1810, in J. C. A. Stagg, et al. (eds.), *The Papers of James Madison* (1984), III, p. 60.
[73] Letter of 16 January 1811, Historical Society of Pennsylvania; cited in J. E. Henderson, note 25 above, p. 44.

In a Case in the Supreme Court of the United States
(The Nereid) it is a Question whether the Prize Code of
Spain <u>does at this Time</u> contain the Rule laid down by its old
Ordinance, that the Goods of a Friend found on board the
Ship of an Enemy shall be confiscated as Prize of War. Proof
of the old Ordinance is found in Azuni and elsewhere; but
full Satisfaction as to the present State of the Spanish Law on
that Stead can perhaps only be obtained from the translation
of D'Abreu by M. Bonnemant in 1802.[74]

I suppose it probable (from what I see on p. 130 of your
Translation of a portion of Bynkershoek – for which we are
all much indebted to you – that you are in possession of
Bonnemants Work – and if so you would perhaps do me the
Favour (instead of Sending me the Book) to cause an Extract to be forwarded to me at Washington of the passage
which touches the matter). – It must necessarily be short –
at least a very short Extract will be sufficient to show M.
Bonnemant's opinion (if he entertained it) that the Old
Ordinance was in force when he wrote. – I incline to think
that you have given an Opinion in the Case of the Nereid
against that which I am bound to maintain; but if this
should be so I venture to believe that my Request is not out
of Rule. – I have the Honour to be – with sincere Respect
Your most obedient Servant.[75]

---

[74] Pinkney refers to Felix Joseph de Abreu y Bertodano (1700-1775), author
of *Tratado juridico-politico sobre pressas de mar*, translated into French by
Guillaume Bonnemant (1747-1820) as *Traité juridico-politique sur les prises
maritime et sur les moyens qui doivent concourir pour render ces prises légitimes*
(2d ed.; Paris, Laurens, 1802), 2 vols.
[75] The Letter was postmarked Baltimore, 3 February 1815, and addressed
simply to "Stephen Peter du Ponceau, Esquire. Philadelphia". Retained in
1815 for the *Nereid* case, Pinkney "contended in vain that the shipment by
the Argentinian merchant of goods from London to South America on a
British vessel justified capture by an American privateer and condemnation of
its cargo". *Dictionary of American Biography*, XVII, p. 548. Pinkney argued 84
cases before the United States Supreme Court. The Supreme Court decided

Joseph Story pleaded with du Ponceau to continue his translation contributions: "why will not Mr. Duponceau increase the public gratitude by translating the works of other learned foreigners, and by a critical account of the writings of those civilians who are best entitled to the attention and study of American lawyers?"[76]

Du Ponceau added notes and commentary to the translation that also influenced the state of the law as it existed when this American translation appeared:

> In his translation of Bynkershoek, he first suggested the application of the distinction between an *absolute* and a *qualified* neutrality, to the case of the United States and France; considering our neutrality not to be absolute, but qualified by the treaty with France, in 1778. His remarks (in the same work) on the doctrine of the *jus postliminii*, present some new and important views, which, if we rightly recollect, have been adopted by Mr. Wheaton, in his valuable work on International Law. We believe, too, that Mr. Du Ponceau was the first to announce the opinion, in the same work, that *piracy* might be committed on land as well as at sea; which principle was afterwards incorporated into the act of Congress on that subject.[77]

The Publisher

If not unique, then Du Ponceau's translation of Bynkershoek must be unusual among works on international law for having

---

the case on 6 March 1816, Pinkney appearing for the respondents and captors. See 14 U.S. 171, 1816 WL 1749 (U.S.N.Y.), 4 L.Ed. 63, 1 Wheat. 171.

[76] See Story, "Literature of the Maritime Law", in W. Story, note 24 above, II, p. 110.

[77] Pickering, note 9 above, p. 167.

appeared first in a journal for circulation in book format to all
subscribers with extra copies offered for sale to the general
public. So Du Ponceau relates in his Preface:

> It is, according to its first destination, published in and for
> the *American Law Journal* and will be delivered to its subscribers
> as the third number of the third volume of that publication; but
> a sufficient number of copies will also be struck off for such as
> may wish to possess it as a separate work.[78]

The publisher of the *American Law Journal*, John Elihu Hall
(1783-1829), originally, according to du Ponceau, expressed a
wish to publish the translation as a part of this periodical. As du
Ponceau relates, "the manuscript was accordingly handed over
to the printers of the Journal ... ".[79] This was the "first law review
ever to appear in the United States".[80] Hall would have appreciated the quality and importance of du Ponceau's translation, for
he himself produced major legal translations, among them: B.
M. Emérigon, *An Essay on Maritime Loans, with Notes, to which is
added an Appendix* (1811); "Commentaries of the Ordonnance
de la Marine", *Journal of Jurisprudence*, I (1821), 176, 123; and
substantial extracts from Justinian's Digest and Code.

His credo was well-stated in an advertisement for his *American Law Journal*:

> However the annals of our domestic jurisprudence
> might fail in the contribution of materials, we should be at no
> loss. The legal lore of former ages and foreign nations is an
> abundant treasury, to which the scientific lawyer can always

---

[78] Preface, pp. v-vi.

[79] Preface, p. v.

[80] Nadelmann, note 9 above, p. 250. The journal appeared from 1808 to 1817
inclusive; in 1821 Hall undertook the *Journal of Jurisprudence*, which did not
survive its first year.

resort for those abstract principles of right which are applicable at all times and in all places.[81]

Hall was born in Philadelphia, the eldest of ten children. He attended Princeton without completing a degree, returned to Philadelphia in 1804 and studied law with Joseph Hopkinson (1770-1842). He was admitted to the Bar in 1805. Six volumes of his *American Law Journal* appeared between 1808 and 1817, specializing in the publication of new decisions and statutes that were not readily available and the texts of foreign legal materials, usually of a commercial or maritime nature. Hall hoped to attract a general readership, not only legal professionals, and encouraged law reform in the direction of the harmonization of State and federal laws and the emergence of a more systematic national jurisprudence. He joined the American Philosophical Society in 1814. Between 1816 and 1827 he also edited the *Port Folio*, which his brother had purchased. Besides his translations enumerated above and a considerable number of literary works, Hall wrote *The Practice and Jurisdiction of the Court of Admiralty* (1809);[82] *Tracts on Constitutional Law, Containing Mr. Livingston's Answer to Mr. Jefferson* (1813); and *Office and Authority of a Justice of the Peace in the State of Maryland, to Which Is Added a Variety of Precedents in Conveyancing* (1815).[83] From 1813 he briefly held a professorship in the University of Maryland.

Du Ponceau contributed the introductory preface to the relaunched *Journal of Jurisprudence* with the hope that Hall would

---

[81] Quoted in P. Stein, "The Attraction of the Civil Law in Post-Revolutionary America", *Virginia Law Review*, LII (1966), p. 415.

[82] Comprised of three parts, the second part consisted of a translation of Francis Clerke, *Praxis Curiae Admiralitatis* (1679).

[83] See M. Bloomfield, "Hall, John Elihu", in *Dictionary of American Biography* (1999), IX, pp. 863-864.

continue his good work of publishing translations of foreign legal materials. Du Ponceau's vision was expressed with his customary eloquence:

> In the preceding volumes we were presented with several translations of valuable foreign works of jurisprudence, the originals of which are difficult to be procured. Among these we observe Bynkershoek's celebrated treatise on the Law of War, a collection of the titles of the Justinian code, which relate to the maritime law, and the ancient and venerable *Consolato Del Mare*, which Mr. Hall has only published in part, but of which he promises to give us soon the remainder, having completed the whole of the translation of that excellent work. We understand that the same plan is to be pursued in the future numbers of the Journal, by means of which, we shall successively become possessed of several interesting legal works which are either out of print, or otherwise not easily obtained in this country. Selected extracts will also be given out of heavy volumes which contain but little that is interesting to the profession, but which little is of value. Thus it has long been a *disideratum* among lawyers to see a separate publication, out of the two huge volumes of sir Leoline Jenkins, of such much of the works of that great judge as relates to admiralty and prize law. This we understand is to be done through the channel of the Law Journal.[84]

William Fry and Joseph Kammerer, Printers of the Bynkershoek and the *American Law Review*, were specialist publishers in Philadelphia of newspapers or periodicals.[85] They rarely, if ever, ventured into the publication of books on

---

[84] Du Ponceau, "Testimon, erudit, viror", *The Journal of Jurisprudence: A New Series of The American Law Journal*, I (1821), p. 5.
[85] See R. Remer, *Printers and Men of Capital: Philadelphia Book Publishers in the New Republic* (1996), p. 70.

their own. Records of the period show them located in Philadelphia at 15 North Seventh Street during 1807 and 1808, next door at No. 13 in 1809, and at Prune near Debtors Apartment from 1810 to 1812.[86]

The "Publishers" of Bynkershoek were bookseller-publishers led by William Powell Farrand (1777-1839) in Philadelphia in collaboration with Charles Nicholas and co-venturers in Boston, Baltimore, Albany, New York, Portland, Maine, and Middlebury, Vermont. This would be characterized in printing history as a "publishing combination" – a "method of financing and producing books that fit specifically the wholesale approach to publishing or the extension of publishing to a national market".[87] Partners in the combination obtained their books a cost or at a price lower than offered to other members of the trade. Literary fairs, commenced in 1802, operated as gatherings where publishers could network and personally meet co-venturers with whom they had corresponded by post. In the instance of Bynkershoek, the co-venturers covered the area thoroughly from Baltimore northwards to Maine and left the New York City and Washington D.C., as well as the southern markets, to presumably any of the venturers prepared to serve them by exchange, commission, or consignment (all methods of distribution widely used at the time by booksellers and publishers).

Farrand and Nicholas, "law booksellers and publishers", were located literally around the corner from du Ponceau's home, with a shop in October 1810 at the corner of Chestnut

---

[86] See H. Glenn Brown and M. O. Brown, *A Directory of the Book-Arts and Book Trade in Philadelphia to 1820, Including Printers and Engravers* (1950), p. 52.
[87] Remer, note 83 above, p. 87.

and Sixth Streets and during 1811-1812 at the northwest corner of Sixth and Chestnut, second door on Sixth Street.[88]

The appearance of Bynkershoek occurred in autumn 1810, commencing with the October/November issue of *American Law Journal*. Farrand and Nicholas, in the District of Pennsylvania, deposited with the Clerk the title of Bynkershoek on 8 October 1810; matters will have moved quickly, for Du Ponceau's Preface is dated October 1810. The book was being advertised in Baltimore by 25 November 1810 at the retail price of $2.50 by Philip H. Nicklin & Co., "opposite Gadsby's" as "Published This Day".[89]

Du Ponceau in the meantime was distributing copies to friends and colleagues. A copy held by the Harvard Law School inscribed from the "Editor to Thomas Cooper" and dated 22 November 1819 bears the bookplates of three subsequent owners: William Bell, Samuel P. Bell, and Samuel Seabury. The copy held by the American Philosophical Society, of which Du Ponceau later became the President, was presented by the author on 7 December 1810. Of an autumn appearance we can therefore be certain.

---

[88] Brown and Brown, note 84 above, p. 47.

[89] *Federal Republican & Commercial Gazette*, III, no. 383 (29 December 1810), p. 1, col. 4.

A
TREATISE

ON

THE LAW OF WAR.

Translated from the original Latin of
CORNELIUS VAN BYNKERSHOEK.

BEING

THE FIRST BOOK

OF HIS

QUÆSTIONES JURIS PUBLICI.

WITH NOTES,

BY PETER STEPHEN DU PONCEAU,

Counsellor at Law in the Supreme Court of the United States
of America.

—— Ne fortior omnia possit.—Ovid.

PHILADELPHIA:

Published by Farrand & Nicholas; also, by Farrand, Mallory & Co., Boston;
P. H. Nicklin & Co., Baltimore; D. Farrand & Green, Albany;
Lyman, Mallory & Co., Portland; and Swift &
Chipman, Middlebury, (Vt.)

Fry and Kammerer, Printers.
1810.

TABLE OF CONTENTS.

† a

TABLE OF CONTENTS.

PREFACE.

THE following translation was made several years ago for my own private use, and without any intention of ever publishing it. But Mr. *Hall*, the editor of the *American Law Journal*, having expressed a wish to insert it in that valuable periodical work, I freely consented to it, having no other idea at the time but that it should appear there as an anonymous performance. The manuscript was accordingly handed over to the printers of the Journal, and the first ten chapters were printed off, without undergoing any other corrections but such as occurred in revising the proof sheets, to which I subjoined a few short notes as I went along.

But while I was engaged in that occupation, I felt my ancient attachment to a favourite author revive; the subject grew upon me; I gave an attentive revisal to the remainder of the manuscript, and added to it a more copious body of notes; and I now, with diffidence, venture to present the result of my labours in my name to my brethren of the American bar. It is, according to its first destination, published in and for the *American Law. Journal*, and will be delivered to its subscribers as the third number of the third volume of that publication; but a sufficient number of copies will also be struck off for such as may wish to possess it as a separate work.

I need not explain to those who are conversant with the works of my author, that his *Quæstiones Juris Publici* are divided into two parts, entirely distinct from and unconnected with each other, otherwise than by being published together under one title, and by their general relation to subjects of public law. The first part, *De Rebus Bellicis*, treats exclusively of the law of war, and forms of itself a complete treatise on that particular subject. I have thought it best, therefore, to translate and publish it separately, under its appropriate title, *A Treatise on the Law of War.*

To expatiate on the merits of this excellent work would be useless. It is known and admired wherever the law of nations is acknowledged to have a binding force. Its authority is confessed in the cabinets of princes, as well as in the halls of courts of justice: to be unacquainted with it, is a disgrace to the lawyer and to the statesman. It ranks its author among the great masters of the law of nature and nations, with *Grotius*, *Puffendorff*, *Wolffius*, and *Vattel*. His range is not indeed so extensive as that of his illustrious colleagues; but he has more profoundly investigated and more copiously discussed than any of them the particular branch which he assigned to himself.

It is extraordinary that a treatise, the merit of which is so generally acknowledged, has not as yet been translated into any of the modern languages (the *Low Dutch* excepted), and that the *English*, particularly, who profess to admire it so much, have not favoured the world with a good translation of it into our common idiom. For we cannot consider as such the incorrect and incomplete version which in the year 1759 was, by the help of some interpolations, published by Mr. *Richard Lee*, as an original work, under the title of *A Treatise of Captures in War*, a second edition whereof appeared at London in 1803, in the preface to which the book is for the first time acknowledged to be an *enlarged translation* of the present work. The insufficiency of that performance to supply the place of our author's text is every where admitted; and the friends of science in this country have long expected that some of the learned civilians of Great Britain, a *Robinson*, a *Ward*, or a *Brown*, would present the world with an English translation of the treatise *De Rebus Bellicis*, executed in a manner worthy of its author. But this fond hope has unfortunately been disappointed.

No person has wished more anxiously than myself to see this translation performed by some one of the able professors whom I have just named, and who are so capable of doing it complete justice. Then my favourite author would have appeared in an *English* dress, with all the advantages which brilliant talents, combined with a profound knowledge of the science of which he treats, could have given him. The translation which I offer to the public cannot boast such high advantages; it claims no other merit but that of correctness, the only one which a translator cannot dispense with. To deserve this humble praise has been the object of my constant efforts. I have endeavoured to discover the precise English expressions which my author would have used, if he had written in our language. If sometimes I have shortened his long *Ciceronian* periods, and divided them into more convenient paragraphs; if sometimes, also, I have connected his phrases in a manner more suited, as I thought, to the idiom in which I wrote, I believe that I have done it without injury to the sense. Where my author narrates, I have endeavoured to state with fidelity the facts and events that he relates; where he argues, to convey the full force of his able and luminous reasoning, and I was sensible that it could not be done better, than by keeping as close to the text as possible. I have but in few instances wandered from this strict plan, and only where our author treats of local subjects, of little or no interest to the *American* reader. Of the few other liberties, which I have thought necessary to take in the course of this work, it is proper that I should give an account in this place.

I have shortened the titles of the several chapters, which in the original are presented in the shape of queries, to suit the modest-title of *Questions,* which is prefixed to the whole work. Considering this first part, as justly entitled to be considered a complete and regular *treatise* on the law of war, I have thought it my duty to present it as such to my readers, and to head its several divisions accordingly.

For the same reason, I have entitled the twenty fifth chapter, which in the original bears the title of " Various Small Questions," (*Variæ Quæstiunculæ*); Miscellaneous Maxims and Observations, for such they will appear to be; and I have headed each of the sections into which that chapter is divided, with the result of the observations that it contains, in the form of an *axiom* or *aphorism*, so that the reader may see at once the proposition which the author means to maintain or to illustrate in each of those subdivisions.

I have omitted the whole of the twenty third chapter and some parts of a few others, which are pointed out in notes in their several places, as treating of subjects which are local in their nature and application, and consequently, are neither useful nor interesting to us. I have, for the same reason, left out a great number of the references, which our author frequently makes to the *Dutch* statute books, and to some other national works, little or not at all known in this country. I have, however, preserved a few to some of the most noted among them, and particularly to *Aitzema*, whose *Chronicle* I consider as an excellent compilation of historical facts and documents, of which I have endeavoured to give a character in a note to page 15.

I have thrown into notes, in the fifteen last chapters, the numerous references which abound in the body of the original work. The first ten chapters being in the press, as I have already mentioned, when I began to revise this translation, I was prevented from doing the same with respect to them by the fear of giving to the printers too much additional trouble.

With regard to the notes which I have subjoined to the body of the work, and which, to distinguish them from those of the author, are marked *T.*, they are principally intended to elucidate and explain the text. Our author often slightly refers to facts which were well known, and some of them even remembered in his day; frequently, also, he alludes to particular texts of the civil law, and to the opinions of writers whose works were familiar to the civilians of *Europe* and of his country, but are little read among us. In every such instance, whenever it has been in my power, I have presented the reader, in a note, with the text or passage referred to; and where that could not conveniently be done, I have given such explanations as I thought would best enable him clearly to understand the scope and meaning of the observations or arguments of our author.

As I progressed in the work, I have added some other notes, which exhibit a comparative view of the

principles and practice of the different states of *America*
and *Europe* on various interesting points. In a few instances I have presumed to advance my own opinions,
and even in some of them to differ from my author himself; but I have done it, I am sure, in the spirit, and, I
hope, in the manner pointed out by the great orator,
quærens omnia, dubitans plerumque, et mihi diffidens.*

I have thought that an account of the life and writings
of *Bynkershoek* would not be unacceptable to the reader,
and therefore it will be found immediately after this
preface. I have added to it a brief alphabetical notice of
those writers on the civil law or the law of nations, whose
works are not generally known, and are quoted or referred to in this book. A list of the American and English
cases cited in the notes, and a table of reference to the
books and titles of the quotations from the text of the
civil law, which occur in the course of the original work,
are also subjoined. I regret that some errors of inadver-
tence have escaped my attention, particularly in the notes,
which I acknowledge, were written with some degree of
haste, though they are the result of much previous study
and reflection. Such of those errors as I have discovered
are noticed in an *errata*, at the end of the book.†

Being about to commit this work to the candour and
indulgence of the public, I have thought it necessary to
premise these few observations. It has long been, as I
have already observed, an anxious wish of the *American*
jurists to see this celebrated treatise correctly translated
into our language, and published in a portable form. It
is very difficult to procure in this country a copy of the

---

* Cic. acad. quæst. 1.

† To which add the following, which was not noticed at the
time: page 155, line 1, of the text, *dele* " whether."

original, which is only to be found in a few of our libraries. Nor can it be obtained from Europe, without purchasing at the same time two folio volumes, which contain a great deal of matter of little interest to those who do not make the civil law the object of their particular study. With the greatest diffidence, therefore, I submit this feeble attempt to the candid and enlightened judgment of my professional brethren; if it shall be thought deserving of their approbation, I shall consider it as an ample and honourable reward of my labours, otherwise I shall endeavour to profit by their censure.

At the present moment, when the fate of *Holland* creates a lively interest in every feeling mind, the public will be disposed to receive with peculiar indulgence, a work which recals to our memory the brilliant epochs of that celebrated republic, once so famed in arts as well as in arms. She has proved to the world, that the republican spirit of commerce, and the honourable pursuits of industrious enterprise are not incompatible with any of those more brilliant attainments by which nations as well as individuals are raised to celebrity. Since her separation from the *Spanish* empire she has produced more great men, and achieved more great deeds, than all the remainder of that once immense and powerful monarchy.

Holland is no more, but the remembrance of her past glory can never die. The admirers of military exploits will with pleasure and pride dwell on the achievements of her *Maurice*, her *De Ruyters*, and her *Van Tromps*. The statesman will still guide his political bark by the lights which her *De Witts*, her *Van Beuningens*, and her *Fagels* have supplied. The astronomer, the philosopher, will explore the secrets of nature and the heavens, with her *'sGravesandes* and her *Huygens*. The physician will improve his theory and his practice by the discoveries

† b

of her *Boerhaaves* and her *Van Swietens.* And the student, who delights in investigating the principles of that law of nations, so much talked of and so little practised, will ever revere the hallowed soil which gave birth to such illustrious men as *Grotius* and our BYNKERSHOEK.

His saltem accumulem donis & fungar inani
Munere.

Philadelphia, October, 1810.

AN ACCOUNT

LIFE AND WRITINGS

OF

THE AUTHOR.

CORNELIUS VAN BYNKERSHOEK was born the 29th of May 1673, at *Middleburgh*, the capital of the province of *Zealand*, where his father was a respectable, merchant. He received his education at the university of *Franeker* in *Friesland*, and his juvenile exercises while there, drew upon him the attention of the celebrated professor *Huberus*,* who in one of his elaborate dissertations, calls him *eruditissimus juvenis* CORNELIUS BYNKERSHOEK.† On leaving the university, he settled at the Hague, where he exercised with great applause the profession of an advocate, and published from time to time ingenious and learned dissertations on various subjects of the civil, and of his own municipal law. In the year 1702, he published his excellent dissertation *De Dominio Maris*, and the next year was appointed a judge of the Supreme Court of *Holland, Zealand*, and *West Friesland*, which sat at the *Hague*. In the year 1721, he published his learned treatise *De foro Legatorum*, and three years afterwards, on the 26th of May 1724, was appointed president of the respectable court, of which he already was a member. He was now fifty one years of age. His

---

* Well known in this country, by his dissertation *De Conflictu Legum*, part of which has been translated into *English*, and published by Mr. *Dallas*, in a note to the case of *Emory* v. *Greenough*, in the third volume of his Reports, page 370.

† *Huber. Eunomia Romana*, ad l. Lecta, D. de reb. cred.

celebrated *Quæstiones juris publici*, are among the last works that he produced, as they did not appear until the year 1737, when he was sixty four years old. He died of a dropsy in the chest, on the 16th of April 1743, in the seventieth year of his age. He was twice married. By his second wife he had no children, but left six daughters by his first wife.

His works consist chiefly of dissertations and treatises (which he modestly calls *questions*) on various subjects of the law of nations, and of the civil law, combined in some instances with the municipal regulations of his own country. They were published separately, in his lifetime, except the *Quæstiones juris privati*, which appeared only after his death. These are only a part of a larger work, which he did not live to finish. He had however prepared the four first books for the press, when death put a period to his labours. He had not even time to write more than the first paragraph of a preface, with which he intended to usher that work into the world, and in which he appears fully sensible of his approaching end.

Eighteen years after his death, his scattered writings were collected together by the learned *Vicat*,* professor of jurisprudence in the college of *Lausanne* in *Switzerland*, and published in two folio volumes at *Geneva*, in the year 1761. This edition is the only one, that we know of, of all the works of our author, though we are informed that some of his treatises have gone through several editions in his own country. The Baron *Von Ompteda*† notices a second edition of the *Quæstiones juris publici*, Leyden 1752, 4to. But this, the best and most complete monument of his fame, was published in a foreign land.

This edition is remarkable for its beauty and correctness, and is adorned with an elegant preface by the learned editor, and an account of the author's life and writings, from which we have in part gathered the information which we now communicate to the *American* reader.

* M. *Vicat* is the author of an esteemed treatise on natural law, entitled: *Traité du Droit Naturel & de l'application de ses principes au Droit Civil & au Droit des Gens.* Lausanne, 1782, 4 vols. 8vo. Baron Von Ompteda calls it a *very useful book.* Litter. des Vœlkerr. p. 389.

† *Litteratur des Vœlkerrechts*, p. 420.

We shall here give a brief notice of the several works of our author, which are contained in the collection of professor *Vicat*, although but few of them can be of any practical use in this country, yet we believe that a general idea of the whole will not be thought altogether uninteresting.

I. The first volume contains:

1. *Observationes juris Romani*, in eight books, in which a variety of curious points, relating to the ancient *Roman* jurisprudence, are ably discussed, several of which are interesting in an historical point of view, as elucidating through the medium of their laws, the manners and customs of that once great people. Among those, we notice the first chapter of the first book, in which the terrible *partis secanto* of the law of the twelve tables is ingeniously and plausibly maintained to have meant no more than that the insolvent debtor should be sold in the public market as a slave, and the proceeds of the sale distributed among his creditors. The 14th chapter of the third book discusses the question, how far and in what cases the military force could among the Romans be called in to the aid of the judicial authority. In the 4th book, chap. 13, the author comments on the 19th law of the digest *De ritu nuptiarum*, by which a father was obliged to give his daughter in marriage with a competent portion, if a suitable match offered; and if he refused, might be compelled to it by the magistrate. Various other subjects of an equally interesting nature to the scientific lawyer, are examined and discussed in the course of that work; of which we think it sufficient to have instanced a few, to give an idea of the general scope and object of the whole.

2. *Opuscula varii argumenti*. This work like the former, consists of dissertations on various subjects of the Roman law. They are six in number, the most interesting of which are the first, on the second law of the digest *De origine juris*, the third on the right which fathers had among the ancient Romans, of killing, selling, or exposing their children, and the fourth on the Roman laws, respecting foreign modes of worship. This last is replete with curious information, particularly with regard to the law which prevailed on that important subject, in the first ages of christianity.

3. This volume concludes with an answer to his learned

cotemporary *Gerard Noodt*, who had controverted some of the opinions which he had delivered in his above mentioned dissertation, on the power which fathers had at Rome over their children.

II. The contents of the second volume are as follow:

1. *Opera Minora*, consisting of six dissertations on various subjects, none of which will be thought very interesting in this country, except the 5th, *De Dominio Maris*, and the 6th, *De foro legatorum*. These, indeed, had he never written any thing else, would have been sufficient to establish our author's reputation as a lawyer, and a publicist. Every one who has read and understood, and of course admired them, cannot help finding fault with the excessive modesty which induced him to publish them under the inappropriate title of *opera minora*. The learned world has long classed them among the best works that have ever appeared on those generally interesting subjects.

In the dissertation *De Dominio Maris*, our author considers the long agitated question of the *Dominion of the Sea*, in a liberal and impartial manner, unbiassed by prejudice, and unswayed by party spirit. He calmly and dispassionately considers in what cases the sea is capable of becoming the subject of sovereignty or exclusive jurisdiction, discusses with candor the various pretensions which different states have set up from time to time to the dominion of that element, or of considerable portions thereof; and upon the whole, his conclusions are such as reason avows, and moderate men will ever be disposed to adopt.

His dissertation, or rather treatise *De foro Legatorum* is in every body's hands, in the excellent translation which Mr. *Barbeyrac* made of it into the *French* language, with notes, in which he has displayed his usual judgment and learning. That translation has not only received the approbation, but the praise of our author himself, with whom Mr. *Barbeyrac* was intimate. We shall therefore dispense with giving a more particular account of a work which is so well and so generally known. To name it is sufficient praise.

2. *Quæstiones juris publici*. This work is divided into two parts; the first of which, entitled *De Rebus Bellicis* is now presented in an *English* translation to the *American* public, under

its appropriate title of " *A Treatise on the Law of War;*" and a more complete one never yet has been written on this inte- resting subject. The *second* part which is entitled *De rebus va- rii argumenti*, treats of various subjects, some of them belong- ing to the law of nations, and others to the constitution and laws of the *United Netherlands.* From the 3d to the 12th chapter inclusive, our author treats of the law of *ambassadors*, and those chapters might well be added to the treatise *De foro Legatorum*, with the subject of which they are more nearly connected than with any other. In the *seventh* chapter he ex- amines the question, whether the acts of a minister are binding when *contrary to his secret instructions*. The 21st chapter treats of the salute to ships of war at sea, and seems to belong more properly to the dissertation *De Dominio Maris*, where the same subject is treated of. The remainder of the chapters, twenty- five in number, do not treat of any subject of general concern, and the whole of this second book is unconnected with the first, which is best exhibited as a separate and independent treatise on the *Law of War.*

The *Quæstiones juris publici* have been translated into the *Low Dutch* language by *Matthias Ruuscher*, in the year 1739. We do not know of any other translation of them into any language whatever, except that of the first book by Mr. *Lee* into *English*, of which we have made mention in the preface.

3. *Quæstiones juris privati.* This work, which was to have contained one hundred chapters, and contains only forty-eight, was left incomplete, as we have already mentioned, by the death of the learned author. It is divided into four books, chiefly on topics of the civil law and the municipal law of *Holland.* The fourth book alone, and the last chapter of the third, may be considered as interesting to the *American* jurist, as they treat of the subject of insurance, and of various points of the mari- time and commercial law. This work closes the second and last volume.

Our author also wrote two other considerable works, the one entitled *Corpus juris Hollandiæ & Zelandiæ*, and the other *Observationes Tumultuariæ* or *hasty notes*, being memoranda which he took from day to day, of the decisions of the court in which he sat for the space of forty years. He gave directions

by his will, to his executors, that those works should not be
published; and they strictly complied with his injunction.
As the ancient laws of *Holland* have been subverted, and the
Napoleon code introduced in their place, it is probable that
those writings, if published, would not be found of any great
use at the present time.

The character of our author's works has long been established among the learned of Europe. *Heineccius*, who, in the
year 1723, published at *Leipsick*, an edition of the four first
books of the *Observationes Juris Romani*, calls him in his preface to that work, " a man of consummate learning and ability,
possessing a sound discriminating mind, and an extraordinary
and incredible fund of legal knowledge."* *Barbeyrac*, in the
preface to his translation of the treatise *De foro Legatorum*,
describes him as one of that superior class of writers, whose
works are only intended for men of learning, and who, disdain-
ing to retail the opinions of others, are unwilling to say any thing
which has been observed before, and endeavour, as much as
they can, to exhibit their subject in some new point of view.
"And he is right;" continues he, " to have taken that ground.
One who possesses, within himself, such a rich fund of knowledge, may well leave it to others to borrow and repeat what
has already been said."† .

In *England*, the great Lord *Mansfield* thought him worthy
of his high commendation from the bench, and recommended
the work which we have translated, to the attention of the members of the *English* bar.* Since that time, our author's works
on the law of nations, (but particularly that which is now before us) have been considered as standard authorities, in *Great
Britain* as well as in the *United States*, and are daily quoted.

* *Admiratus præcipuè viri eruditissimi judicium acre, ingenium solers, juris
scientiam inusitatam ac denique incredibilem.*

† *Notre auteur est un de ces écrivains du plus haut vol, qui n'écrivent que pour
les savants, et qui ne veulent dire, autant qu'il se peut, rien que du nouveau. Et il a
raison de se mettre sur ce pied là. Quand on est si riche de son propre fonds, on
fait très bien de laisser à d'autres le soin d'emprunter ce qui a été déjà dit.*

* Lord *Mansfield* spoke extremely well of *Bynkershoek*, and recommended
especially, as well worth reading, his book of prizes, *Quæstiones juris publici*.
2 Bur. 690. *in margin*.

with respect by the bar, and relied on by the bench as the ground of their decisions.

Nor have our American statesmen been behindhand in commending the merit and talents of this eminent writer. Among them none has bestowed upon him more correct and judicious praise, than the great character, who is generally understood to be the author of the excellent *Examination of the British doctrine, which subjects to capture a neutral trade, not open in time of peace.* " *Bynkershoek,*" says he, " treats the subject of belligerent and neutral relations with more attention, and *explains his ideas with more precision* than any of his *predecessors.*"† How honourable to our author is this testimony, when we consider, on the one hand, by whom it is given; and reflect on the other, that in the list of those predecessors whom Mr. *Madison* speaks of, are found the celebrated names of *Puffendorff* and of *Grotius!*

It ought to be a great inducement to the study of the law of nations, that the fame of those who devote themselves to that important branch of science, extends throughout the civilized world; while the most excellent works on mere municipal jurisprudence, are hardly known or spoken of out of the country which gave them birth. Thus the writings of *Grotius, Bynkershoek,* and *Vattel,* are read and admired in all *America* and *Europe,* while the very names of *Coke* and *Dumoulin*‡ are unknown out of the countries where the particular systems of law are in force, which they took so much pains to methodize and elucidate. Of the truth of this observation, a striking instance is to be found in the works of our author, who from an opinion of lord *Coke,* which he had found quoted and misrepresented in Dr. *Zouch's* treatise *De jure inter gentes,* conceiving him to be a writer entirely ignorant of the law of nations, treated him and his opinion with the most marked contempt, calling him *a certain Coke,* (*Cocus quidam*); and punning upon his name, declared that he could not *concoct* his opinions,

† Examination, &c. p. 22.

‡ Styled the prince of the French Law—*le Prince du Droit François. Vie de Dumoulin, par* Blondeau.

† c

nor could they be *concocted* by the other writers on the law of nations.*

It is to be wished that this passage were expunged from our author's writings, particularly as it is, perhaps, the only time that he has indulged in such undignified language; and unfortunately he has applied it to a man whom of all others he would have admired, had his studies but led him to a perusal of his writings. Little did he know that that *Cocus quidam*, whom he so unjustly despised, was one whose powerful mind was in every respect congenial to his own; and yet he thought him unworthy of his serious notice, while he paid an unmerited attention to the works and opinions of such an inferior writer as Dr. Zouch. But *Zouch* had written on the law of nations, which is studied every where, and the great *Coke* had only elucidated the municipal law of *England*, which is not any where an object of attention, except in those countries where it is the established system of jurisprudence.

Unfortunately many of the works that have appeared on various subjects of the law of nations, are some of them polemical writings, written in the heat of a particular controversy, and on the spur of the occasion; and others, though professing to be on a more liberal scale, do nevertheless betray the partiality of their authors to the system adopted by the country in which they lived, or the governments under whose patronage they wrote: it is not so with the work which we now present to

---

* —— *eamque sententiam tuetur* Cocus QUIDAM *apud Zoucheum*, De jur: fec. p. 2. § 4. Q. 19. *Sed ego tàm difficilis stomachi sum, ut eam sententiam* concoquere *non possim, neque etiam* concoxit *Albericus Gentilis neque Zoucheus. Quæst. jur. pub.* l. 2. c. 5. The opinion that our author could not assent to is that which is expressed by Lord Coke in 4th Inst. 153. "*If a banished man* " *be sent as ambassador to the place from whence he is banished, he may not be* " *detained or offended there; and this also agreeth with the civil law.*" But he had not well considered that opinion, which appears a very sound one, and perfectly agrees with his own, which is, that such a minister indeed, may be sent out of the country; but that it would be a violation of good faith, to detain him and punish him for having returned, notwithstanding his sentence of banishment. But *Bynkershoek* viewed Lord *Coke* in the light in which he was exhibited to him by *Zouch*, who represented that great man as learned, indeed, in the municipal law of *England*, but ignorant of the law of nations. *Juris patrii consultissimus noster Eduardus Cocus; ejus quod cum exteris obtinet* NON ADEÒ PERITUS. Zouch, ubi supra.

the public; it was written at a time when *Europe* was in a state of profound peace, when there was no particular point warmly controverted between the *European* governments, and although the author was a Dutchman, and wrote in the bosom of his native country, yet we see that he did not even adopt the favorite doctrine, for which his government had been struggling during the space of near a century, that *free ships make free goods;* so that although many among us may not agree with him on this particular point, still we cannot withhold from him the praise of a strict and honest impartiality; and upon the whole, very few propositions will be found in the present treatise, to which all moderate and impartial men will not give their cordial and unfeigned assent.

ALPHABETICAL NOTICE

OF

SEVERAL WRITERS AND WORKS

ON THE

CIVIL LAW AND THE LAW OF NATIONS:
Not generally known, and which are quoted or referred to in this book.

ABREU *(the chevalier de)*. See note, p. 130.

AITZEMA *(Leo* or *Leeuwe)*. See note, p. 15.

BELLUS *(Petrinus)*, a *Venetian* writer, author of a dissertation *De re militari*, printed at *Venice* in 1563, 4to. It is to be found also in the 16th vol. of *Tractatus Tractatuum, seu Oceanus Juris;* an enormous work, being a collection of legal tracts, in 18 folio volumes, published at *Venice* in 1584, under the auspices of pope *Gregory* the 13th. It contains a multitude of writings on the civil and canon law, by jurists of the middle ages; some of them of so early a period as the sixth century. In this curious collection, there are several tracts which relate to subjects of the law of nations.

BOLAÑOS *(Juan de Hevia)*, a *Spanish* writer, a native of *Oviedo*, in the province of *Asturias*; author of an excellent institute of the law of *Spain*, entitled *Curia Philippica;* the last part of which treats of commercial and maritime law, and has been the foundation of many subsequent works upon that subject. *Roccus* has borrowed liberally from it. This work is remarkable for its clearness, brevity and precision, and lays down very sound and correct principles on the subject of maritime and commercial jurisprudence. The author informs us, that it was finished at the city of *Los Reyes*, in the kingdom of *Peru*, on Christmas eve, in the year 1615. It may therefore be considered as an *American* production. The edition before us, was printed at *Madrid*, 1783, in folio. It is a book of very great authority throughout the *Spanish* dominions, and in our territories of *Orleans* and *Louisiana*, and is often quoted by foreign writers, on subjects relating to maritime law.

BUDDÆUS (*John Francis*), a *German* professor at *Halle*, and afterwards at *Jena*, where he died in 1705. He was the author of several works, and among others, of a book entitled *Elementa Philosophiæ practicæ, instrumentalis & theoreticæ*, 3 vols. 8vo. the same which is so contemptuously referred to by our author, and was nevertheless formerly so celebrated, that the professors of the protestant universities of *Germany*, took it for the text of their lectures. He also wrote the great *German* historical dictionary, printed several times at *Basil* and *Leipsig*, in 2 vols. fol.

CLEIRAC, a *Frenchman*, author of a valuable work on maritime law, entitled *Les Us & Coutumes de la Mer*. It contains, 1. The text of the laws of *Oleron*, *Wisbuy*, and the *Hanse Towns*, with learned notes. 2. *Le Guidon de la Mer*, an ancient *French* treatise on maritime contracts, and principally on *Insurance*, divided into sections, in the form of an institute, and enriched with notes fraught with much curious learning. 3. The laws or ordinances of *Antwerp* and *Amsterdam*, concerning insurance. 4. A treatise on the *French* admiralty jurisdiction, and a copious index to the whole work. There have been several editions of this book; the first that we find any mention of, was printed in 1647; and the last at *Amsterdam*, in 1788.

CODE DES PRISES. This *French* work is well known in this country, but it is not generally understood that there are four editions of it, or rather four different works, all nearly on the same plan, but published at different periods; and containing more or less information on the important subject of *maritime captures.*

The first is the *Old Code des Prises*, by M. *Chardon*, who was secretary, under the monarchy, to the council of prizes at *Paris*. It is entitled *Code des Prises; ou recueil des Edits, Declarations, &c. depuis* 1400, *jusqu' à présent; Imprimé par ordre du Roi;* 2 vols. 4to. Paris, imprimerie royale, 1784.

The second is entitled *Code des Prises maritimes & armements en course, par le Citoyen G., homme de loi;* 2 vols. 12mo. *Paris, Garnery, an* 7.

The title of the third is *Nouveau Code des Prises, par le Cit. Le Beau*, 4 vols. 8vo. *Paris, Imprimerie de la République, ans* 7, 8 & 9. It is brought down to the 3d Prairial, 8th year, (23d of May, 1800.)

The fourth is entitled *Code des Prises & du Commerce de terre & de mer*, par F. N. Dufriche Foulaines, jurisconsulte; 2 vols. 4to.

small close print. *Paris, Duprat du Verger,* 1804. It is more copious and complete, and is brought down to a later period, than any of the others.

Consilia Belgica is a collection of official opinions given to the states general of the *United Netherlands,* by the law officers of that government.

Consilia Hollandica, are the opinions of the law officers of the provincial states of *Holland* and *West Friesland,* collected in like manner.

Consolato del Mare. This celebrated work is but little known in this country, owing to the difficulty of procuring it from abroad, and to its being written in languages not generally understood. The forty three first chapters have been translated from the *Amsterdam* edition, by *Westerveen,* and published in the *American Law Journal,* (vol. ii. p. 385, and vol. iii. p. 1.) but they relate only to the form of judicial proceedings in the maritime courts of the kingdom of *Majorca,* and are thought by many not to belong to the ancient *Consolato.*

The oldest edition of this work has lately been discovered by Mr. *Boucher,* in the Imperial library at *Paris.* It is embodied with the marine ordinance of *Barcelona,* of which it constitutes the principal part, and was printed in that city, in the *Catalonian* language, in the year 1494, thirty-seven years only after the discovery of the art of printing. Mr. *Boucher* has favoured the public with a translation of it into the *French* language, printed at *Paris* in 1808, several copies of which have already made their way into this country. Mr. *Hall,* of *Baltimore,* (to whom the profession is already indebted for a very good translation of the *Praxis Curiæ Admiralitatis,* enriched with learned and useful notes,) is, we understand, at present employed in translating it into the *English* language, which will entitle him to the thanks, not only of the scientific, but also of the *practical* lawyer. That excellent book has been styled, with great propriety, the *Pandects of maritime law.*

A copy of the beautiful edition of the *Consolato,* published at *Madrid,* in 1791, in the *Catalonian* language, with a *Spanish* translation, by *Don Antonio de Capmany y de Monpalau,* is in the library of the *American Philosophical Society,* to whom it was presented by his excellency, the marquis de *Casa Yrujo.*

Cunæus or *à Cunæo* (*Gulielmus*) author of a small treatise on *Suretiship* (*De materia securitatis*). See Mercatura (*De*).

Curia Philipica, See Bolaños.

CYNUS or *Cino*, was a learned *Italian* lawyer, who flourished in the beginning of the 14th century. He died at *Bologna*, in 1336. He wrote a commentary on the *Code*, and some parts of the *Digests*.

GALIANI (the abbé *Ferdinando*), is a celebrated *Neapolitan* writer. He was secretary to the *Neapolitan* legation at *Paris*, and afterwards a member of the Royal Council of Commerce in his own country. In the year 1782, he published at *Naples*, his treatise *De' doveri de' Principi neutrali verso i Principi guerreggianti, e di questi verso i neutrali; (Of the duties of neutral and belligerent princes towards each other.)* It was translated into *German* by professor *Kœnig*, and published at *Leipsick*, in two octavo volumes, in 1790, under the title of *Recht der Neutralität (the law of Neutrality.)* The life of *Galiani* has been written and published at *Naples*, by *Diodati*, in 1788. See LAMPREDI.

GAMA (*Antonio de*), born at *Lisbon* in 1520; was counsellor of state, and high chancellor to the king of *Portugal*. He wrote, among other things, a book of reports of *Portuguese* decisions, entitled, *Decisiones Supremi Lusitaniæ Senatus*, in folio. He died in 1595, at the age of 75 years, greatly respected for his immense erudition.

GENTILIS (*Albericus;*) born in the marquisate of *Ancona*, in the *Roman* state, about the year 1550; was professor of the civil law at *Oxford*, and died at *London* in 1608. He published a treatise, *De jure belli*, in three books, which has not been useless to *Grotius*, and in which, at that early day, he supported the belligerent claims of *Great Britain*, against the pretensions of neutrals. *Lampredi*, in his preface, says, that he was the first who endeavoured to introduce a system of jurisprudence amidst the din of arms. Although he may be properly considered as an *English* writer, it is remarkable that his name does not appear in the *Bibliotheca Legum Angliæ.*

GRONOVIUS (*John Frederick*), was born at *Hamburgh*, in 1611, and was professor of literature at *Deventer*, and afterwards at *Leyden*, where he died in 1672. He published many valuable editions of Latin authors, and among others of *Grotius*, *De jure belli ac pacis*, with learned annotations. His son, *James Gronovius*, distinguished himself likewise, by several works of learning and erudition.

GUIDON DE LA MER (*Le*). See CLEIRAC.

HORNE (*Thomas Hartwell*), an *Englishman;* is the author of an useful work, entitled: *A compendium of the statute laws and regulations of the court of admiralty, relative to ships of war, privateers, prizes, recaptures and prize money; with an appendix of notes, pre-*

cedents, &c. 168 pages, duodecimo; *London, Clarke,* 1803. This book is scarce in *America.*

IMOLA (*Joannes de*), was professor of the civil law, at *Bologna,* in the *Papal* states, and a disciple of the elder *Baldus.* He composed a great number of professional works, which were much admired in his day, but are at present no longer read. He died in 1436.

KOCH, a *Frenchman,* professor of law at the university of *Strasburgh,* and member of the national institute, is the author of an excellent work in the *French* language, entitled, *Abregé de l'Histoire des Traités de paix entre les puissances de l'Europe, depuis la paix de Westphalie, Basil* 1796. 4 vols. 8vo.

LAMPREDI, was a professor of the law of nations, at the university of *Pisa* in *Tuscany.* He published at *Florence,* in the year 1788, his *Trattato del commercio de' popoli neutrali in tempo di guerra,* (*a treatise on the commerce of neutral nations in time of war.*) It has been translated into *German,* by professor *Kœnig, Leipsig,* 1790; and into *French,* by M. *Peuchet, Paris,* 1802, one vol. octavo. M. *Peuchet* tells us, that the ministry of Louis XVI. had ordered a translation of this work to be made, but it was not executed during his reign.

Lampredi combats on many points, the doctrines of *Galiani,* whose book is written in favour of the freedom of the neutral flag, while his opponent supports the opposite doctrine, so strenuously contended for by *Great Britain.* These two works were written at the close of the *American* war; the one at *Naples,* which was at that time under *French,* and the other in *Tuscany,* which was under *British* influence. See GALIANI.

LOCCENIUS (*Johannes*), author of a valuable treatise in three books, entitled, *De jure maritimo & navali.* It has been published by *Heineccius,* together with *Stypman's Jus maritimum & nauticum,* and *Kuricke's Diatribe de Assecurationibus,* under the title of *Scriptorum de jure nautico & maritimo Fasciculus,* in two vols. 4to. *Hal. Magdeb.* 1740.

MARQUARDUS (*Johannes*), a *German,* is the author of a very learned treatise on mercantile law, in the Latin language, entitled, *Tractatus politico-juridicus de jure mercatorum & commerciorum singulari,* in 4 books, printed at *Frankfort,* in 1662, *folio,* 1316 pages. It contains a number of public documents, historical facts, and other valuable information.

MENOCHIUS (*James*), a lawyer of *Pavia,* in *Italy,* was so learned, that he was called the *Baldus* and *Bartholus* of his age; no contemptible names among the civilians. He was president of the superior court of *Milan*, and died in 1607, at the age of 75. Among a variety of professional works which he published, and were much read in his time, he wrote a treatise in folio, *De arbitrariis Judicum quæstionibus & causis conciliorum,* which is the work to which our author refers in his 25th chapter, page 196.

MERCATURA (*De*), a large and valuable collection of treatises and dissertations, by various authors of different nations, on subjects of maritime and commercial law. It is entitled, *De Mercaturâ, Decisiones & Tractatus varii & de rebus ad eam pertinentibus,* 1 vol. fol. *Colon.* 1622. It contains, amongst other things, the treatises of *Straccha* and *Santerna*, and the little tract of *Cunæus,* mentioned in this book; (See STRACCHA, SANTERNA, CUNÆUS.) It contains also, a collection of the decisions of the court of *Rota* of *Genoa*, on subjects of mercantile law, to the number of 215, much in the manner of our common law reports: *See Ingersoll's Roccus, p. 53. in not.* The remainder consists of a number of other tracts on similar subjects, by various authors, which, as they are not mentioned in this book, we think it unnecessary to notice here.

MORNAC (*Anthony*), a *French* advocate, who died in the year 1619. He wrote a great number of professional works, which were published at *Paris*, in 1724, in four vols. *folio.* He was a man of great erudition.

NOODT (*Gerardus*), of *Nimeguen*, was a *Dutch* professor, whose writings on the *Roman* law, are in very great repute among the civilians. His works have been edited by *Barbeyrac*, the celebrated commentator of *Puffendorff* and *Grotius*, and printed at *Leyden*, in two *folio* volumes, under the title of *Gerardi Noodt, Noviomagi, Jurisconsulti & Antecessoris, opera omnia. Lugd. Bat,* 1760.

OMPTEDA (*Henry Lewis*, Baron *von*), was ambassador of the king of *Great Britain*, as elector of *Hanover* and duke of *Brunswick-Lunenburg*, to the Diet of *Ratisbon*, and his minister plenipotentiary to the electoral court of *Munich*. He is the author of an excellent work in the *German* language, entitled, *Litteratur des gesammten sowohl natürlichen als positiven Völkerrechts,* or *Literature of the natural and positive law of nations; Munich,* 1785, 2 vols. 8vo. It is a biographical, critical and bibliographical notice of the various authors who have written on the law of nations, and of their works, down to the time of its publication, arranged in a very methodical order.

ROCCUS (*Franciscus*), a *Neapolitan*, author of the celebrated

NOTABILIA *de navibus et naulo; item de assecurationibus*. An excellent *English* translation of this well known work, the original of which is very scarce, has been lately published, with valuable notes, by *Joseph Reed Ingersoll*, esq. counsellor at law of this city; one vol. 156 pages, octavo; *Philadelphia, Hopkins and Earle*, 1809. This translation is executed with great judgment and accuracy, and may, in our opinion, well supply the place of the original.

SANTERNA, (*Peter*) a *Portuguese* writer, author of a treatise upon Insurance, entitled, *Tractatus de assecurationibus & sponsionibus Mercatorum*. See MERCATURA (*De*).

STRACCHA (*Benvenuto*), an *Italian* writer, author of a valuable treatise on the law of merchants, entitled, *De Mercaturâ, seu Mercatore*. See MERCATURA (*De*).

US ET COUTUMES DE LA MER. See CLEIRAC.

VALIN (*René Josué*), was born at *Rochelle*, in *France*, where he exercised the profession of an advocate, and was king's attorney, in the court of admiralty, and in the municipal court. He was also a member of the academy of that city, where he died in 1765. His celebrated commentary on Louis XIV.'s *Ordonnance de la marine*, published at *Rochelle*, in 1760, in two vols. 4to. is well known in the *United States*; but few are acquainted in this country with his *Treatise on Captures*, published at the same place, in 1763, in one vol. 8vo. This excellent work, worthy of the high reputation of its author, is unfortunately out of print; the copy which we have in our possession, was the last which remained two years ago in the bookseller's store, at *Rochelle*. It is to be hoped that a new edition of it will soon be published.

VERWER (*Adriaan*), author of a work in the *Low Dutch* language, entitled, *Nederlants See Rechten, Averyen en Bodemeryen* or *The maritime law of the Netherlands, and the law of average and bottomry*. It contains, 1. The laws of *Wisbuy*, and the ordinance of *Amsterdam*, with notes. 2. Several ordinances of the *Spanish* kings, sovereigns of the *Netherlands*. 3. A treatise on the law of bottomry. 4. A treatise on average, by *Quintijn Weijtsen*, with an index to the whole. The edition before us was printed at *Amsterdam*, in 1764.

ZENTGRAVIUS (*John Joachim*), was professor of divinity at *Strasburg*, and wrote in 1684, a dissertation, entitled, *De origine, veritate & obligatione juris gentium*, in which he maintained against *Puffendorff*, the existence of a *positive law of nations*; a controversy which called forth the abilities of several writers at that time, but at this day appears little more than a dispute about words. *Zent-gravius* also wrote a dissertation on *Commerce between neutrals and belligerents.* Strasb. 1690.

ZOUCH (*Richard*), an *Englishman*, born in 1590, in *Wiltshire*, was professor of civil law in the university of *Oxford*, and was made judge of the high court of admiralty, by Charles II. at the restoration, in 1660. He wrote some elementary tracts on the civil law, and distinguished himself in the celebrated controversy which took place in that reign, on the subject of admiralty jurisdiction, and was principally managed on the part of the civilians, by himself, Dr. Exton, and Dr. Godolphin. He wrote a treatise on the law of nations, entitled, *Juris & Judicii Fecialis sive juris inter gentes & quæstionum de eodem explicatio*, in which he does little more than retail the opinions, and often copies the very words of *Grotius.* Although this work is frequently quoted by our author, he appears to have been sufficiently sensible of its want of real merit. It was published at *London*, in 1650, in 4to.; and at the *Hague*, in 1659, in 16mo.

A TABLE

AMERICAN AND ENGLISH CASES,

CITED OR REFERRED TO IN THE NOTES.

Note: Those printed in italics are *American* cases.

	Page
AMITIE (L')	145
Atlas (the)	111
Bell v. Gilson	167
Blaireau (the)	156
Brandon v. Curling	172
———— v. Nesbitt	167
Bristow v. Towers	167
Cheline's case	134
Casseres v. Bell	195
Dempsey v. Ins. Co. of Penn.	169
Diana (the)	105
Donaldson v. Thompson	169
Emmanuel (the)	111
Flore (the)	145
Fortuna (the)	105
Franklin (the)	99
Furtado v. Rogers	172
Glass & Gibbs v. the Betsey	136
Grange (the)	61
Henckle v. Royal Exch. Ass. Co.	166
Hendrick & Maria (the)	38, 115
Herstelder (the)	38
Hollingsworth v. the Betsey	136
Hoop, Cornelius, (the)	166, 167
Hudson v. Guestier	38
Immanuel (the)	111
Jonge Tobias (the)	96, 99
Kellner v. Lemesurier	172

TABLE

REFERENCE,

To enable the reader to find in their numerical order, and by the books to which they respectively belong, the several titles of the *Institutes*, *Digests*, and *Code*, quoted in this work.

INSTITUTES.

De rerum divisione & adquirendo ipsarum dominio. Lib. 2. tit. 1.

DIGESTS.

☞ *The titles in italics are translated into English in the American Law Journal.*

De adquirendo rerum dominio, lib. 41. tit. 1.

captivis & postliminio, lib. 49. tit. 15.

collegiis & corporibus, lib. 47. tit. 22.

distractione pignorum, lib. 20. tit. 5.

exercitoriâ actione, lib. 14. tit. 11. (2 *Am. Law Journ.* 462.)

institoriâ actione, lib. 14. tit. 3.

jure Fisci, lib. 49. tit. 14.

nautico fœnore, lib. 22. tit. 2. (3 *Am. Law Journ.* 158.)

noxalibus actionibus, lib. 9. tit. 4.

origine juris, lib. 1. tit. 2.

publicanis & vectigalibus, lib. 39. tit. 4.

ritu nuptiarum, lib. 23. tit. 2.

Locati, conducti, lib. 19. tit. 2.

Si quadrupes pauperiem fecisse dicatur, lib. 9. tit. 1.

CODE.

De legibus, & constitutionibus principum, lib. 1. tit. 14.

naufragiis, lib. 11. tit. 5.

Ne uxor pro marito, &c. conveniatur, lib. 4. tit. 12.

☞ The four works which compose the body of the civil law, to wit: the *Institutes*, *Digests*, *Code* and *Novels*, are divided into *Books*, *Titles*, *Laws* and *Sections* or *paragraphs*, and are generally quoted by the *English* civilians, by referring to those divisions, as for instance, *Dig. l.* 1. *tit.* 4. *l.* 5. § 7., and sometimes *Dig.*, *D.*, or *ff.* 1. 4. 5. 7., for *Digest*, *Book* 1., *Title* 4., *Law* 5., *Section*, or *Pa-ragraph* 7. The civilians on the continent of *Europe*, on the con-trary, quote the heading of each title, and then refer only to the numerical subdivisions of *law* and *paragraph;* sometimes even, they quote the first words of the *law*, and refer to the *paragraph* only by its number. Thus our author, page 41, refers generally to the law *non omnium*, which is the twentieth *law* of the third *title* of the first *book* of the *Digests*. The references in this work being all by the heading of the *title*, and not referring to its *number*, or to that of the *book* in which it is contained, the foregoing table is presented to our readers, that they may with greater ease turn to the several titles of the books of the *Roman* law, which are quoted, or referred to in the course of this work.

ON THE

LAW OF WAR.

CHAPTER I.

Of War in general.

WHEN *Cicero* said, l. 1. *de Offi.* c. 11., *that there are two kinds of contests between men, the one by argument, and the other by force,* by the latter of these he undoubtedly meant *war;* though he did not intend, as *Grotius* would have it,* to give thereby a definition of that state of things. Such a definition would be imperfect, as is clearly that of *Albericus Gentilis*, who defines war, l. 1. *de Jure Bell.* c. 2., *a just contention of the public force.* Both these definitions, although the first and the least perfect is approved of by *Grotius*, are defective; and the reader will be convinced of it by attending to the following which I have myself attempted, and which, if I mistake not contains all the ingredients which constitute a state of war. WAR, then, *is a contest carried on between independent persons, by force, or fraud, for the sake of asserting their rights.* Let us now proceed to examine it in detail.

I have said that war is *a contest.* By this word I have not meant to express merely the act of fighting, but that state of things which is called war; for if the thing itself be defined with sufficient accuracy, its incidents will necessarily follow. Thus jurists have defined slavery, not merely the act by which freemen are subjected to the dominion of others, but the very state and condition of servitude. *Grotius* himself has attended to this distinction in his definition of war, which he borrowed from *Cicero.*

* De Jure B. ac P. l. 1. c. 1. § 2. n. 1.

† A

War is also a contest *between independent persons.* This applies not only to nations, but to individuals not living in a state of society; for both are equally independent. Nor can this war between individuals be called a private war; because the word *private* can only be used in contra-distinction to the word *public,* which cannot apply where there exists no society. Wherever men are formed into a social body, war cannot exist between individuals; the use of force between them is not *war,* but a trespass, cognisable by the municipal law. Thus, if I extort from my debtor the ten pieces which he owes me, I incur the penalty of the Julian law against private force; because beating and wounding do not alone constitute *force* in the sense of the prohibition, but it applies to every case in which a man obtains even what belongs to him, by any other than legal means. *L. 7. ff. ad L. Jul. de vi privatâ.*

War is a contest *by force.* I have not said by *lawful force,* for in my opinion, every force is lawful in war. Thus it is lawful to *destroy* an enemy, though he be unarmed and defenceless; it is lawful to make use against him of poison, of missile weapons, of firearms, though he may not be provided with any such means of attack or defence; in short, every thing is lawful against an enemy. I know that *Grotius** is of a different opinion with regard to the use of poison, and that he distinguishes between the different kinds of missile weapons.† I know that *Zouch,* who hardly ever decides upon any point, is in doubt upon this question.‡ But if we take for our guide nature, that great teacher of the law of nations, we shall find that every thing is lawful against an enemy as such. We make war because we think that our enemy, by the injury that he has done us, has merited the destruction of himself and of all his adherents. As this is the object of our warfare, it is immaterial what means we embrace to accomplish it. A judge will not be called unjust who orders a convicted criminal to be put to death by the sword of the executioner, though he be unarmed and bound with chains; for if

* L. 3. c. 4. § 15.   † § 18.   ‡ Part 2. § 10. Q. 5 & 6.

he should unbind and arm him, it would no longer be the
punishment of a crime, but a trial of courage and good fortune. If you think that you ought only to make use of the
same weapons against your enemy that he himself makes use
of against you, you must at the same time be of opinion, that
his cause is equally good with your own, and therefore that he
is entitled to the same advantages. But on the contrary, your
enemy stands with respect to you, in the situation of a condemned culprit; and so indeed you stand with respect to
him; though in the eyes of third persons, who are friends to
both parties, your cause and his are equally just, and you are
both equally in the right.

Nor ought *fraud* to be omitted in a definition of war, as it
is perfectly indifferent whether stratagem or open force be
used against an enemy. There is, I know, a great diversity of
opinion upon this subject: *Grotius* quotes a variety of authorities on both sides of the question.* For my part, I think
that every species of deceit is lawful, perfidy only excepted;
not that any thing may not lawfully be done against an enemy,
but because, when a promise has been made to him, both parties are devested of the hostile character as far as regards that
promise. And indeed when the reason of war admits of every
mode to destroy an enemy, we cannot account for so many
authorities and precedents against making use of fraud or deceit, but that as well the writers on the law of nations as the
leaders of armies improperly confound *justice*, which is the
object of our present inquiry, with *generosity*, which is not
uncommon among warriors. Justice in war is indispensable;
but generosity is altogether a voluntary act. That leaves us at
liberty to destroy an enemy by every possible means; this
grants to him every thing that we would wish to be granted to ourselves in the like case; and thus war is carried on as
a duel formerly was in those countries in which that mode of
terminating differences was admitted. Justice permits the use
of numerous armies, of machines, firearms and other imple-

* L.. 3. c. 1. § 6. &c.

ments of war, that the enemy is not possessed of; while generosity, on the other hand, forbids it. Justice permits every
kind of deceit, except perfidy, as I have before mentioned;
generosity does not admit of it, perhaps even though it be employed by the enemy; for cunning is a token of fear, while the
magnanimous mind is never afraid. St. *Augustine* says,*
" that when a just war is undertaken, it is of no consequence
whether it be carried on by fraud or open force." This
clearly applies to justice, and it is in fact justice that he treats
of. But when the *Roman* consuls wrote to king *Pyrrhus:*
" *We do not wish to contend with you by means of bribery or
fraud,*"† and at the same time gave him notice of the offer that
had been made to them to poison him, they certainly did an
act of the greatest generosity.‡ Many nations have often
preferred generosity to justice; others have preferred justice
to generosity: the *Romans* themselves sometimes displayed
the one, sometimes the other. If then, as I have said before,
authorities and precedents are reconciled, the point will be
clearly settled by recollecting that *justice* may always be insisted upon, though *generosity* may not.

Lastly, the definition says, *for the sake of asserting their
rights.* That is to say, in order to defend or recover what is
our own; for that is the sole *cause*, though I do not mean to
say that it is the *end* or *object*, of war. A nation which has injured another, is considered, with every thing that belongs to
it, as being confiscated to the nation that has received the injury. To carry that confiscation into effect may certainly be
the object of the war, if the injured nation thinks proper; nor
is the war to cease as soon as she has received a reparation or
equivalent for the injury suffered. The whole commonwealth,
and all the persons as well as the things contained within it,
belong to the sovereign with whom we are at war, and in the
same manner as we may seize upon the person and upon all

* Quæst. 10. in Josua.   † Aul. Gell. l. 3. c. 8.

‡ The *British* government acted with equal generosity, when, by their
minister, Mr. *Fox*, they gave notice to the first consul of *France*, of the offer
which had been made to them to assassinate him.   *T.*

the property of our debtor, so a sovereign in war may seize
the whole of the subjects and dominions of his enemy. It is
true that we can recover no more of a debtor than what he actually
owes us; but in war all social ties are dissolved between
states. We make war to subdue the enemy and all that belongs
to him, by occupying every thing which belongs to the sovereign
of the hostile country, and exercising dominion over all
the men and things that are contained within his territories;
for war is of so general a nature that it knows no measure or
bounds.*

* The Translator has taken the liberty to transpose this paragraph for the
sake of perspicuity. As it stands in the original, it ought to come in at the
beginning of page 2, of this translation, but as it explains the *last* member
of our author's definition, it seems best placed at the end.　　*T.*

CHAPTER II.

Of a Declaration of War.

MANY things are required by writers on the law of nations in order to make war lawful, and particularly, they
think it necessary that it be publicly declared, either by a special proclamation or manifesto, or by sending a herald. This
opinion certainly accords with the practice of the modern nations of *Europe*, and it is perfectly clear, that before recourse
can be had to arms, a demand of satisfaction should be made
for the injury complained of. But this is not the question now
before us; it is whether after a reparation has been demanded
and-refused, war can be immediately made without a previous
declaration?

*Albericus Gentilis** is of opinion that it cannot; that a
war ought not to be secretly commenced, and that the
adverse party's friendship is to be publicly renounced. It
is true that by the law of nature there is no necessity for a
declaration of war. *Grotius*† is of that opinion and quotes
several authorities in support of it. He contends only that the
law of nations requires that a demand should be made, by
which it may appear that the party is forced into a war by the
refusal of a satisfaction which cannot be otherwise obtained.
As to declarations of war,‡ he thinks they have been introduced in order that it should appear that the hostilities which
are committed are the acts of the whole nation, or of the sovereign, and not merely of daring individuals. *Puffendorff*§ and
Huberus‖ are of the same opinion, and support it by the same
arguments. Other writers, and among them *Gentilis*¶ and
Zouch,** think that a declaration of war is necessary, but that
it may be dispensed with in certain cases. *Hertius*†† does

---

* De Jure Bell. l. 2. c. 1.——† L. 3. c. 3. § 6. n. 1, & 2.——‡ C. 3. § 11.——
§ De Jure N. & G. l. 8. c. 6. § 9. 15.——‖ De Jure Civitatis, l. 3. § 4. c. 4. n.
27.——¶ De Jure Belli, l. 2. c. 2.——** De Jure int. gent. P. 2. § 10. Q. 1.
——†† Adnot. ad Pufend. l. 8. c. 6. 9.

not deny that the custom of declaring war has been handed down to us by the *Germans*, but at the same time he is of opinion, that that custom is not obligatory, and that nothing can be said of those who do not conform to it but that they are not to be considered as the most civilized nations.

Christian Thomasius,* a man of sound judgment, considers, in my opinion very properly, a declaration of war as an act of mere humanity, to which no one can be compelled; and he asks, with reason, what difference there is between a war that has and one that has not been declared, and whether there is a different law for the one and for the other? He does not agree with *Grotius*,† who, quoting a passage from *Dion Chrysostom* "that wars most frequently take place without a previous declaration," is of opinion that such wars are lawful only by the law of nature. On the contrary, he asserts that they are justified by the law of nations, and immediately afterwards he adds, that this is a question of so interesting a nature that it deserves to be made the subject of a special dissertation.

I shall not, however, undertake to write a dissertation upon it, but I shall devote to its investigation the contents of the present chapter. My opinion is that a declaration of war is not necessary, and that it is one of those things which may very properly be done, but which cannot be insisted upon as a matter of right. A war may begin by mutual hostilities as well as by a declaration. The states-general appear to have understood it so, when by their ordinance of the 17th of *January* 1665 they declared, that the *Dutch* ships taken by the *English* might be claimed, because they had been captured before a declaration of war, and *before the commencement of hostilities on the part of the Dutch*. War may be justly begun upon the denial of a just demand; for how does that differ from actual hostility? I admit, in the fullest extent, that it is necessary in the first instance to make a demand of what we conceive to be due to us, but not that we are to accompany that demand with threats of hostility, or with an actual de-

* Ad Huberum de Jure Civitat. l. 3. § 4. c. 4. n. 27.   † Ibid. § 6. n. 1.

claration of war. What *Grotius* says about *interpellatio* applies
to a demand only; but what he says afterwards about a public
declaration, *denunciatio*, cannot be applied in like manner. Nevertheless, it was from his and other's prejudices, although not
at all consonant to reason, that this subject, otherwise very clear,
began to become obscure. Yet it must have been evident, that
where there is no judge between the parties, as is the case
with princes, every one may forcibly retake that which belongs to him and has been unjustly taken away from him by
another, who refuses to make restitution. This being the case,
every one is at liberty to make or not as he pleases a declaration of war; the necessity of such a solemnity can only have
been established by an agreement which between nations has
no obligatory force.*

Nations however, and princes, who are impressed with
sentiments of magnanimity, are not willing to make war without a previous declaration. They wish by an open and manly
attack to render victory more glorious and more honourable. But here I must repeat the distinction between justice and
generosity, which I have laid down in the preceding chapter: the former permits the use of force without any previous
notice; the latter considers every thing in a nobler point of
view, deems it inglorious to subdue an unarmed and unpre-
pared enemy, and considers it an unworthy act to attack and
despoil of a sudden those who have come among us on the
faith of the public peace, which happens to be suddenly
broken, perhaps without their fault. Hence *Polybius*, l. 13.
c. 1., praises very highly the custom of declaring war, which
was peculiar to the *Achaians* and to the *Romans*, and he
praises them in the same manner for abstaining from fraud
and deceit in war; but his praise in both instances is due only
to their generosity.

Speaking of the *Achaians*, *Polybius* adds, that they had also
appointed a particular place to fight their battles in, precisely

---

* *Non nisi conventione, quæ inter Gentes nulla est.* Our author probably
means here that such an agreement has no force, *except between the parties
to it;* otherwise, he would appear at variance with himself. See pp. 3. 13. 17.
           T.

as we read of certain counts of *Holland,* who in ancient times, when they intended to go to war, not only gave notice of it by a public declaration, but appointed the time and place of combat. This appointment of time and place *Grotius** himself acknowledges to be unnecessary, and yet he urges a declaration as if it were indispensable. If you inquire into the reason of this difference, you will find no other but that it is not at present customary in *Europe* to appoint the time and place of combat. Whence it appears, that *Grotius,* in writing his book on the law of war and peace, has not so much written of the universal law of nations, as of the customs and manners of most of the *European* countries, which, as he himself teaches us,† do not constitute the law of nations. But on other points as well as on the present he has extracted the law of nations from customs and manners alone; so that when he has found these to differ on any particular question, he has hardly ever ventured to decide upon it.

From what *Polybius* said, however, that it was an honour peculiar to the *Achaians* and *Romans* that they did not make war without a previous declaration, we sufficiently understand that what is said by *Dion Chrysostom,* that war is *most frequently* NOT *declared*‡, is certainly true; not merely because it is not required by the law of nature, but because such is the custom or usage of nations. And indeed a declaration of war was not so frequent among other nations, as among the *Romans* and *Achaians.* Nor was such a declaration made by either party when the other nations of *Greece* waged war with the barbarians or with one another; nor do we read of the *Jews,* who went to war by *God's* command, that they ever declared war against their enemies. Neither did the *Macedonians* make a public declaration of *war when they destroyed

---

* L. 3. c. 3. § 11.　　　　† L. 2. c. 8. § 1. n. 1 & 2.

‡ In the original, this passage from *Dion Chrysostom* is quoted so as to mean, that *war is most frequently* DECLARED, (*bella indicta ἐπὶ τὸ πλεῖσον, ut plurimùm*) but from the context it appears evidently to have been an error of the press. The words of *Chrysostom* are: πόλεμοι ὡς ἐπὶ τὸ πλεῖσον 'ΑΚΗΡΤΚΤΟΙ γίγνονται. *Wars are most frequently made* WITHOUT *a public declaration,* and so our author translates them very correctly above, page 7.　　　*T.*

† B

with so much glory the empire of the *Persians*. Even at this day, as far as I have been able to learn, none but the *European* nations declare war; nor even do they all or always do it, but they are accustomed so to do after the example of the *Romans*, for no other reason perhaps than because the *Romans* did so before them. For such was the estimation in which the *Romans* have been held among the nations of *Europe*, that not only their laws, but their manners and customs have been adopted among us, although those customs, as for instance that of declaring war which we are speaking of, differed from those of the rest of the world. Wherefore, if any sovereign of *Europe* should make war without previously declaring it, as was done by *Gustavus Adolphus* upon the *Germans* in the last century, he would certainly act contrary to the general *custom* of *European* nations, but none would say that he acted in opposition to the *law* of nations, except those who call by that name every thing which they see done in their own country.

But let us consult reason, whose authority is of so much weight in the law of nations. Reason, as I have before said, does not require any other formalities than that we should demand in a friendly manner what has been taken from us; nor perhaps will it even require that amicable demand; because all laws permit the repelling force by force, nor do I know that any solemnity in order to repel force is known to the law of nations. But admitting that among good men it may be proper or necessary to make a previous request; yet if that should be denied, will it be prohibited to make use of force? I surely do not prohibit it, though *Grotius* and others do, unless a declaration of war be previously made. But the arguments which are commonly made use of in support of the necessity of declaring war amount in fact to nothing. That which is adduced by *Gentilis* is reprobated by *Grotius* himself,* while he gives another, which I have already quoted, and which if not the worst of all is certainly a very bad one.

When two sovereigns commit hostilities against each other without having declared war, can we doubt that it is their mutual

* L. 3. c. 3. § 11.

will to make war? If we cannot doubt it, to what purpose would
their declaration be? When a thing is public and notorious, it
certainly requires no proof. That is not therefore a sufficient
argument, and yet *Grotius* has preferred making use of it in
order to deduce the necessity of declaring war, from its being
commonly done among *European* nations, though he well
knew that that was not sufficient to constitute the general
law. Reason alone, reason is the soul of the law of nations,
and if we take her for our guide in the present discussion, no
argument will be found to prove the necessity of a declaration
of war, but many on the contrary, which I have adduced, to
shew that it is not necessary.

But even if this question were to be decided by the customs of *European* nations, authorities can also be quoted from
that source. To recur back to the precedents of ancient times
would be an endless task. That war of extermination which
was carried on between *Spain* and the *United Provinces,*
from the time of the foundation of our republic until the
year 1648, was begun by mutual hostilities, without any
public declaration. Because therefore no such declaration
was made, will the legality of the war, of the victories and of
the peace which followed in 1648 be doubted? I do not think
that it will. But the states of *Holland* seem to have thought
otherwise, when on the 4th of *March* 1600 they published an
edict declaring that the owners of the ships which *Philip* III.
had confiscated in *Spain* in 1658 should have satisfaction, because the *Dutch* before that time resorted freely to *Spain*, and
those ships had been confiscated without any previous warning. I do not approve of this edict, for who could justly
have required the king of *Spain* to declare war, when the
Dutch since the year 1581 had not ceased publicly to commit hostilities against him? War, in fact, properly begins from
the mutual use of force, not to speak of other cases* mentioned by the publicists which fall within the same reason.

In the preamble of this edict, as well as in the edict itself,
the states-general add, that formerly, that is to say prior to the

---

* Zouch, *De Jure inter gentes*, part 2. sect. 10. § 1.

year 1598, the *Belgians** were allowed a free intercourse with
Spain. But of the truth of this fact I have never been able to
satisfy myself, and admitting it to be true, I cannot see how
it applies to the justice of the present case, as I shall shew
hereafter. If the *Belgians* thus carried on a free trade and intercourse with *Spain,* it could not be by force of the laws of
war, but rather by the negligence of the magistrates. Indeed
it is stated in the preamble to the edict, by which on the 4th of
April 1586, the earl of *Leicester,* with the advice of the states-
general and their counsellors, prohibited the *United Belgians*
from trading with the *Spaniards,* that the king of *Spain* had
already condemned and sold *Belgic* vessels, both in *Spain* and
Portugal. And in the first section of the said edict of 1586,
as well as by another edict of the 18th of *July* in the same
year, the earl of *Leicester* actually forbids all commercial intercourse with the *Spaniards.* It is true, that by the first section of the edict of the 4th of *August* following he restricted
the prohibition to trading with those places within the *Belgic*
territory, which were in the possession of *Spain,* and permitted carrying on trade with *Spain* proper; but this was done
for no other cause than for the advantage of the *Belgic* merchants, which brought no alteration in the laws of war, which
could not be changed without the consent of the *Spaniards.*

Even if a declaration of war had been necessary, it would
not have availed the *Belgians* any thing to prevent the condemnation of their vessels. For what if the *Spaniards* in that
very year 1598 had solemnly declared war against the *Belgians,*
and immediately afterwards condemned their vessels, perhaps
the same day? They might have done this conformably to the
laws of war; nor indeed are the *Belgians* or any other power,
when a war suddenly breaks out, in the habit of giving notice
to the subjects of their enemies to withdraw their effects and
property, or otherwise that they shall be forfeited. No one
ever required this; on the contrary, *Tryphonius,* in l. 12. pr.

* Our author, when referring to the times of the *Dutch* revolution, calls
indiscriminately *Dutch* and *Belgians* those *Netherlanders,* who were in insur-
rection against *Spain.* Several of the now *Belgic* provinces were at times in
possession of the insurgents.   *T.*

ff. *de Capt.* & *Postlim. Revers.*, lays down the contrary position. And such is the practice of all nations, unless there be a
special convention to the contrary, which is sometimes the
case. There are a few examples of similar compacts. In the
fourth article of the treaty of *Utrecht* with *Muyden* and
Weesp,* of the 1st of *July* 1463, it was agreed that the
peace should last fourteen days, *after we the said city and
cities shall have written to each other, within which fourteen
days it shall be lawful for our respective subjects to withdraw
their goods and effects from the territory of their enemies.*
In the sixteenth article of the treaty of peace between the king
of *Portugal* and the *States-general*, of the 6th *August* 1661,
it is stipulated, that if differences shall arise between the
said king and states, it is so to be declared, and within two
years from that declaration it will be unlawful to do an
injury to the property of the subjects of either party. After it
had been agreed in the year 1662 between *France* and the
states-general, that in case of a war taking place the subjects
of either party should be allowed six months to withdraw their
property from the territory of the other, the king of *France*
having declared war against the *Dutch* in the year 1672
issued a special edict declaring that the convention of 1662
should be observed. The same term of six months was
granted for the same purpose by the same powers to each
other by the fifteenth article of the peace of *Nimeguen*, of
the 10th of *August* 1678, nine months by the thirty-ninth
article of the marine treaty of the 10th of *August* 1678,
nine months again by the fourteenth article of the treaty of
peace of the 20th of *September* 1697, and again nine months
by the thirty-sixth article of the treaty of peace of the 11th of
April 1713. And in the thirty-second article of the treaty of
peace between *England* and the states-general, of the 31st of
July 1667, it was stipulated, that if war should arise between
the parties, the effects of their respective subjects found in the

---

* *Muyden* and *Weesp*, or *Wesop*, are two towns of *South Holland:* the
former is situate at the mouth of the river *Vecht* (a branch of the *Rhine*)
and the latter a few miles above it on the same river.   *T.*

territories of each other should not be condemned, but six
months should be allowed to take them away. If these examples should not be sufficient, I could adduce several others
mentioned by *Zentgravius*, *de Orig. Verit.* & *Oblig. Jur. Gent.*
art. 7. § 9. Where, however, there do not exist similar conventions for suspending the state of war, whatever others may
say, hostilities may commence immediately. *Grotius*, who
requires a declaration, does not require any interval between
it and the beginning of hostilities. See l. 3. *De Jure B. & P.*
c. 3. § 13. *Zouch* and *Zentgravius* are of the same opinion.
Zouch, *de Jur. int. gent.* part 1. § 6.* and *Zent.* d. loc. The
king of *Spain*, therefore, might in the year 1598 have declared
war and immediately afterwards taken the *Dutch* ships, as
there was no convention between the two powers to the contrary, nor indeed could there be any between that sovereign
and a people whom he considered as his subjects.

Here then is a remarkable instance of a war carried on for
a great length of time without ever having been declared.
Indeed, I do not know how the *Belgians* could have required
a declaration of war from the *Spaniards*, when they themselves
never issued any, either at the commencement of hostilities,
or when they were resumed after the expiration of truces.
Nay, even admitting that such a declaration was indispen-
sably required by the law of nations, the *Spaniards* might
perhaps have objected that it was only necessary when war
took place between independent princes, but that it was never
used in a civil war, in which case it was perfectly lawful for a
sovereign to take the property of his rebel subjects. But I do
not urge this argument. It is sufficient for my purpose if I
make it appear that the edict of the 4th of *March* 1600 was
not predicated on the laws of war, but on the interest of the
Dutch merchants. It was the same interest which influenced
the *Hollanders* in the year 1639, and set them improperly at
variance with the states-general, in another case which was
no less dependent on the laws of war. For the governor of the

---

* Our author here quotes *Zouch*, § 3. Q. 10. without referring to the part.
It is evidently a misquotation. The true reference (which we have restored)
is to part 1. § 6.   *T.*

Canary Islands having been taken by treachery and brought
into this country, and the states-general being desirous of
detaining him as a prisoner, the *Hollanders* opposed it; but,
says *Aitzema*,* merely on the ground of its being detrimental
to their trade. For my part I think that they might well have
founded their opposition on the merits of the case itself: as
this was a much more shameful act than the condemnation of
the *Dutch* vessels by *Philip* II. in 1598; for although an
enemy's property may be taken and hostilities may be committed immediately upon a declaration of war, if there are no
treaties to the contrary, yet it is in no case lawful to betray a
friend. The *Dutch* had hitherto been admitted to trade freely
with the *Canary Islands*, and there was on both sides a free
commercial intercourse. A *Dutch* captain, who had been thus
admitted to trade, persuaded the governor to go on board of
his vessel, under pretence of carrying him from one island to

---

* Lib. 19. As this writer is frequently quoted in the course of this work,
we think it proper to give some account of his writings to the *American*
reader. Leo van Aitzema is the author of an excellent Chronicle of the
events which took place during the middle part of the seventeenth century,
from 1621 to 1668. This work is published in six thick folio volumes,
(with an additional volume containing political tracts,) and contains an
immense collection of state papers, during the period to which it refers,
which are connected together by the author's narrative. It is divided
into books, each book containing a recital of the public events and a copy
of the public documents of one year. It has been ably continued on
the same plan by *L. Sylvius*, in four folio volumes, down to the peace
of *Ryswick*, in 1697. This book, as well as its continuation, is entitled *Saken
van Staet en Oorlogh*, (*Of matters of State and War*). Unfortunately it is
written in the *Low Dutch* language, which is understood but by few among
us. A translation of it into *English* would be a great acquisition to literature, and prove an invaluable mine of historical knowledge. From the
manner in which the public documents that it contains are connected and
introduced by short historical narratives, it is superior to any collection of
state papers that has ever appeared. It combines the advantages of such
a collection with those of a chronicle of the times, which, we believe, are
not to be found together in any other work extant. There are two editions of
Aitzema, one in *folio*, the other in *quarto*. The latter is that from which
our author has taken his quotations, to the paging of which he refers.
Being possessed only of the *folio* edition, we have thought it best to refer
merely to the *book* in which each particular passage is to be found.   *T.*

another, instead of which he carried him to *Rotterdam* in order to make him a prisoner. This appears to me to be precisely the same as going to an enemy under the protection of a flag of truce, with an intention however to seize upon the first favourable opportunity to take away his life.

But let us pass on to other wars commenced and carried on without any declaration. It is well known that when *Gustavus Adolphus* invaded *Germany*, the emperor *Ferdinand* II. complained that he had done it without a previous declaration of war, upon which *Gustavus* replied that the emperor himself had before invaded *Prussia* without any such declaration. It is thus that princes, though bound by no positive law, enforce upon each other the law of reciprocity. The same thing happened in the year 1657; for the *French*, in the midst of peace, having detained the goods of *Dutch* subjects which they had in their own country, the *Dutch* detained in like manner the goods of *French* subjects. See the edict of the states of *Holland* of the 26th *April*, and the decree of the states-general of the 6th of *May* of that year. Indeed the states-general lay it down in their said decree that such a detention among friends is unlawful, unless for a just cause, and unless there has been a previous demand and denial of justice. But no prince will detain the property of foreigners, unless for a cause which he himself thinks just. Certainly I would admit of a demand, because a cause of complaint cannot otherwise be known; but since the common use of resident ambassadors, which now obtains, there can be but few cases of injury of which a complaint is not made; for ambassadors are in the habit of making frequent representations, if the smallest thing happens by which their sovereign may be offended. But let us proceed.

We read of the *Portuguese*, that in the year 1657 they seized the ships of the *Dutch* before any war declared or hostilities commenced. And in the war which took place between the king of *England* and the states-general, which ended in the peace of 1667, the states-general, in the letter which they wrote to the king of *England* on the 16th of *September* 1666, complained that a great deal of property was taken from them and their subjects; unlawfully, said they, because war had not been declared. But of this the reader will judge from the reasonings which I here adduce. *Louis* XIV. also, in the year 1667, did not declare war against the *Spaniards*, and yet, as it were, without breaking the peace, he ordered the king of *Spain* to be expelled from dominions that he was pos-, sessed of, being of opinion that there was no need of a declaration to take what belonged to him. Now, if a declaration is necessary in any case, who, I ask, will put up with such a pretext? For to make war is nothing else than to take forcibly from an unwilling prince or people what we think to be justly due to us. There is a long complaint on this subject in the edict of the states-general against *France*, of the 9th of *March* 1689,* because the same king of *France* had, in the year 1688, without any declaration of war, detained the *Dutch* subjects and their ships and merchandize, and afterwards, immediately on the declaration of war being published at *Paris*, he took up arms, and seized on the goods of *Dutch* subjects.

The first part of this complaint was indeed just; for that detention was a violation of the fifteenth article of the peace of *Nimeguen* and of the thirty-ninth article of the *Marine* treaty of the 10th of *August* 1678, the period stipulated by those several instruments, as above mentioned, for carrying off the effects of the respective parties, not being expired, so that the state of war was in this respect suspended. It was therefore an act of injustice to capture such goods as might have been carried off within the limited time. As to other goods, there was no treaty concerning them, and therefore I doubt whether the second part of the complaint was equally well founded. But however this may be, the instances which I have adduced are sufficient to prove that there is no reason why we should think so favourably of *European* manners, as to refer to them for a convincing proof of the necessity of declaring war.

* Sylv. contin. of Aitzema, b. 25.

† C

CHAPTER III.

Of War considered as between Enemies.

IT may be said that a state of war ought rather to exist among princes for whose interest alone in most cases it is carried on, than among their subjects, who, unless the war is made for their own quarrel, are not actuated by so hostile a spirit. Yet when hostilities are to be waged against another nation, no one can expect that we shall compliment our enemies and wish them well. The grave majesty of the *Roman* people displayed itself in the conduct of *Caius Popilius*, who, although he was saluted by king *Antiochus*, then his enemy, refused to return the salutation while the war continued. So we are told by *Plutarch, Apophthegm,* p. m. 364.: *Livy,* b. 45. c. 12., and *Polyb. Excerp. Legat.* c. 92., relate likewise, that *Antiochus* offered his hand to *Popilius*, who refused to take it.

The *Roman* consuls however, in their letter to king *Pyrrhus,* with whom they were at war, as related by *Gellius,* b. 3. c. 8., wished him health. This perhaps was necessitated by the state of *Roman* affairs at that time, but so addicted to flattery has the last century been, as well as the present, that princes omit none of the usual adulatory forms even in the midst of war. Hence enemies now wish to each other every kind of prosperity, call each other friends, and are almost sorry for their mutual losses. This is exemplified in the letters of the states-general to the king of *England*, of the 10th of *July,*[*] 16th *September,*[†] and 26th of *November,* 1666; and again in the letters of the king of *England* to the states-general of the 4th of *August,*[‡] and 4th of *October* 1666. Although the two nations were at that time at open war, and bent upon mutual injury, yet the states-general write in their said letter of the 10th of *July* 1666, *que les offices de civilité ne*

---

[*] Aitz. b. 46.   [†] Aitz. ibid.   [‡] Aitz. ibid.

sont pas incompatibles avec les devoirs de la guerre,—that an interchange of civilities is not incompatible with the duties of war. And the king of *France*, in the year 1666, who was then at war with the king of *England*, sent an ambassador to condole with him on the conflagration of the city of *London.* It is certainly noble to practise the duties of humanity, clemency, piety and other magnanimous virtues in the midst of war; but I think it disgusting to trifle with mere words, for what else is it than trifling when you express sorrow for the conflagration of a city to which you would wish to set fire yourself?

As the conqueror may lawfully do any thing that he pleases with the vanquished, no one can doubt his having on that account over him the power of life and death. There are so many instances on record of the exercise of this right amongst all nations in ancient times, that a large book would not be sufficient to contain an account of them all; and the publicists have already exercised their industry upon this subject. But although the right of killing has almost become obsolete, yet it is to be attributed merely to the will and to the clemency of the victor; nor can it be denied but that it might be exercised even at this time, if one should chuse to avail himself of his right. That there still exist some remains of this right is in full proof; for in this sense alone is to be taken and on this ground alone is to be defended the edict of the states-general of the 1st of *October* 1589, which inflicted the penalty of death on those who should be found with the traitors of *Gertruydenberg;* and also their other edict of the 24th *February* 1696, by which they inflicted the same penalty on those enemies who should approach the shore nearer than the buoys, or should land on the coast for the sake of plundering.

One who is in company with his fellow soldiers is not guilty of any crime by the laws of war, though they be traitors, nor is he who invades a hostile shore in hopes of making booty. Drive him away if you can, but if you cannot, why will you treat him differently from other enemies? It is on the ground of the same right of life and death that I defend the conduct of the *Dutch,** who sometimes hanged the

* Aitz. b. 6.

Spaniards because they were not ransomed, for so it is related to us. It is lawful to hang prisoners; but if it were not lawful, there is no reason or authority for doing it because they are not ransomed, but the contrary is practised, as will be seen hereafter.

To the right of killing our enemies has succeeded that of making them slaves, which was formerly exercised during many ages. But this custom of making slaves of prisoners has now fallen into disuse among most nations, in consequence of the improvement of their manners. *Cujacius*, indeed has said, *Comment. post. ad* l. 5. *ff. de Just. et Jur.*, that even among *Christians*, prisoners were still made slaves of; but that their servitude was milder than formerly. He however does not prove his position otherwise than by the right of redeeming. But why should the custom of redeeming prisoners and their detention until they are redeemed be considered as a species of servitude, any more than for instance the imprisonment of *foreign** debtors, until they pay what they owe to us? For in those cases such debtors are never discharged, unless they pay the money due, or give security for it, precisely as in the case of prisoners of war. Nay, prisoners of war, if they are not redeemed, are very often released, even without a ransom. Thus the supreme military council of the *United Provinces* on the 14th of *December* 1602, permitted the release of twenty-four prisoners, taken at the siege of *Boisleduc*, because they were not redeemed, and lest those unfortunate wretches should perish by the miseries of a gaol. It would have been very unexpected indeed, and quite contrary to the manners which now prevail, if the council had ordered those prisoners to be either hanged or made slaves of. Hence, when the rhingrave of *Solms*,† who served in the *British* army in *Ireland* in the year 1690, had ordered prisoners to be transported to *America*, there to be made slaves, the

---

* In *Holland*, foreigners alone and transient persons, who have no domicile in the country, are imprisoned for debt.   *T.*

† Aitz. b. 30.

duke of *Berwick** gave him notice, that if this should be done, all the prisoners that he should make would be sent to the galleys in *France.* But as slavery itself has fallen entirely into disuse among christians, we do not inflict it upon our prisoners. We may however, if we please, and indeed we do sometimes still exercise that right upon those who enforce it against us. Therefore the *Dutch* are in the habit of selling to the *Spaniards* as slaves, the *Algerines, Tunisians* and *Tripolitans,* whom they take prisoners in the *Atlantic* or in the *Mediterranean;* for the *Dutch* themselves have no slaves, except in *Asia, Africa* and *America.* Nay, in the year 1661, the states-general gave orders to their admiral to sell as slaves all the pirates that he should take. The same thing was done in the year 1664.†

To the slavery of prisoners succeeded the custom of exchanging them according to their respective grades and ranks, and detaining them until redeemed.‡ And the necessity of redeeming them is sometimes expressed in treaties, with a specified sum, according to the dignity of each person that may be taken, which sum being paid, there is an end of that *summum jus* which belongs to the victors over their prisoners. Among the *Romans* the right of capture was exercised upon those who at the breaking out of the war were found in each other's territory, l. 12. ff. *de Capt. et. Postlim. Revers.;* but in modern times it rarely takes place, although the right still exists. Nay, *Louis* XIV. himself, king of *France,* when on the 26th of *January* 1666, he had declared war against *England* by sea and land, and interdicted all commerce between

* The duke of *Berwick,* a natural son of *James* II. of *England,* commanded at that time the *French* army in *Ireland.* He was afterwards commander in chief of the *French* forces in *Spain,* during the succession war, while the *British* troops were commanded by the earl of *Galway,* a Frenchman. *T.*

† Aitz. b. 41. 44.

‡ We are informed by the public papers that by a late cartel which has been settled between the *British* and *French,* sixteen *French* prisoners are to be given for every nine *British,* until the whole are regularly exchanged; it having been ascertained that the number of *French* prisoners in *England* exceeds that of the *English* in *France* in that proportion. *T.*

the two nations, in consequence of which the *English* who were in *France* were in fears for their persons and property, issued on the 1st of *February* 1666, another edict, telling them that their fears were vain; for that by the edict of the 26th of *January* 1666, he had merely declared war against those of the *English* who should be found thereafter on the high seas, or who should commit hostilities on the *French* territory, but not against those private individuals who had established their domicil in *France;* that however, it was his pleasure that *English* subjects residing in *France*, and who were not naturalized, should depart within three months, and go whithersoever they should please.

But that this is to be attributed solely to humanity, if there exist no treaties suspending the state of war, I have endeavoured to shew in the preceding chapter.* Because, however, there are many such treaties, the laws of war are seldom exercised upon those who have come in time of peace to a country where war afterwards has arisen, and have been found there at the time of the war's taking place. But after the expiration of the time which has been granted to them either by humanity or by treaty, those who remain in the country, or come into it without permission, may lawfully be arrested. On this principle, the states-general on the 4th of *April* 1674 issued an edict, that if any enemies should tarry within the *United Provinces* or the dominions of the states-general, without having obtained liberty to come, they should be arrested, and not be restored until redeemed.

But although the right of killing prisoners has fallen into disuse, it is made a question, however, whether it may not be, without the least imputation, exercised upon those who defend themselves too obstinately; and there are some who maintain the affirmative. But I think it would be a shameful action, unless the weak and defenceless girl, who obstinately

* On this principle, probably, the first consul of *France* arrested and detained, without any previous notice, all the *British* subjects who were found in *France* at the commencement of the present war. The principle may be correct; but if it is, it must be acknowledged that the *summum jus* of war is very near akin to barbarism.   *T.*

resists the attempts of a libertine, should also be deemed deserving of punishment.

Every thing is lawful against an enemy, but nothing can be more cruel than to punish him for his courage. Nay, we even admire the courage of our enemies, and we are indignant at their cowardice. I remember to have read, that the *Algerine* corsairs tore to pieces and loaded with every kind of ignominy a certain captain who had meanly given 'up his vessel when she was in a condition very fit for defence, and had only stipulated for the liberty of his own person. For even with enemies fortitude is glorious and cowardice contemptible. If you wish to read what others have written upon this subject, you may be gratified by reading *Gentilis*, *de Jure Belli*, l. 2. c. 16.; *Grotius*, *de J. B. ac Pac.* l. 3. c. 4. § 13., and *Zouch*, *de Jur. Fec.** part 2. § 10. **Q.** 9.

We have laid down what it is lawful to do with living enemies, but what shall we say of the remains of those who are dead? In ancient times their bodies were abandoned to beasts and birds of prey, but now the conquerors either bury them themselves, or deliver them up to be buried. Sometimes even more is done for the sake of humanity. On the 16th of *September* 1666, the states-general caused the body of an *English* admiral which was in their power to be embalmed, and sent it over to *England.* They had before, viz. on the 10th of *July* 1666, written to the king of *England*, to know whether he wished that corpse to be sent thither or be buried in *Holland*, and on the 4th of *August* 1666 he chose the former. The *French* did the same thing in the year 1692.

There can be no doubt but that from the nature of war itself, all commercial intercourse ceases between enemies. For to what purpose will trade be carried on, if, as is clearly the case, the goods of enemies brought into our country are liable to confiscation? And if he who having obtained the right of killing his enemy should go with merchandize into the hostile country, and the enemy should kill him in the midst of

* This work is sometimes referred to by the title *De Jure Feciali*, sometimes by that *De Jure inter gentes*, which is indifferent, as it bears both titles.   *T.*

commercial intercourse, would you think it justly done? But
every commercial intercourse ceases. Hence in declarations
of war commerce with the enemy is prohibited, and it is often
done by subsequent edicts. By the eleventh section of the
edict of the earl of *Leicester* of the 4th of *April* 1586, interdicting trade with the *Spaniards*, it is enacted that those who
should carry on such commerce contrary to that edict should
be hanged and their ships and goods confiscated, if they were
subjects, but if foreigners, they should only be punished by
the confiscation of their ships and merchandize. The same
was enacted by the twelfth section of the edict of the said earl
of the 4th of *August* 1586. And by the thirteenth section of the
edict of the 4th of *April*, and the fourteenth of that of the 4th
of *August*, the intention to carry on trade with the enemy was
punished in the same manner as the fact itself, and thus the
states of *Holland* had formerly enacted on the 27th of *July*
1584. It was moreover added to all those edicts, that there
should be no prescription or limitation against the charge of
having traded with the enemy, whether they were taken in the
fact or not. And by the same edict of the states of *Holland*
of the 27th of *July* 1584, the pecuniary penalties which it
inflicts were to be recovered not only from the delinquent but
from his heirs, which I do not believe to be conformable to
the *Roman* law: for the offence provided against by these
edicts does not, if we will be candid, amount to the crime of
treason, but is a particular species of offence, to which one is
instigated by cupidity and the love of gain rather than by a
treasonable intent.

But although trading with the enemy be not specially prohibited, yet it is forbidden by the mere operation of the law
of war. Declarations of war themselves sufficiently shew it;
for they enjoin on every subject to attack the subjects of the
other prince, seize on their goods, and do them all the harm in
their power. The utility, however, of merchants, and the mutual
wants of nations, have almost got the better of the law of
war as to commerce. Hence it is alternately permitted and
forbidden in time of war, as princes think it most for the
interest of their subjects. A commercial nation is anxious to

trade, and accommodates the laws of war to the greater or
lesser want that it may be in of the merchandizes of others.
Thus sometimes a mutual commerce is permitted generally;
sometimes as to certain merchandizes only, while others are
prohibited, and sometimes it is prohibited altogether. But in
whatever manner it may be permitted, whether generally or
specially, it is always, in my opinion, so far a suspension of
the laws of war. And in this manner, there is partly war and
partly peace between the subjects of both princes.* The herring
fishery was permitted on both sides by the edicts of the *French*
and *Dutch* of the year 1536, and formerly by the edict of the
latter of the 22d of *December* 1552. To which is to be added,
what was done during the whole of the *Spanish, Portuguese*
and *English* war, in the years 1653, 1665 and 1672, and also
during the *French* war in the years 1672, 1689 and 1702,
for it would be too long to commemorate every thing.

It is a question whether our friends are to be considered as
enemies, when they live among the latter, say in a town which
they occupy. *Petrinus Bellus, de Re Milit.* part 2. tit. 11. n.
5., thinks that they are not. *Zouch, de Jure Fec.* part 2. § 8. **Q.**
4., gives no opinion. For my part I think that they must also
be considered as enemies, certainly as to the goods which they
have within the hostile territory, and therefore those goods
may properly be taken by us by the law of war, if they have
been before taken by our enemies. We may lawfully take all
that belongs to the enemy, and those goods are a part of the
enemy's dominion, which as they may be useful to them, may
be hurtful to us. But if the goods of friends are within our
territory, although their owners may be within that of the
enemy, being detained there as prisoners by the law of war,
I would then speak differently; because it is true that these are
not the enemy's goods, nor can they be at all useful to him.
Again, as we are to do to our enemies all the harm that we can,

* How is it, when, as in the present *European* war, the belligerents trade
with each other, and prohibit neutrals from trading with their respective
enemies? According to our author's opinion, it seems that such belligerents
are *so far* at peace with one another, and at war with the neutral nations. *T.*

why shall we not take from them goods which they themselves
have occupied by the law of war, and which they make use of as
of their own? I know upon what principle others are of a different
opinion.* They say that our friends, although they are among
our enemies, yet are not hostilely inclined against us; for if
they are there, it is not from their choice, and the *quo animo*
only is to be considered. But the thing does not depend only
on the *quo animo;* for, even among the subjects of our
enemy, there are some, however few they may be, who are not
hostilely inclined against us; but the matter depends upon the
law, because those goods are with the enemy, and because
they are of use to them for our destruction.

* Our author here distinguishes between the goods of a friend which are
within our territory, while the friendly owner is a prisoner with the enemy,
and those which having been captured by the enemy, as well as the person
of the owner, are *retaken* by us. The latter, he contends, are, though the
former are not, liable to confiscation.   *T*

CHAPTER IV.

Of the Capture of movable property, and particularly of Ships.

WE have in the former chapters treated of the persons of enemies, we shall now speak of their goods and actions. It is evident that the enemy's property, whether movable or immovable, may be lawfully taken. To whose benefit the capture enures, whether to the private captors or to the state, I shall not now examine, as I am to consider this subject in the 20th chapter. But I shall at present attend to another question, which is not less important and which occurs every day, From what time is property changed by capture? I shall not distinguish here between the different species of personal property; whether a man be taken, or a ship, or merchandize, or furniture, or any thing else which may be properly the object of capture. By the *Roman* law, as *Grotius* very properly observes, the things taken are said to become the property of the captors, when they are carried *intra præsidia*,* for which doctrine there is no other reason, but that now every hope of pursuing and recovering the thing taken is at an end. " Whence," says the same author,† " it seems to follow, that ships and other things taken on the high seas, are considered as effectually captured, when they have been carried into a port or harbour, or in a place where the whole fleet is, for now their recovery begins to be despaired of. But," he adds, " by the modern law introduced among *European* nations, such things, in order to be considered *as captured*, must have been twenty-four hours in the power of the enemy." Which doctrine he applies in his notes to those things which

---

* Grot. De J. B. ac P. l. 3. c. 6. § 3. n. 1.   † Ibid. n. 2.

are taken upon land. *Zouch* has stated *Grotius's* doctrine very fairly,* and *Loccenius*† has done the same. What *Grotius* says of the doctrine of twenty-four hours, that it is now observed among all nations, without any distinction, whether a captured ship has been carried or not into a port of the captors, the attorney-general in the court of admiralty of *Amsterdam*, has formerly answered,‡ and others are of the same opinion.

But I never have been able to find that this custom was observed. I have found, indeed, that the military judges decided thus on the 24th of *December* 1624,§ and also at another time, but of what weight is the decision of men, mostly ignorant of law, who either have not been guided by any authority or perhaps have been seduced by that of *Grotius.* What I shall say in this and the next chapter will abundantly prove that this custom is repugnant to the laws and manners of the *United Provinces.* I know, that in the year 1631, the ambassador of the states-general in *England,*¶ requested the states-general to sanction by their authority that principle of jurisprudence, which vests the property in a prize after twenty-four hours' just possession; but I do not find that the states ever did so. It is indeed contrary to all reason; for if you consider the thing by the mere light of common law, the true reason of a change of property consists in a real possession. But a real possession is that which may be safely retained. Then what signify the twenty-four hours, if there may be a real possession within that time, and if on the contrary a possession may even continue longer and not be real? Certainly it has been impossible to lay down a general rule upon this subject, on account of the great variety of cases that may happen; but every case is to be considered by itself, and from every case it will result, that the property of the thing taken will not vest in the captor, unless he is able to keep and defend it. Things taken in war, says the digest, belong to him who has first taken possession of them. L.1.§1. *ff. de Acquir. vel Amitt. rer. Possess.*

* De Jure Fec. part 2. § 8. Q. 1.——† De Jure Marit. l. 2. c. 4. n. 4.——
‡ Consil. Belg. vol. 2. Cons. 66.——§ Consil. Holland. vol. 2. Cons. 151.——
¶ Aitz. l. 11.

And he is not considered as having the possession of a thing, who is not able to retain it. L. 22. *ff. Eod.* Such is the opinion of the most eminent jurists, which is dictated by the law of nations itself. When, however, we have such a possession that we may or may not retain the thing taken, the variety of cases is such, as I have said, that it is not possible to give any definition. We may, however, be considered as having a firm possession, when we have carried the thing taken *intra præsidia*, to use the language of the *Roman* law. By *præsidia*, we understand castles, ports, towns and fleets; for in any one of these the thing taken may be considered as safe, and in a situation to be defended.

But how can the twenty-four hours be sufficient, if it is not even sufficient, in order to change the property, that the captured thing should have been carried *intra præsidia?* For such is the mistaken idea of some, nay, of those whose authority otherwise is of the greatest weight. They are of opinion, that captured ships do not become the property of the captors, unless they have been carried into one of his ports and condemned there, and afterwards have freely navigated to a neutral port. Of merchandizes and other things, which are within the same reason, they might have said the same thing, but I believe they were ashamed. I well know what the states-general decreed concerning captured vessels on the 27th of *November* 1666: " That if ships, taken by the enemy and carried into *England,* and the kingdoms thereto belonging, and there condemned as prize, and purchased by neutrals, should be captured by *Dutch* ships on their way from the enemy's ports, either *in ipso actu* or afterwards, before arriving at their port of destination or at some other free port, such ships should then and therefore be declared good prize, as was usual in ancient times, and agreeably to the disposition of the fourth point of the *case stated** of the 26th of *June* 1630, *mutatis mutandis.*" I have quoted the precise words of the decree, that I may not be thought to relate incredible things. You will wonder, indeed for my part I

* See the next page.

certainly do wonder, what it can signify, whether the ships have
arrived or not into one of the ports of the purchaser, or into
some other friendly port. This national or friendly port must
then give, I know not how, I know not what, to I know not
whom. It would not give a right of property to the enemy,
who already had taken and sold the prize, nor to the purchaser,
who had thus purchased our own property from one who was
not the rightful owner thereof. Then that certain port of the
neutral purchaser or of his friend would actually be the thing
that would take the property of the vessel from us. If recourse
was to be had to a fiction, it would have been better to suppose that the vessel became enemy's property by the enemy's
capture, remained such until it was purged of that taint, and
that it could not be so purged until it had entered the port
of the neutral or of one of his friends, until which time it
might be lawfuly retaken. But such a fiction would not have
been legal, because by the act of purchase the thing belongs to
the purchaser, nor is it material whether it was originally
his, or whether it became his property by capture and condemnation.

But observe how improperly ancient custom is appealed to,
and see that other decree of the states-general of the 26th of
June 1630, which is supposed to have given rise to that
custom. That decree was made on a *case stated* by the admiralty of *Amsterdam*, which contained several questions, to
the fourth of which the states answer thus:

" On the fourth point their high mightinesses declare, that
ships taken by the enemy, carried into *Flanders*, and purchased by neutrals, but which shall be taken in the very act of
coming out of the enemy's ports or on their way from them,
before they have been into their own or in other free ports,
shall be lawful prize, as has always been the custom in ancient
times, by virtue of the right herein before alleged as to the
first point; and likewise such vessels, which being so captured and purchased, and having run out of the said *Flemish*
ports into other ports under the dominion of the king of
Spain, and coming from thence, shall be captured by *Dutch*
ships."

That this decree is very foreign to that cause appears from the case stated itself; and the states-general themselves, by referring to the *first head* of the decree,* sufficiently make known what was their reason for enacting it. The fact is, that for the sake of preventing commercial intercourse, the states-general had blocked up the ports of *Flanders* with ships of war, so that all vessels, to whomsoever belonging, bound to those ports, or sailing from them, were condemned by them as lawful prize; because by the law of nations and according to the principles of reason it is not lawful to carry any thing to a blockaded port, nor to take any thing away from it. Therefore the admiralty said, and the states-general decreed, that the same law applied to vessels which had been before taken from us and afterwards sold, because it was lawful to take even the ships of friends when trading with blockaded ports; which is true so far, that is, if they are taken before their voyage is ended, and while employed in the illicit trade, for the voyage is not considered as completed until the vessels have entered into their own or a friendly port.

This and nothing else was what the states-general had in view by the said decree of the 26th of *June* 1630, and on these principles, that of the 27th of *November* 1666 would have been very proper, if in that year the whole of *England, Scotland* and *Ireland,* and all the *British* dominions in *Asia, Africa* and *America* had been blockaded by the fleets of the states-general. It is indeed related, that in the year 1652 they boasted of a similar thing with regard to the *English,* having prohibited all trade with them to all the world.† But upon what foundation they so boasted I do not now inquire. I content myself with observing, that the same states-general in 1663 denied to the *Spaniards,* who pretended to blockade the whole of *Portugal,* that same right which they had before arrogated to themselves against the *English.* These facts are so recorded in *Aitzema's* chronicle.‡

* That is to say, the *first point* of the case stated, on which the states made their decree. What that *first point* was, does not precisely appear, though it may be gathered from the context of our author's observations on the whole decree.   T.

† Aitz. B. 32.——‡ Aitz. B. 43.

From thence it appears, that the said decree of the states-general of the 27th of *November* 1666 cannot be defended. And indeed if we once admit the principles of that decree, a number of monstrous consequences will necessarily follow: for as the poet says,

" Si prava est regula prima,
" Omnia mendose fieri atque obstipa necesse est."

It will manifestly follow, that all enemy's goods, without exception, will be placed in precisely the same predicament; for whatever enemies have by capture is as much their own as what they have by succession, purchase, or by any other title. Therefore the same is to be said, not only, as I observed before, of merchandize and other things which enemies have taken from us, but also of ships, and every thing else which they have otherwise than by taking it from us, and which our friends have purchased from them. If this be admitted, we must also admit that it is lawful for princes to interdict their enemies from the use of fire and water, and to forbid all the world from carrying on a commercial intercourse with them, which hitherto has only been done so far as relates to those things which are called *contraband:* for all things of that kind which our friends may purchase of our enemies, may lawfully be taken and confiscated, unless they have been carried into a neutral port.

But it is unreasonable to infer a general rule from a law which, against the principles of reason, has been established in a particular case, by which means a pretence will be given to every sovereign to commit injustice. On this and no other ground was founded the edict of *Louis* XIV. king of *France*, of the 17th of *September* 1672, by which he ordered the capture and confiscation of all vessels, even purchased by his friends in the *United Provinces* and found coming from thence. In consequence of that edict, on the next day a certain vessel was condemned which had been taken coming from *Holland*, where she had been built and purchased by *Hamburghers*, manned with a *Hamburgh* crew, and was going to *Hamburgh*. To that edict of the king of *France*, the states-general, that they might not appear to do less harm to their

friends, (for such things fall upon the heads of friends)
replied by an edict in which they decreed " that all ships
purchased by neutrals within the dominions of the king of
France, although manned with a neutral crew, which sailing
for the first time from the enemy's ports, and not yet having
been in the neutral port to which they were bound,
should fall into the hands of *Dutch* cruizers, should be
lawful prize." One would think that this edict was founded
on the law of retaliation; but retaliation is only to be exercised
on him who has committed the injury, and not against a
common friend. Therefore the edict of the states-general of
the 29th of *November* 1666 cannot be defended on the ground
that the *English* had before acted with a greater degree of injustice when their ambassador, on the 23d of *December* 1664,
gave notice to the *Hanse-Towns,* who were in amity then both
with *England* and the states-general, that all the ships which
they should purchase in the territory of the *United Provinces*
should, without distinction of voyage, be considered as enemies.* He who has done no injury ought not in justice to
suffer.

Moreover, from those decrees of the states-general of 1630
and 1666, one might think that it appears that those things
which our friends have purchased from our enemies cannot
be taken from them, if they have once been carried into a
neutral port, as they say that such things may be lawfully
condemned, " *before they have been into their own or some other
neutral port:*" but so much does not even sufficiently appear.
The admiralty of *Amsterdam* had consulted the states-
general upon this subject, but nothing was decided upon it;
for the states simply answered by their letter of the 26th of
June 1630, " As to ships taken by the enemy from the inhabitants of this country, carried into *Flanders* and there condemned, which without being taken should be carried into
England, France, or other neutral countries, and should be
captured by our ships on their way from thence on other free

* Aitz. b. 44.

† E

voyages, we ought to have some short time to consider, whether or not they should be declared lawful prize, requesting that in the mean time you will communicate to us the sentences that have been given in similar cases, and the decisions that have taken place thereon in other countries." On this same question I find that the court of *Holland* was consulted in the following year, 1631; but I do not know what answer they gave. But although the *Dutch* lawyers, requested to give their opinions on the same point, on the 25th of *January* 1636, answered very properly and upon true legal principles, " that our ships, taken by the enemy and purchased by neutrals, became by the very act of capture the property of the enemy, and therefore lawfully belonged to those who purchased from him," there have nevertheless been since that time disputes upon that subject.* But that this doubt of the states-general in the year 1630 may not hereafter occasion any prejudice, when similar cases shall arise, I must repeat what I have said above, that they had a special case before them, that the question was concerning the blockaded *Flemish* ports, which not being attended to, has involved the point in obscurity; but that from thence it would not be proper to argue as to ports which were not blockaded, and to and from which a free ingress and egress was permitted. The decree of the 27th of *November* 1666 is sufficiently iniquitous, let us not therefore add to it another injustice, which was not in fact such, because founded on a special case.

But if the states-general had meant to say, that the property of a prize is not altered, unless it has been carried into the enemy's port, and has afterwards freely sailed from thence and arrived into the port of a friend, what ground or reason would there be for their edicts, by which, in case of recapture of our vessels taken by the enemy, they allow a part to the recaptor and a part to the original owner? If mere capture transfers the property, what right remains to the former owner? if not, what right has the

* Aitz. b. 21.; Id. b. 28.

recaptor to a certain part, when the former owner may reclaim his property? I should think for my own part with many others, that no right remains in him, and so is the usage among all nations. These are things that can neither.be reconciled with the decree of the 27th of *November* 1666, nor with law, nor with common sense.

CHAPTER V.

Of the Recapture of movable Property.

WHAT I have lightly touched upon at the end of the last chapter, I am now going to consider and discuss more at large. Whereupon it is to be observed, that immovable property, when recaptured, returns to the former owners by postliminy, but that movables which we now treat of do not so return. It is thus laid down by *Labeo*, in l. 28. *de Capt. & Postlim. Revers: Si quid bello captum est, in præda est, non postliminio redit.* " If any thing be taken in war, it is a prize, and does not return by postliminy." As to ships, however, although they are considered as movables, he distinguishes, *l. 2. pr. ff. eod.*, that such ships as may be of use in war return by postliminy, but others not. But this and other distinctions of the *Roman* law between movable things have become obsolete by the gradual change of manners, as *Grotius* justly observes.* Hence now movable goods, without any distinction, are prize, without any right of postliminy. As a consequence from this it has been inferred that goods taken by the enemy, and afterwards recaptured, vest in the recaptors; because, as capture, in time of war, transfers the property, so recapture must of course transfer it in like manner. But we do not recapture for ourselves, except those things which have *pleno jure* become enemy's property; for if they have not, the former owner may still vindicate his right. As to the time when movable goods are considered *pleno jure* as having become the enemy's property, it depends on the circumstances which I have treated of in the preceding chapter.

Although the definition of this thing is very uncertain, so much, however, is most true, that movable goods carried *intra præsidia*† of the enemy, become clearly and fully his

* De Jure Belli ac Pac. l. 3. c. 9. § 15.——† Within the places of safety. *T.*

property, and consequently, if retaken, vest entirely in the recaptors. The same is to be said of ships, carried into the enemy's ports, and afterwards recaptured, so that no property or right to them remains in the former owner, as I mentioned at the end of the preceding chapter. On these principles, the agreement which was made on the 22d of *October* 1689, between the king of *England* and the states-general, then allies in war, that each other's ships when recaptured should be restored to the former owner, on payment of a certain salvage, has been construed to apply only to cases where the ships had not been carried into the ports of the enemy, for otherwise they are to be entirely the property of the recaptors.

So far is sufficiently clear, but what is not equally so is what is to be understood by *præsidia*, or ports? Is it the ports of those who have taken the ship, or of their allies? It may be said that it is enough if they are carried into the ports of the latter, provided they are their allies in the existing war, and equally with themselves the enemies of those whose vessels have been taken. Prizes are equally safe in the ports of such an ally, as in those of the captor himself, and there is no hope of retaking them, unless they should sail again out of that port. But when the *French* had taken two *Hamburg* ships, on the 28th of *December* 1675, in which were the goods of *Amsterdam* merchants, and had had them fourteen days in their possession, and afterwards carried them into the port of *Hull* in *England*,* I find that the states-general entertained a different opinion. The admiralty of *Dunkirk*, before the return of the *French*, had condemned the said ships and their cargoes, and the *French* had even sold a part of the goods at *Hull;* and as the ships, with the remainder of the goods, were on their way to *Dunkirk*, they were taken by the *Zealanders*, carried into *Zealand*, and there condemned. But the states-general, being applied to by the *Amsterdam* merchants, did, on the 23d of *October* 1676, decree, that the recaptured goods should be restored to their former owners, because they had not yet been carried into the ports of the enemy and there con-

* *England* was at that time in alliance with *France* against the *United Netherlands.*　　　　　　　　　　　　　　　　　　　　T.

demned and distributed. By the ports of the enemy, the states-general understood those of the captors, for they say " *of the aforesaid enemy*," thereby implying that it was not sufficient that the ships had been carried into another port, either of a *friend* or of an ally in the war. It appears to me that the *Zealanders* had the *law*, and the *states-general* had *power* on their side.*

Ships therefore become the property of the enemy, which have been taken by them, and carried into their ports. But what if they have not been yet carried thither, and should have remained some time in the port of a friend or ally, or navigated in company with the capturing ship? Certainly, if we consider the laws of our country, and the authority of publicists, it can hardly be said, that the length of time that ships have been captured, or the place into which they have been carried, though ever so safe, can transfer the property, unless they have been carried into port. Hence jurists simply say, that every thing which is retaken before it is carried into the enemy's ports, is entitled to *postliminy*, although it may have been taken for several months, and although it may have remained in the ports of a common friend, and that it does not vest in the enemy, unless he has carried it into his

---

* From this, and what our author says afterwards, page 41, it seems that *he* was of opinion that a belligerent might lawfully condemn enemy's property, while lying under capture in a *neutral port*. Such appears also to have been the opinion of that able civilian sir *William Scott*, (while *advocate-general*) and of the whole court of *king's bench* in *England*, in 1789. (*Smart* v. *Wolff*, 3 *Term Rep.* 329.) But political considerations have since induced that learned judge to maintain the opposite doctrine, contrary to the ancient, nay, inveterate practice of his own country, which probably, however, continues the same, the superior court not having appeared disposed to controvert the established principle and to adopt the new rule which was pointed out to them. (The *Herstelder*, 1 *Robinson's Reports*, 100.; the *Hendrick* and *Maria*, 5 *Rob.* 35. 6 *Rob.* 138. *Amer. edit.*) The supreme court of the *United States* have sanctioned what appears to be the opinion of our author on this point, by their decisions in the cases of *Rose* v. *Himely* and *Hudson* v. *Guestier*, 4 *Cranch's Reports*, 241. 293. These decisions are conformable to the universal practice of *Europe* for more than one hundred years, which is, indeed, sufficiently justifiable, on principles of convenience to neutrals as well as to belligerents. See *Lampredi, del commercio de' popoli neutrali in tempo di guerra*, part 1. § 14.　　　　　　　　　　*T*.

own ports. The word *postliminy* is very *improperly* used here, because those who know what *postliminy* is, know also, that it does not take place except in regard to those things which had before become the property of the enemy. They should have said, that before prizes were carried into port, they did not become the property of the enemy, but remained the property of the former owner, and that therefore when recaptured they returned to him, and did not go to the recaptor.

It will not be unprofitable to consider what laws have been made on this subject in this country, taking them in their chronological order. There are some who think from the edict of the states of *Holland*, of the 4th of *March* 1600, that there existed a right in favour of former owners to claim their captured property, wherever they might find it, even though it had been carried into the enemy's ports. This is correct as far as the edict goes, but it speaks only of those vessels, which the states of *Holland* considered as having been condemned in violation of the laws of war, as I have said before; (c. 2.) therefore the edict does not apply to the present question. If the ships have been lawfully taken, carried into port and condemned, every claim must cease; and if they sail afterwards, there remains nothing but a right to recapture, and whoever retakes them will be their full and complete owner. But it is important to know, before the carrying of the ship into port and her subsequent condemnation, what right belongs to the former owner, and what to the recaptor? If we know what belongs to the one, we know at the same time that the remainder belongs to the other.

The oldest law that I know of on this subject, is the edict of the states-general of the 4th of *July* 1625, by which it is enacted, that if a vessel be retaken within twenty-four hours, one eighth goes to the private recaptors; if within forty-eight hours, one fifth; if afterwards, one third. This law the same states-general on the 22d of *July* 1625, applied to ships of war, recapturing private vessels. There followed afterwards another law also enacted by the states-general, of the 11th of *March* 1632, by which, without any distinction of time, private recaptors were entitled to two

thirds of their recapture. But afterwards, on the 1st of
September 1643, the states-general altered this disposition,
for by the fifty-eighth section of their edict of that date, if
a ship be recovered within twenty-four hours, the recaptor is
to have one eighth; if within forty-eight hours, one fifth, and
if afterwards, one third, as in former edicts, which, I think,
were made on the 4th and 22d of *July* 1625. Afterwards
they returned to two thirds, without any distinction of time
with regard to privateers, agreeably to the edict of the year
1632. The 16th section of the edict of the states-general of
the 8th of *February* 1645, gave two thirds to the recaptors, and
added that the value of the vessel and cargo should be amicably
estimated between the owner and the recaptor, otherwise that
the admiralty should decree on the amount of salvage. They
again changed their minds on the 19th of *April* 1659, for
by a decree of that date, they gave to the recaptors, whether
of public or private ships, but one ninth part of the vessel
and cargo retaken, thus again abolishing every distinction of
time. This decree, however, was never published, but I have
found it among the acts of the states-general, and it is mentioned somewhere else. At last, the states-general, saving, as
they say, the ancient laws as to ships of war (what ancient
laws they meant I cannot say, as they have so varied) did on
the 13th of *April* 1677, decree as to private recaptors as follows, to wit: that they should have by way of salvage, one
fifth of the ship and goods retaken, if the same had not yet
been forty-eight hours in the possession of the enemy; if forty-
eight hours and less than ninety-six hours, then one third; if
more than ninety-six hours, one half.

The king of *England* and the states-general were pleased
to establish between them the same distinction and division of
time, and the same rates of salvage, by the treaty above mentioned of the 22d of *October* 1689, in case a privateer of
one nation should retake the ships or goods of a subject of the
other party, but if the recapture should be made by a ship of
war, the recaptor was to have only one eighth, without any
distinction of time.

Now, why so much variety? why these distinctions of time and those greater and lesser shares in proportion thereof? Whence again, if the distinction of time must be had, so much diversity in the proportion of the salvage? Why also, rejecting all distinction of time, is now so large a proportion as two thirds and now so small a one as one ninth allowed to the recaptor? Certainly it is difficult to give a reason for things that have been established without any reason, and here, if any where, it will be proper to refer to the law *non omnium**—the reader knows the rest. The public tranquillity of nations however, and the repose of our own subjects, require that something certain should be established upon rational principles. The whole depends upon this question: when do we consider that captured ships and goods vest absolutely in the enemy? The law indeed has decided that they so vest by a true and complete occupation. But the variety of cases and circumstances does not always permit us to know, whether there is actually a firm possession, that is to say, such a one as the captor may retain and defend. What the enemy has taken on the high seas, at a great distance from his territory, he may lose, and often loses by recapture. If he carries what he has taken into his own ports and territory, no one can doubt that it has then become his absolute property. I *would say the same* if he had carried it into the port of a neutral or of an ally, but *if this*, as I said above, *cannot be admitted*,† I *must* grant, that whatever is taken at sea, is to be carried into the captor's own port or fleet, and that it cannot be until then considered as fully his.

What then, if it be recaptured before that time? Then the former owner will have a right to claim his property, as the property has neither vested in the captor nor in the recaptor; I say the *former* owner, because there has been an intermediate possession of some kind. But shall the owner claim his property from the recaptor, without paying him any salvage or reward for the recapture? without any remuneration for his

---

* *Non omnium, quæ à majoribus constituta sunt, ratio reddi potest.* A reason cannot be given for every law which our ancestors have established. *Dig.* 1. 1. tit. 3. 1. 20.   *T.*

† See note, p. 38.

‡ F

labour and expense in and about the said recapture? this, equity, the supreme law of nations, will not permit. It requires that a salvage, premium, reward, something, in short, by whatsoever name it may be called, should be given. The recaptor has saved the ship and goods, which otherwise would have been lost to the owner, and why should he have exposed himself to danger without any hope of reward? why should he have fought for the property of another as if it were his own? why should he have employed his arms and his men to no purpose whatever? He has beneficially managed the business of the owner, and he is entitled for his labour and expenses to the action *negotiorum gestorum*.* I do not know of any other action in the *Roman* law proper for the recaptor; if the thing is to be decided by the rules of the *Roman* jurisprudence, for this action is the only proper one when a reward is sued for, either for work and labour done or for money laid out. But upon what law or principle it has been thought proper to give to the recaptor a part of the thing retaken, I do not myself understand; much less do I understand how that proportion can be greater or less according to the quantity of time that the thing taken has been in the hands of the enemy. What have 24, 48 or 96 hours to do here? The greater or lesser duration of the enemy's possession, when the thing taken has not been carried into a place of safety, cannot, in my opinion, give a greater or a less right.†

Wherefore, if the subject is to be considered according to the rules of reason, every distinction of time is to be abolished, and in lieu thereof is to be the proportioned value of the recaptor's labour and expenses, taking into consideration the danger that he has been exposed to, and the value of the things saved. From all these considerations taken together, impartial men are to settle and determine what reward he is entitled to. Nor should the allowance be dealt with a sparing, but

---

* This action in the civil law is analogous to our *general assumpsit* founded on an implied contract, for work and labour done and money laid out and expended.   *T.*

† See the case of the *Santa Cruz*, 1 Rob. 44. *Philad. edit.* in note.   *T.*

with a liberal hand, in order to encourage the industry of recaptors. For, is it to be of no consequence whether the recapture
has been made with great or little trouble or labour? whether
the recaptor has fought bravely? whether he has expended a
great deal? whether the things saved are of great or of little
value? If it should be observed that the valuation of such things
is so uncertain that it might occasion a great deal of litigation,
I answer, that as the matter stands, there will not be less controversy, and that there have often been great contestations
about the value of a ship and goods, and what ought to be de-
ducted from it,* before the true value thereof has been determined.

But afterwards, if you still chuse to give a part of the
thing saved, give it; not, indeed, in proportion to the time that
the prize has been in the possession of the enemy, but
to the labour employed upon it, as is usual in other cases
of salvage. Thus the *Rhodian* law has allowed a reward to
those who have saved property from shipwreck, varying according to the degree of labour, as is said by *Harmenopulus*,
Προχ. l. 2. tit. 11. § 18. agreeably to which I interpret the
reasonable salvage which *Mary* of *Burgundy* allowed to the
salvors of shipwrecked property, by her law made for *Holland*
and *Zealand*, on the 14th of *November* 1476. A proportion of
the thing saved from shipwreck was also allowed by the edict
which *Philip* II. on the 15th of *May* 1574 issued in the name
of *William* of *Orange*, which has been often since reenacted,
and lately, on the 2d of *April* 1676; but the salvor is allowed
there a greater proportion than is therein expressed, if he has
been at a greater labour and expense. I conceive that the
states of *Holland* had a view to this, when on the 22d of *July*
1677, they decreed a *reasonable* salvage to those who should
take up timbers floating down the rivers without any guard,
and deliver them up to the company of ship-builders at *Dordrecht.* Those laws do not distinguish, how long the things
shipwrecked, and the timbers found drifting may have been

---

* In the *United States,* salvage is generally allowed on the *gross* value of
the property saved.   *T.*

floating at the mercy of the sea, rivers and wind, as there is no reason for that distinction, but left it to the arbitration of impartial men, to determine the amount of the reward for the labour and expenses. Nor do I think that any other rule should be followed, with respect to ships and goods retaken from the enemy.

Indeed, in the book called *Il Consolato del Mare*, the point is determined exactly as I have said; for there the recaptor is ordered to restore the vessel and cargo to the former owner, saving however, a salvage, which, in order to be just, is to be liquidated in proportion to the labour and expense employed in and about the recapture,* without making any distinction about the time that the vessel and cargo have been in the possession of the enemy. It is very properly added in the same book, that this restitution only takes place when the ship has not yet been carried into a place of safety, but that if it has been so carried, the property having thus clearly vested in the enemy, if the ship and goods are afterwards retaken, they belong entirely to the recaptor.† Which agrees perfectly with the doctrine that I have contended for in this chapter. I wish that all the principles which are contained in that *farrago* of nautical laws were equally correct; but every thing that is there is not so sound.

---

* *Dando à quelli che a i detti nimici tolta haveranno,* BEVERAGGIO *conveniente, secondo la fatica che ne haveranno havuta, e secondo il danno che ne haveranno sofferto.* Giving to the recaptors a sufficient *beverage* or *drink-money,* in proportion to their labour and damage suffered. *Il Consol.* c. 287. In the late *French* translation by *M. Boucher,* it is c. 290. § 1136.   *T.*

† *Anzi debba essere tutta di loro.* Il Consol. Ibid.—Fr. Transl. *Ibid.* § 1138. *T.*

CHAPTER VI.

Of the Possession of Immovables taken in War.

WE must now consider, for the subject is worthy of it,
how far extends the possession of immovables acquired in war, and the property arising out of such possession. *Grotius** simply says, that every kind of possession
is not sufficient, but that it must be a *firm possession*, which he
explains thus: " as if a country is so provided with permanent
fortifications, that the adverse party cannot enter it openly
without first making himself master of them by force."
What then if the fortified town is taken; shall the country
be considered as taken also, and for how long? *Grotius*
decides absolutely nothing about this, and yet he often
proposes this question when he speaks of the capture and
occupation of places. An example will make the thing more
clear. The *French* had taken *Casal* and *Turin* in *Piedmont;* a
truce was afterwards made, during which it was agreed that
each party should keep what he had taken on the principle of
uti possidetis. A question was made about the territory and
villages which owed services and duties to the cities which
were held by the *French.*

There were lawyers who decided that question against the
French, on the ground that the law of nations requires
actual possession, acquired by natural means, and that the
part occupied does not draw along with it the part not occupied. Therefore they were of opinion that the obligation of
those inhabitants did not enure to the use of the *French*, as
the citizens themselves submitted to their dominion against
their will. It is thus contended by *Petrinus Bellus*,† with
whom I do not know whether *Zouch* agrees.‡ But I think
Bellus was mistaken: he was certainly so in the case of

* De Jure B. ac P. l. 3. c. 6. § 4.——† De re militari, part 5. t. 3. n. 7.——
‡ De Jure Fec. part 2. § 9. Q. 48.

a truce like the present, because the general words *uti posside-tis* embrace an implied as well as an actual possession. That implied possession consisted in the performing and receiving services and duties, which were usually rendered only to the master; but what actual possession is will be seen from what I am about to say.

Reason, therefore, is to point out to us, what may be properly called a possession of immovables, taken in war, which is that the whole is occupied and possessed, if such has been the intention of the captor; and thus *Paul* defines it in l. 3. § 1. *ff. de Acquir. vel amitt. rer. poss.* That this is not a principle merely of civil law, but also of natural law, the thing itself, and custom which is an excellent teacher, abundantly demonstrate. Possession extends to every thing that is occupied, and what is occupied is placed within our power by the law of nature; but even that is considered as occupied, which is not touched on all sides with our hands or feet, if the occupant so chuses, or the nature of the case requires it, as is the case with lands. On another principle it would not be easy to say what is possessed or occupied, for if every thing is to be touched, it is not even sufficient to touch the surface of the land; it will be not only necessary to walk round, but to dig into every field.

But although it be true, that a part being taken, the whole is taken, when the taking is made with that view or intent, yet it will not otherwise obtain, than if no other person possesses another part of the thing in question. For if another possesses a part of the same whole, he would by the same reason possess the whole. This cannot be said with propriety, for as *Paulus* very truly says in *D.* l. 3. § 5. two persons cannot at the same time possess the whole of the same thing, because the ownership of one would exclude the ownership of the other. If then one is in possession of a thing, and another takes a part of it which the other does not corporally occupy, he has taken nothing but what he has occupied by natural means, nor can the thing be possessed *pro ratâ*, in proportion to the parts which each actually occupies, because the possession of the first occupant is paramount, and

cannot be excluded by another, which is only similar, each of
them having the same force and effect as the other. And the
latter occupant has done away what is called the *legal
possession* of the other in that part which he detains, for no
other reason than because he possesses it by natural means;
for the natural possession has taken away the *legal* one. It
is the same thing that *Celsus* says in l. 18. § 4. *ff. Eod.* " *Si
cum magna vi ingressus est exercitus, eam tantùm modo
partem quam intraverit obtinet.* If an army has entered a
territory with great force, it has possession only of that part of
the country which it has entered upon." When he says, *with
great force,* he means that there was a resistance made, and
that there were those who defended by force the possession of
the first owners. An army, therefore, does not further occupy
a country than it has compelled the opposite army to recede.
Perhaps *Paulus* is to be thus understood, in *D.* l. 3. § 1. when
he says that a part being taken with intent to take the whole,
the whole is occupied, but to a certain extent only, *usque ad
terminum;* which I take to mean, so far as to that part which
another possesses, whether it be a neighbour on an adjoining
land, or some other person on the very land which is contended
for.

Hence it is not difficult to discern what may be considered
as properly occupied in an occupied country. The metro-
politan law of itself has nothing to do with this case, for
it is a municipal law which the sovereign may establish
wherever he pleases. If so, it is easily understood that if from
the occupation of a strong place, dominion is exercised over
the whole country, yet by that occupation, the victor is not
considered in possession of those cities, walled towns and fortresses which the sovereign still detains, but all these things are
to be judged of by the fact itself of occupation and possession.

According to this principle we say, that if a part of a country be occupied, the whole is considered as occupied, if the vanquished party has retained no other part of it; but if he has, then
nothing is occupied, but what the victor has taken by force
from the vanquished, and is actually in possession of. But in
regard to several distinct countries under the dominion of the

same prince, it may be asked, whether the same distinction can apply, which is used with regard to contiguous private estates? If *Titius* is the owner of three contiguous plantations, *A*, *B* and *C*, and *Gaius* occupies part of the plantation *A*, he will be considered as occupying the whole of it, but not the plantations *B* and *C*. For when we possess an estate, our possession goes as far as its extent, or its boundaries, but no farther; *fundo enim possesso, ad terminum quidem, sed ad terminum duntaxat, neque ultrà possidemus. D.* 1. 3. § 1. *ff. de Acquir. vel amitt. rer. poss.* He who has entered on part of the plantation *A*, is not supposed to have entered upon it with any other intent than to possess himself of the whole of that of which he has occupied a part, but he is not considered as having thought in the least of the manor *B* or the manor *C*. When we occupy a part of a whole which is distinguished from all other things, that distinction marks the boundaries of our possession, whether it be a house, a piece of land, a store or warehouse, or any other thing which comes under the denomination of *immovable property*.

But in my opinion there is another principle as to immovables which are occupied by right of conquest.

The intention of the conqueror is not merely to invade one district, but the whole of the hostile empire, and to make his own all the countries belonging to it. Nor is there here any boundary, but that part of the country which the vanquished still retains. If there is nothing that the conqueror cannot possess, if he pleases, what hinders him from proceeding on and actually possessing the whole? If no one district is retained by the vanquished, the occupation of a single one by the conqueror, nay, of the metropolis alone, will give him possession of the whole empire. Here we must acknowledge the truth of what the ambassador of the emperor *Justinian* said to *Chosroes*, king of *Persia*, according to *Menander Protector, Hist. Byzant.* tom. 1. p. 143. 'Ο γάρ δισπόσας 'Ηγιμονικῦ, πῶς ἐκ ἔχει τὸ ὑποβεβηκὸς? *Shall not he, who is the master of him who commands, also be the master of what is subject to him?* But if the conquered party still retains something, it will not be considered as a conquest of the whole of his dominions that his metropolis has been taken and is occupied by force of arms.

Those princes therefore have justly been laughed at, who because they had taken *Rome* or *Constantinople* arrogated to themselves the whole *Roman* empire, while other princes occupied several large parts of it. Of this kind was the arrogance of *Belisarius*, as related to us by *Procopius, de Bello Vandal.* l. 2. c. 4.; for he, after *Justinian* had taken *Carthage* and her king *Gelimer*, boasted publicly, that every thing belonged to him which *Gelimer* possessed in *Sicily*. Here he was altogether wrong, for the right which he had over *Carthage* and the person of her king, could not transfer to him the possession of what was in *Sicily*. *Sicily* defended itself by its own force, and by taking the king, the whole of his dominions was not taken. Actual occupation is necessary, or a cession, if it be so agreed by the treaty of peace.

Let us now see what the states-general have decreed upon this subject. When by the 3d section of the truce between the archduke of *Austria* and the states-general of the 9th of *April* 1609, it was agreed that each should continue to possess what he was in possession of at the time of the truce, and the archduke had posted up his edicts in the territory of *Kuyck*, which he occupied, the states-general on the 20th of *August* 1609 decreed, that that territory belonged to them, because they possessed the town of *Grave*, to which it was subject, and prohibited all others from exercising jurisdiction therein. When also the states-general had taken some fortresses in the *Overmaze*, and the *Spaniards* had nevertheless prohibited the inhabitants from submitting themselves to the jurisdiction of the council of *Brabant*, sitting at the *Hague*, the states, by way of retort, opposed that interdiction by their edict of the 8th of *March* 1634. Again, when *Boisleduc* belonged to the states-general, and the *Spaniards* made great disturbances respecting the territory thereof, the states obviated them by various edicts, viz. of the 20th of *January* and 3d of *August* 1630, 13th of *May* 1631, 20th of *June* 1634, 2d of *February* and 2d of *December* 1636, and again on the 24th of *December* 1642, in which edicts, of the

† G

8th of *March* 1634, and 2d of *February* 1636, is also recited the edict of the king of *Spain* of the 10th of *July* 1628, in which that sovereign asserts, at great length, that the territory subject to a town follows the conquest of the town itself. The states availed themselves of the same principle, and very properly too, because those are considered as being in possession of a territory, who command there at their pleasure. But if there is in that territory a fortress not yet occupied, so far as that fortress commands the territory, the possession and dominion of the occupier of the remaining part of the country does not take place.

If the principles which I have contended for are correct, as indeed they appear to me, the council of *Brabant*, which legislates at the *Hague* for those parts of *Brabant* which the states have taken by the right of war, has justly enacted by its edict of the 26th of *October* 1629, that the investiture of the fiefs situate in the territory of *Boisleduc*, was to be asked of them, and not of the council of *Brabant*, sitting at *Brussels*. And it also appears, that the king of *Spain* had no right to issue, as he did, a contrary edict on the 15th of *November*1629, as *Aitzema* relates in detail.* For, by the capture of *Boisleduc*, the whole adjacent territory belonged to the states-general, and therefore they were the lords of the fiefs situated there; as the conquered vassal owes fealty and services to the conqueror, not to the conquered prince.

There is still less doubt, that if a province be ceded, all its parts are ceded likewise. On this subject there is extant an edict of the states-general, of the 22d of *December* 1610, concerning *Twent*, a district of the province of *Over Yssel.*

* Aitz. b. 9.

CHAPTER VII.

Of the Confiscation of the Enemy's Actions and Credits.

IF there are treaties between princes about taking away their goods within a certain time in case war shall take place, several of which treaties I have above mentioned, c. 2.; it is true that they may remove their goods and effects as well as their actions and credits. But if there are no such treaties, or if the goods and actions are not taken away within a limited time, it is asked, what is the law in that case? And surely, such being the state of war, that enemies are on every legal principle proscribed and despoiled of every thing, it stands to reason that every thing belonging to the enemy, which is found in the hostile country, changes its owner and belongs to the *fisk.** It is besides customary in almost every declaration of war to proclaim that the goods of enemies, as well those found among us, as those taken in war, shall be confiscated.

There are also now extant on this subject separate acts of state, whether preceded or not by a declaration of war. The prince of *Orange*, on the 25th of *August* 1572, inserted in the form of government which he then made for *Holland,* " that the goods of all those who acted publicly as his enemies, should be immediately registered by the magistrate of the place where they were found, and their rents and profits should be taken for the benefit of the commonwealth." I understand this to apply to real estates, which it is usual to register, that the rents and profits in time of war may go to the public. If we follow the strict law of war, even immovables may be sold, and their proceeds be lodged in the public treasury, as is done with movables; but throughout almost all *Europe*, immovables are only registered, that the treasury may receive during the war their rents and profits.

---

* As we make use of the words *fiscal, confiscate, confiscation,* why should we not adopt in *America* the word *fisk,* from the Latin *fiscus,* which is the root of all those derivatives?   *T.*

At the termination of the war, the immovables themselves are by treaty restored to their former owners.

On the 2d of *April* 1599, the states-general again issued an edict with regard to all kinds of enemy's property, wherever found, which is in these words: " We declare lawful prize all persons and goods situate or being under the jurisdiction of the king of *Spain*, wherever the same may be taken." There exists also a letter from the states-general to the court of *Holland* dated the 25th of *November* 1672, by which they are simply ordered to detain and confiscate the goods of those who *reside* among the enemies, on which there issued an edict of the court of *Holland* of the same day, declaring that the goods could not be restored to their owners after the date thereof. I am not now inquiring whether this be agreeable to the treaty made in the year 1662, between the states-general and *France*. But as estates of inheritance are principally to be included under the denomination of goods, (*bona*)* it is clear that an enemy cannot acquire such an estate situate in our country, even though it came to him by succession or by will. Agreeably to this principle, when in the year 1695, a person died intestate in *Holland*, whose next of kin and heirs at law were in *France*, I remember that the inheritance was confiscated.

As the edicts which I have recited speak in general terms, they are to be taken to apply to all kinds of goods, whether corporeal or incorporeal. Of incorporeal goods, however, such as actions and credits, I see that doubts exist, and that the states-general themselves have doubted,† nay, and have some-

---

* At the civil law the word *bona* includes every kind of property, real, personal and mixed, but chiefly, as our author says, applies to *real* estates, *chattels* being generally distinguished by the words *effects, movables*, &c. The *English* civilians translate the word *bona* by *goods*, which we employ here in the same sense, though very different from that of the common law.　　　　　　　　　　　　　　　　　　　　　　　　*T.*

† Not only doubts have been entertained on this subject in the *United States* and *Great Britain*, but the two governments by the treaty which was made between them in 1794 have expressly recognised the opposite principle. By the tenth article of that treaty, it is stipulated " that neither the debts due from individuals of the one nation to individuals of the other, nor shares, nor moneys which they may have in the public funds or in the public

times acted in contradiction to the principle. When the king of *France* and the bishops of *Cologne* and *Munster*, in the year 1673, confiscated even *actions*,* and gave orders to call in what their subjects owed to the citizens of the *United Provinces*, the states-general, by their edict of the 6th of *July* 1673, reprobated it, and decreed that payment could not be made but to the true creditor, and that they would not ratify such an exaction, whether made by force or by consent. But in fact it appears that by the common law† actions may be confiscated, for the same reason that corporeal goods may. Actions and credits are by the law of nations not less under our dominion than other goods; why, therefore, might we pursue these and not those by the law of war? and if there is no ground here for a rational distinction, reason alone supports the principle of the common law. But examples and authorities are not wanting in support of it.

It appears from *Polybius, Excerpt. Legat.* c. 35. n. 4., that it was agreed between the *Romans* and *Antiochus*, that actions, as well as every thing else which had been confiscated during the war, should be restored. Therefore it follows, that actions had been confiscated on both sides. That the kings of *France* and *Spain* also exercised this right towards each other, appears by the twenty-second article of the treaty of peace made between them, on the 17th of *September* 1678, for by that article it is stipulated that credits which have been actually confiscated shall not be restored. And the king of *Denmark*, having declared war against the *Swedes*, did on the 9th of *March* 1676 issue an edict ordering that the goods of *Swedes* within the *Da-*

or private banks, shall ever in any event of war or national differences be sequestered or confiscated, it being *unjust and impolitic* that debts and engagements contracted and made by individuals, having confidence in each other and in their respective governments, should ever be destroyed or impaired by national authority on account of national differences and discontents."   *T.*

* Here we again use the technical language of the civil law. The common law term is *things*, or *choses in action*.   *T.*

† The civil law and the law of nations are very frequently styled " the common law" (*jus commune*) by writers on the continent of *Europe*. They are, in fact, in many respects, the *common law* of the civilized world.   *T.*

nish empire, and all the debts due to *Swedes*, should be brought within six weeks into the public treasury, there to be confiscated, under a penalty of double the value and discretionary punishment against those who should not obey. The king of *Denmark* had decreed something similar against the *English* in 1667, as is related by *Aitzema*.*

Nor does it appear that the *Dutch* have always been averse to that doctrine from the edict of the 18th of *July* 1536, from that of *Philip* II. against the *French* of the 27th of *March* 1556, and that of the states of *Holland* of the 29th of *January* 1591. There is also an edict which the prince of *Orange* and the court of *Holland* issued on the 7th of *December* 1577, under the assumed name of *Philip* II. king of *Spain*, by which they ordered the confiscation of all the movable and immovable property, and of all the actions and credits, not only of those who had gone over to Don *John* of *Austria*, but of all their enemies. The states-general also, on the 4th of *June* 1584, declared those of *Bruges* and *Vrye*, who had gone over to the *Spaniards*, to be their enemies, and ordered all their goods, actions and credits, public as well as private, to be confiscated. And afterwards, when those of *Venloo* had also gone over to the *Spaniards*, the earl of *Leicester*, by his edict of the 9th of *July* 1586, declared them guilty of the crime of high treason, and ordered all their goods, movable and immovable, and all their actions and credits, to be confiscated. Nor must it be believed that these things were decreed concerning those of *Bruges*, *Vrye*, and *Venloo*, merely because they were not so much enemies as they were traitors, as they had previously bound themselves by the confederation of *Utrecht;* for I must observe, that the penalties of the edict of the 4th of *June* 1584 are expressly applied to all *who hold themselves to be our adversaries, in whatever manner it may be*, precisely as in the abovementioned edict of the 7th of *December* 1577, traitors and enemies are classed together, as to that particular purpose.

Under this head are also to be noted the decrees of the states-general of the 2d, and of the states of *Holland* of the 29th of

---

* Aitz. b. 47.

October 1590, in both of which the following sentence is contained: " That those who come into these provinces out of the enemy's territory, although provided with proper passports, shall not be qualified to bring any personal or real action, either in the petitory or in the possessory, but shall be dismissed from court, in order that hostility against the enemies, and the confiscation of their goods, rights and actions, may subsist in their fullest extent." By these decrees they are not permitted to bring even personal actions, and the reason publicly given for it clearly shews that they cannot do it, because not only the goods of enemies but their actions are liable to confiscation. And when once the king of *France* had ordered the goods of *Dutch* subjects to be seized, the states of *Holland*, on the 26th of *April* 1657, ordered the same thing with regard to the goods of *French* subjects, and prohibited any body from paying to them, on pain of being compelled to pay the amount a second time, for the indemnity of the *Dutch* subjects who had suffered by the seizure of their goods in *France*, and of paying moreover half the amount of the debt by way of punishment, and they ordered the goods and credits of *Frenchmen* to be brought under a penalty to certain officers appointed in each town for that purpose. Wherefore, if the subject of a prince who has confiscated the credits of his enemies, should pay to his government what he owed to the enemy, it has been very properly held that he is discharged.

These things, however, do not take place when war is carried on with so much mildness that commerce is permitted on both sides: for there cannot be any commerce without contracts, contracts without actions, actions without courts of justice, nor courts of justice without parties to litigate before them. Who will sell and carry goods to an enemy without the hope of recovering the price of them? and what hope can there be of recovering that price, if one cannot judicially compel payment from his enemy purchaser? Although, therefore, an enemy has no *persona standi in judicio*,* as it is

---

* No right to be heard as plaintiff in courts of justice. *T.*

simply expressed in the decrees of the 2d and 29th of *October* 1590, and although it has been thus held and adjudged in this country in various instances, yet the case of commerce is properly excepted, that is to say, when there is a mutual liberty of trade; for if there is not, actions, though arising out of commerce, may justly be confiscated. But is the case of commerce to be so distinguished from all other cases, that in this we grant, and in others we refuse to the enemy the *persona standi in judicio?* It has undoubtedly been so adjudged, and if the distinction is proper here, it must also obtain as to the confiscation of actions. But if the enemy be once permitted to bring actions, it is difficult to distinguish from what causes they arise, nor have I been able to observe, that this distinction has ever been carried into practice.

Moreover, if you do not permit your enemy to bring actions, neither can you with justice suffer them to be brought against your enemy, if perchance he should tarry within your territory, and thus the decree of our supreme senate, of the 18th of *September* 1590, confirming the sentence of the inferior judge and of the court of *Holland* is unjust, to wit, that an enemy, who had come with a safe conduct into this country, might be arrested and held to bail in a civil action. For it is manifestly unjust to hinder an enemy from bringing actions, (as he is plainly forbidden by the said decrees of the 2d and 29th of *October* 1590,) and not to allow him the same privilege. Whatever right one arrogates to himself by the law of war, he must also allow to his enemy.

What I have said about the legality of confiscating actions, obtains only in case the prince has really made his subjects pay what they owed to the subjects of his enemies. If he has exacted it, they have lawfully paid, if not, when the peace takes place, the former right of the creditor revives, because the occupation which is had by war consists more in fact than in law. Therefore credits not exacted are in some manner suspended during the war, but at the peace they return to their former owners by a kind of postliminy. Upon this principle it has been agreed among almost all nations, that actions which have been confiscated during the war, and have been called in by the sovereign, are considered at the peace as lost, and are for ever extinct; but if they have not been exacted they revive and return to the real creditors. It was thus agreed by the fifth article of the treaty of peace between *Frede-rick* III. king of *Denmark* and *Charles* II. king of *England*, of the 31st of *July* 1667, the thirty-seventh article of the treaty of peace between the kings of *Spain* and *England*, of the 21st of *September* 1667, and the twenty-second article of the treaty of peace between the kings of *France* and *Spain* of the 17th of *September* 1678, which twenty-second article I have mentioned above in this chapter, in order to establish what is proved by the said 5th and 37th articles, that actions have not less than other goods of the enemy been confiscated in time of war, and have often been exacted.*

Let it not, however, be supposed, that it is only true of actions that they are not condemned *ipso jure;* for other things also, belonging to the enemy, may be concealed and escape condemnation. So that it has been very properly held that those things which we had in the enemy's country before the war began, and which during the war have been concealed, and therefore not condemned, if they are afterwards retaken by our countrymen, do not become the property of the re-captors, but return to the former owners.

* *Vattel,* though he acknowledges the legality of confiscating in war the enemy's actions and credits, yet tells us that a more liberal practice has generally prevailed in modern times. "*Mais aujourd'hui, l'avantage et la sûreté du commerce ont engagé tous les souverains de l'Europe à se relâcher de cette rigueur.* But at this day, the advantage and security of commerce have induced *all the sovereigns of Europe* to relax from this severity." *Vatt. Law of Nat.* b. 3. c. 5. § 77.   *T*

† H

CHAPTER VIII.

Of Hostilities in a neutral Port or Territory.

WE only exercise the rights of war in our own territory, in the enemy's, or in a territory which belongs to no one. If we take the enemy in our own territory, and he has come to it without a safe conduct, there is nothing that prohibits our treating him in a hostile manner. To enter the territory of an enemy, and there to make captures, is permitted by the law of war. The same may lawfully be done on the high seas, as being the territory of no one. But he who commits hostilities on the territory of a friend to both parties, makes war upon the sovereign who governs there, and who by his laws coerces every violence, by whomsoever it may be committed. Therefore the *Carthaginians*, though with a superior naval force, did not dare to attack the *Romans* in a port of the king of *Numidia*, as *Grotius* (after *Livy**) relates in l. 3., *De Jur. Bell. ac Pac.* c. 4. § 8. n. 2., and *Zouch*, *De Jur. Fec.* part 2. § 9. Q. 7., transcribes it out of *Grotius*. *Zouch* there states some contrary arguments, but *Grotius* had already mentioned and refuted them.

But as all the publicists (without any exception that I know of) prohibit the use of force in the dominions of another, it deserves to be considered, whether the usage of nations and the edicts of our princes† and states‡ are conformable to this opinion, and whether on this subject the right to pursue ought to be distinguished from the right to attack? To begin with the princes. *Philip* II. king of *Spain*,§ in the nautical laws

---

* *Liv* l. 28. c. 17.

† The counts of *Holland*, who were the sovereigns of that province before the *Dutch* revolution. 　　　　　　　　　　　　　　*T.*

‡ The states-general of the *United Netherlands*, and the provincial states of *Holland*. 　　　　　　　　　　　　　　　　*T.*

§ Who was also *count of Holland*, and sovereign under different titles of the seventeen provinces of the *Netherlands*. 　　　　　　　　*T.*

which he gave to the *Belgians* on the last day of *October* 1563, (tit. 1. § 27.) ordered, on pain of death, that no violence should be done on the sea, by reason of war or for any other cause, on his subjects or allies, or on *foreigners*, within sight from land or from a port. He therefore understood the dominion of the continent to be extended as far as the sight can reach from the shore, and there are authors who are of that opinion. But I have shewn this to be too vague, in the second chapter of my Dissertation *de Dominio Maris*, being of opinion that the dominion of land ends where the power of arms terminates. And that the states-general and the states of *Holland* were of the same opinion, I think I have sufficiently proved by the two decrees made concerning the salute at sea, quoted in the said chapter 2, and also in chapter 4.*

Certainly it is by no means lawful to attack or take an enemy in the port of a neutral who is in amity with both parties. If it be done, it is the duty of the neutral state to cause the thing taken to be restored, either at its own expense or at the expense of the injured party. That it should be done at the expense of the latter has been agreed by the twenty-second article of the treaty of peace between the commonwealth of *England* and the states-general of the 5th of *April* 1654, the twenty-first article of the treaty of peace between the king of *England* and the states-general of the 14th of *September* 1662 and again by the 29th article of the treaty of peace between the same powers of the 31st of *July* 1667. The same is stipulated by the forty-eighth article of the commercial treaty between the king of *France* and the states-general

---

† The states of *Holland* decreed on the 3d of *January* 1671, that their ships of war should salute those of other sovereigns on their coasts within reach of the cannon of batteries and forts, precisely in such manner as the government of the country should require, leaving it entirely to its discretion to return or not the salute; adding, that every government is sovereign within its own jurisdiction, and every foreigner is a subject there. *Bynk. de Dom. Mar.* c. 2. On the 16th of *May* 1670 the same states decreed that the *Danish* fort of *Croneborg* situate on the shores of the sound in the *Baltic* sea, should be saluted in such manner as the king of *Denmark* should require. *Ibid.* c. 4.　　　　　　　　　　　　　　　　　　　　　*T.*

of the 27th *April* 1662, but there is no mention made therein
of the expenses being to be borne by the injured party, which
appears to me to be very unjust, as it is the duty of the sovereign of the territory to revenge the injury done to himself; for
it is an injury done to him to violate a port which is equally
open to all his friends. And what if he who committed the violence goes away immediately? Is the individual, whose vessel,
perhaps, has been taken, to make war at his own expense?
Therefore the mention of the expense is properly omitted in
the thirty-fifth article of the treaty of commerce which was
made between the same powers on the 10th of *August* 1678,
in the fortieth article of the treaty of commerce between the
same of the 20th of *September* 1697, and again in the thirty-
ninth article of the treaty of commerce between the same of
the 11th of *April* 1713, for later treaties are generally without
any further examination copied from the former ones, as we
have seen just now to have been the case with the *English*.
Those articles of treaties between *France* and the states-
general only stipulate that the sovereign of the port, bay or
river in which a prize shall be made from a friend, shall use
his utmost endeavours that the captured property be fairly
and justly restored. If it be the duty of the sovereign to use
his utmost endeavours to effect that purpose, it follows that
he must do it at his own expense, nay, by going to war, if
other means are not sufficient. Such is the law which is observed among all nations, and there is no other reason for it
than that it is not lawful to commit violence within the territory of another, and that ports, *bays*,* and rivers, are also
within the territory of the sovereign of the country. Thus the
grand duke of *Tuscany*, in the year 1695, caused the *French*,

---

* In the year 1793 the *British* ship *Grange* was captured by the *French*
frigate *L'Ambuscade*, in the waters of the bay of *Delaware*, and brought
into the port of *Philadelphia*, to which she was bound. The *British* minister
demanded her restitution of the government of the *United States*. In vain
did the *French* minister, *M. Ternant*, allege that the bay of *Delaware* was
an open sea, not subject to the exclusive jurisdiction of the *American*
government. His arguments had no effect, and the *Grange* was very properly restored.   *T.*

who had taken near the port of *Leghorn* a ship of the powers
allied against *France*, who were friends to the grand duke,
and carried her into that port, to restore her immediately; for,
as I have said, the sea which is near to the ports of a sovereign
is a part of his territory. These principles may easily be applied to the following cases:

In the year 1639, while admiral *van Tromp* was blockading in
the *Downs* the fleet of the *Spaniards*, who were in amity with
England, the states-general, on the 21st and 30th of *September*
1639, issued decrees by which they ordered him " to destroy
the *Spanish* fleet, without paying any regard to the harbours,
roads, or bays of the kingdoms where it might be found,
even though the *English* should make resistance," and the
admiral immediately carried that order into execution, and
was praised and approved for it by the states-general, as is
commemorated by *Aitzema* in various places.*

This can hardly be defended, neither can the conduct of
the *English*, who, on the 12th of *August* 1665, took some
ships of our *East India* company, in the port of *Bergen*, in
Norway,† not without great indignation in the *Danes*, who
repelled the *English* with all their might. In order, however,
that the case of *van Tromp* may not be considered as too out-
rageous, two things are to be attended to; the one, that the
English, in the year 1627, had taken out of *Holland* a ship of
the king of *France*, then at war with *England*, but in amity
with the states-general;‡ the other, that the *Spaniards* themselves, in the year 1631, were charged with having committed
hostilities against the ships of the states-general, in the ports
of the king of *Denmark*, then a common friend to both, as I
read in *Aitzema*.§ Otherwise, if nothing can be charged that
gives just cause to exercise the right of retaliation,¶ it is manifestly unjust to attack an enemy in the port of a common
friend. And thus the states-general decreed in the year

---

* Aitz. l. 19.——† Ibid. l. 45, 6, 7.——‡ Ibid. l. 7. 9. 19. 20.——§ Ibid. l. 11.

¶ But see page 33, where our author justly contends that retaliation is
only to be exercised directly against the enemy, and never through the
injury of a friend.   *T.*

1623,* on a memorial of the *English* ambassador. The ships of the states-general had committed hostilities against the ships of *England*, in the river *Elbe*, a neutral river. Great complaints were made on this subject, not only by the *English*, but by the *Hamburghers*, and various ambassadors of the *Germanic* empire.† As to the complaints of the *English*, they could easily have been silenced, by reminding them of what had happened the preceding year at *Bergen*, in *Norway*, but it was not so with the others, for this aggression was solely founded on the right of retaliation. Nor can it be doubted that the *French* acted very unjustly, when in the year 1693 they set fire to certain *Dutch* ships in the port of *Lisbon*, at that time neutral, which the king of *Portugal* would not either permit to be fired at nor to be taken away. This fact I assert from my own memory.

It might be more doubted, whether it is lawful to pursue in the heat of battle an enemy met with on the high seas, into a neutral river, station, port or bay? The weight of argument is in favour of permitting it, on taking certain precautions which I shall enumerate by and by. Such certainly was the opinion of the states-general in the year 1623,‡ when they answered to the *English* ambassador that it was not lawful to commit violence in a neutral port, " with this understanding, however, that it was hoped his majesty would not take it amiss, if any *Dunkirkers* were met with on the high seas, that they might be pursued even along the king's coasts and into the king's ports." The same opinion of the states-general appears expressed in their decree of the 10th of *October* 1652,§ but so, however, as is very properly added in it, that the castles of neutrals be spared, even though violence should be committed from them, and that the enemies also be spared, if they should have already entered the neutral ports. Both of these exceptions are right, for it is better to suffer within the dominions of another than to act, and if we act, we are to be very careful that the force used against our enemy shall not

---

* Aitz. l. 3.——† Ibid. l. 45, 6, 7.——‡ Ibid. l. 3.——§ Aitz. l. 32.

hurt our friend. If therefore two fleets fight in the open sea, I do not pretend that the conqueror may not justly pursue the conquered fleet, even though it should be driven to the territory of a neutral. But I approve the direction of the states-general in their decree of the 10th of *October* 1652, to abstain from violence in the port itself, because violence could not be done there without danger to the neutral. On this principle it is not lawful to begin an attack on the sea near the land, within shot of the cannon from the fortresses, but it is lawful to continue an attack already commenced, and pursue the enemy into a jurisdictional sea even close to the land, or into a river, bay or creek, provided we spare the fortresses, though they should assist the enemy, and provided there be no kind of danger to our friends.

From facts which afterwards took place, the states-general appear to have approved even thus much; for when in the year 1654 a *Dutch* commander met an *English* vessel on the high seas and pursued her flying into the port of *Leghorn*, where he took her at the moment she was coming to anchor, the grand duke of *Tuscany* complained of it to the states-general, but we read that he complained in vain.* He, however, afterwards took satisfaction, by condemning the *Dutch* vessel that had made the pursuit and occasioned the capture of the *English* one.† Again, when the *Ostenders* had fired at a *Dutch* ship which was pursuing an *English* vessel into the port of *Ostend*, the states-general‡ complained of it to the court of *Spain* as of an illegal act, because the *Dutch* ship had not fired at the *English* vessel in the port of *Ostend*. But this reason is not good, except to aggravate the injury done to the *Ostenders*, for it is not of any consequence what kind of hostility you commit on your enemy, but whether you attack him in a hostile manner. Upon the whole, it appears that the states-general approved both the pursuits that I have mentioned, because the force was begun before, and was only continued.

* Aitz. l. 4.——† Ibid.——‡ Aitz. l. 45.

The law is the same at land as it is on the sea; so that there as well as here we may justly pursue an enemy flying from a recent fight into the dominion of another. I think the states-general acted in conformity with this opinion when they decreed, in 1653,* that the *Lorrain* soldiers, who had ravaged the *Dutch* dominions, might be pursued even into the dominions of the king of *Spain;* but this cannot be defended, unless it is a fresh pursuit from a conflict or devastation immediately preceding. Otherwise, we may not any more make use of the territory than of the port of a friend, to destroy our enemy. And the states-general very properly, at the request of the king of *France*, who was at peace with the king of *Spain*, forbade upon pain of death, that any one should commit hostilities against the *Spaniards*, in the dominions of the king of *France*.†

The states-general also justly complained of the *Spaniards*, when in the year 1666, those of *Munster* passed through their territory to commit depredations in the dominions of the states-general, and they demanded of *Spain* an indemnity for the damage which they had suffered from them. This demand‡ might have been just, if the *Spaniards* had willingly and knowingly permitted those of *Munster* to pass through their territory, in order to go and commit depredations; but it does not any where appear that the case was so. If they knew it, it was their duty to prevent any hostility being committed against their friends from their territory.

Therefore I do not approve of the conduct of those of *Wolffenbuttel*, who, in the year 1700, being, as is said, neutral, permitted the *Saxons* to commit depredations from their territory on those of *Lunenburg*, and in like manner permitted the allies of the *Lunenburgers* to kill the *Saxons*. At the utmost it is lawful, after a recent fight, to pursue the flying enemy into another's dominion; for the same reason that *Philip* II. king of *Spain*, by the seventy-sixth section of his criminal edict of 1570, gave permission to pursue a criminal immediately and *flagrante delicto* into a territory not our own. But it is one thing to begin

* Aitz. l. 33,——† Aitz. l. 2.——‡ Aitz. l. 46.

a hostility, and another to pursue the force while the thing is yet warm. For it is not a new doctrine, that an act lawfully begun may be continued where it would not have been lawful to give it a beginning. In short, it is not lawful to begin force within the territory of a neutral, but if begun out of that territory, it is lawful to continue it there in the heat of action, *dùm fervet opus.*

Thus it seems that this distinction may be made and contended for without absurdity. Yet I have never seen it mentioned, either in the writings of the publicists or among any of the *European* nations, the *Dutch* only excepted. Nevertheless, reason both persuades and commands it, and it is made use of in other analogous cases. If we attend to it, we shall without difficulty decide on the following fact: A *Spanish* ship pursued by a *French* ship (the two nations being at war) fled into *Torbay*, was run aground there, and concealed her cordage, tackle, sails, &c. in the houses of the inhabitants. The *French* mariners went on shore and took those articles from the houses they were in, and carried them on board of their own ship. Now was it lawful for the *French* to attack the houses of the *English*, and to take away the things that were protected there? It could not be done without injury to the *English;* therefore the king of *England* in the year 1668 very properly ordered every thing to be restored, and recommended the prosecution of the national injury to his ambassador in *France*, as we are told by *Aitzema.** The same author relates† other complaints of the *English* for the violation of their ports by the *French*, and informs us of the damages which they paid therefor, but I shall not particularise those cases; the reader will judge of them by attending to the distinction which I have just now suggested, if he is as satisfied with it as I am.

* Aitz. l. 48.   † Ibid.

† I

CHAPTER IX.

Of Neutrality.

I CALL neutrals (*non hostes**) those who take part with neither of the belligerent powers, and who are not bound to either by any alliance. If they are so bound, they are no longer neutrals, but allies. *Grotius* has called them middle men, (*medii*) l. 3. *De J. B. ac P.* c. 9. Of these it is asked what is lawful for them to do or not to do between two belligerent parties? Every thing, perhaps it will be said, that it was lawful for them to do or to omit doing when they were all at peace, for the state of war does not seem to extend farther than to those who are at war with each other. Does reason require, will you say, that the enemies of our friends should be considered as our own enemies? If not, why shall not our friends carry to their friends, though they be our enemies, those things which they were in the habit of carrying to them before? nay, arms, men, and every thing else? It militates, indeed, against our own advantage, but we are not considering what is advantageous, but what is reasonable. The injury suffered is alone the cause of the war, and it is evident that that injury has no effect beyond the person of him who has suffered it, except, that if he is a prince, it extends also to all his subjects, but not to those who are not subject to his dominion. Whence it must follow, that my friend's enemy is not my enemy, but that the friendship between us subsists precisely as it did before the war.

* It is remarkable that there are no words in the *Latin* language which precisely answer to the *English* expressions, *neutral, neutrality;* for *neutralis, neutralitas,* which are used by some modern writers, are barbarisms, not to be met with in any classical author. These make use of the words *amici, medii, pacati,* which are very inadequate to express what we understand by *neutrals,* and they have no substantive whatever (that we know of) for *neutrality.* We shall not here inquire into the cause of this deficiency. Such an inquiry would carry us too far, and does not comport with the object of this work.   *T.*

We find that the counsellors of the states-general adopted this doctrine, when on the 3d of *March* 1640 the states issued an edict on their report, declaring that *agreeably to ancient custom and to the law of neutrality*, it was lawful for neutrals to fight for us or for our enemies as they might think proper. And when the *Spaniards*, on the 30th of *March* 1639, issued an edict declaring that if any of the people of *Liege* had enlisted in the service of the states-general, they should return within one month, having first taken an oath that they would no more fight against *Spain* or the house of *Austria*, otherwise, every pardon would be denied to them, a similar edict was made in retaliation on the 3d of *March* 1640, in the name of the states-general, of which I remember that it was to be in force as long as that of *Spain*, which in the said edict of the 3d of *March* 1640 was represented as an innovation, entirely devoid of reason, and stigmatized in these words: " *an un-reasonable edict—such novelty and unreasonableness—so long as the Spaniards shall continue in force their unreasonable edict*," &c. Such also was the opinion of certain *Dutch* citizens, expressed in the states of *Holland*, on the 26th of *February* 1684, when they urged the sending of auxiliary troops to the *Spaniards*, to be employed against the *French*, which they said could be done without injury to the peace then subsisting with *France, salvâ pace et amicitiâ cum Francis.*

But certainly this opinion is not to be approved, if we speak of those who are simply neutrals. It is their duty to be every way careful not to intermeddle at all with the war, and not to do more or less justice to one party than to the other. It is the same thing that we read in *Livy*, b. 35. c. 48. *Bello se non interponant*, let them not intermeddle with the war, that is to say, *in causâ belli*, as to what relates to the war, let them not prefer one party to the other, and this is the only proper conduct for neutrals. I do not know whether what *Grotius* says, *De J. B. ac P.* c. 7. § 3., will be satisfactory: " The duty of those, says he, who abstain from the war, is to do nothing by which he who supports an unjust cause shall be made stronger, or whereby the motions of him who carries on a just war may be impeded." If I judge rightly, a neutral has nothing at all to do with the justice or injustice of the war, it is not for him to sit as judge between his friends who are at war with each other, and to give or deny more or less to the one or to the other as he thinks that their cause is more or less just or unjust. If I am a neutral, I cannot be useful to one that I may hurt the other, *alteri non possum prodesse, ut alteri noceam.*

But, will you say, may not I send to each of them whatever I may think proper? It is what friendship requires. If one power makes use of what I shall send him for the destruction of the other, what is that to me? But you must not adopt such an opinion: you must rather believe, that the enemies of our friends are to be considered in two points of view; either as our friends; or as the enemies of our friends. If we consider them only as our friends, then it is proper to assist them with advice, soldiers, arms, and all that they may want to carry on the war. But inasmuch as they are the enemies of our friends, it is not lawful for us to do so, because we thus would prefer, *in causâ belli*, one of them to the other; and this the equality of friendship, which is first to be attended to, forbids. It is more important to preserve friendship with both, than by favoring one of them *in causâ belli*, thus tacitly to renounce the friendship of the other.

And indeed, what I have just now said is not only conformable to reason, but to the usage admitted by almost all nations. For although it be lawful for us to carry on trade with the enemies of our friends, usage has so ordered it, as I shall shew more at large in the next chapter, that we should not assist either of them with those things by which the war against our friends may be carried on. It is therefore unlawful to carry to either party those things which are necessary in war, such as cannon, arms, and what is most essentially useful, soldiers; nay, soldiers are positively excepted by the treaties of various nations, and sometimes also materials for building ships, which might be used against our friends, have been excepted. Provisions likewise are often excepted, when the enemies are besieged by our friends, or are *otherwise* pressed by famine.* The law has very properly forbidden our supplying the enemy with any of those things; for it would be, as it were, making war against our friends. Therefore if we consider the belligerents merely as our friends, we may lawfully carry on trade with them, and carry to them any kind of merchandize, but if we consider them as the enemies of our friends, those merchandizes must be excepted, by means of which they might injure those friends; and this reason is stronger than the former, for in whatever manner we may assist one against the other, we do interfere in the war, which is not consistent with the duties of neutrality. From these reasons may be seen which had the most justice on its side, the edict of the *Spaniards* of the 30th of *March* 1639, or that of the states-general of the 3d of *March* 1640, of both of which I have spoken above.

Thus I have shortly laid down what has appeared to me to be the duty of those powers which are not bound by any alliance, but are in a state of *perfect* neutrality.† These I have

---

* It was probably on the principle which this vague word *otherwise* seems to indicate, that the *British* government issued their *provision order* against *France*, or rather against *neutrals*, on the 8th of *June*, and signed their convention with *Russia*, on the 25th of *March* 1793. If such is the *strict* law of nations, we must again repeat what we have said in a former note, that it is very nearly allied to *barbarism*. *T.*

† There are two kinds of neutrality, which some writers distinguish by the words *perfect* and *imperfect*, and others by *absolute* and *qualified*. *Absolute* neutrality is when the neutral is bound to neither of the belligerents by a treaty, the execution of which may affect the other in case of war, otherwise, his neutrality is no longer *absolute*, but *qualified*. Thus if a neutral is bound by treaty to admit the prizes of one party into his ports and not those of the other. At the beginning of the war of 1793 the *United States* were neutrals between *France* and *Great Britain*, and so our government declared them to be by that proclamation which at the time excited so much sensation; our neutrality, however, was not *absolute*; it was *qualified* by the treaties made with *France* in 1778, which, independent of the mutual guaranties and eventual alliance, contained several articles that applied only to a time of war. Between a *qualified neutrality* and an *alliance* there are many shades, and it is often difficult to draw the line which separates the one from the other. Our author, however, seems here to confound them together, and to consider every *qualified neutrality* as an *alliance*. *T.*

simply called neutrals, in order to distinguish them from allies and confederates. If the doctrine which I have contended for be correct, I cannot agree to the principle which I have seen advanced by many writers upon public law, to wit, that I may and ought to support and assist that one of my friends whose cause appears to me the best and the most just, not only by supplying him with military stores, but by going openly to war for him, if the case require it. This is not correct, for it is never right to interfere with the business of others. When neither of my friends has entered into any engagement with me, why shall princes, who are independent, and masters of their own actions, stand or fall by my judgment? It does not belong to me to avenge the injuries of every sovereign; it is sufficient if I avenge my own, and those of my allies. If, however, the injury done to another is such, that I may fear for myself, and there be no other hope left, but of being the last devoured, it may perhaps be admitted, that I ought to assist my oppressed friend; for it cannot be otherwise than impious to make war upon a friend, while he continues to be called such, and unless your friendship with him has been first dissolved.

As to allies and confederates, the thing is quite different. If two sovereigns with whom I am allied, are at war with other nations, I shall administer to both the succours which I am bound to give by treaty; but if they are at war with each other, shall I assist both, or only one of them, and which of them in preference? On this question the interpreters of the law are at variance with each other, not less so than nations themselves. *Gentilis, De Jure Belli*, l. 3. c. 18. relates various opinions, and adds his own; *Grotius, De Jure Bell. ac P.* l. 2. c. 15. § 13., and after him *Zouch, De Jure Fec.* part 2. § 4. Q. 28., lay down various distinctions. Certainly auxiliary troops shall not be sent to each ally, even though they be due by treaty; for it would be most absurd to send my soldiers to both, that they may fight against each other. Those who hire out their soldiers are often in that predicament, but this does not belong to the present disquisition. As to myself, I think that whether my allies are at war with a foreign nation, or with each other, the only thing to be distinguished, is which of the two has the most just cause of going to war. If they are both engaged in a just war with foreigners, I shall render to both that aid which I am bound by treaty to give: if only one of them, I shall deny it to the other. If two of my allies are at war with each other, I shall perform the obligation of my treaty with respect to him who has the best cause, of which I shall be myself the judge, as you will hear by and by. And thus we may easily do without the opinions and distinctions of others.

But what if I have promised succours to my ally and confederate, and he is at war with my friend? I think that promises are to be performed, and may be performed, because allies constitute, as it were, one society to be defended by mutual assistance. But here I must distinguish, whether my ally has received an injury, or has inflicted one; if he has received it, I shall perform my promise: if on the contrary he is the aggressor, I shall not perform it, because I am not bound to assist my ally in an unjust cause. But whether the cause be just or unjust, is to be determined by the judgment of the party bound.*

I wish indeed, that what I have said of the justice and injustice of a cause, was clearly and roundly expressed in treaties between nations; but those which I have seen simply express, that the one ally shall furnish to the other, when attacked, so many naval or land forces, and no more is said. But when the treaties say *when attacked*, there can be no other interpretation, but that succours are to be given to that ally, who is unjustly made war upon; to him who is attacked by, not to him who attacks the enemy. However, I do not find that expression, *when attacked*, sufficiently clear. For what if he who is *attacked* should have done an injury to the other, and thus have afforded him a cause of

* Our author seems here to be at variance with himself. See the preceding page and page 66, where he says that " a neutral has nothing *at all* to do with the justice or injustice of the war," *belli justitia* NIHIL QUICQUAM *pertinet ad communem amicum.* Much less does it concern an *ally,* or one who is bound by the solemn engagements of a treaty. See on this subject the able reasoning of Lord *Hawkesbury,* in his *Discourse on the conduct of the government of Great Britain in respect to neutral nations. Lond.* edit. 1794, p. 68.   T.

war? shall I send succours to that unjust ally? No, I shall not. It should be said then, that to him who is *unjustly attacked*, succours should be sent, as likewise to him who has not afforded a cause of hostility, and whose fault or injury has not begun the war. Although, however, it be not openly expressed, that exception is always tacitly understood in treaties, which *Grotius* has proved, *De Jure B. ac P.* l. 2. c. 15. § 13. n. 1., and I do not know any who differ from him.*

He who has promised succours, and he alone, as I have just now said, judges also of the justice of the cause, and whether the *casus fœderis*, as is commonly said, has taken place or not. For the contracting parties are not in the habit of submitting that to the decision of arbitrators; which indeed would be very right, as treaties might not then be made sport of, as they now are. Otherwise, who is there, who will not interpret treaties as he may think will suit best his own interest? who will not evade them by a false interpretation?† The ancient *Greeks* and *Romans*, even in public matters, often left the justice or injustice of their cause to be determined by others, as is proved by many examples quoted by *Grotius*, l. 2. c. 25. § 4.; and it was right to do so. But this part of the law of nations is now disused, and hence hardly any thing now-a-days remains of treaties but an empty name.

This is only applicable to treaties made before the breaking out of the war, by which supplies have been promised; for in my opinion, after the beginning of the war, succours cannot be properly promised or sent to either friend, and he who will promise or send them to one, will violate his neutrality with the other.

As to those states which are tributary to us or under our protection, they constitute a kind of intermediate description of states; for, from the very nature of protection, they are not considered as enemies, nor also as subjects, as they belong to another prince. They may therefore assist their sovereign, though he is our enemy, but not with arms and men, wherewith

* See, however, the notes in the preceding page and page 75. *T.*
† Does not this militate against our author's doctrine in the preceding paragraph? See notes, p. 71. 75. *T.*

he may make war upon us. Therefore the counsellors of the states-general, on the 17th of *March* 1641, and afterwards on the 18th of *July* 1746, very properly decreed, that those of the territories of *Luxemburg* and *Namur*, who were under the protection of the states, and generally, on the 14th of *August* 1645, that no neutral under our protection should fight for the king of *Spain*, even though he had fought for him before, and that no one, who had quitted the service should be recalled into it. The same counsellors, on the 23d of *February* 1636, issued an edict, that none of those who were under our protection should assist the enemy's camps with horses, wagons, or ships: and very properly, because, by acting thus, they would have afforded assistance to the enemy. The law is different, as to those things which are carried to an enemy, for other purposes than for war; and therefore the states-general, although they had before generally prohibited the exportation of corn, decreed however, on the 23d of *May* 1631, that those who were under our protection might carry their corn to the *Spaniards* or to the *United Dutch*, as they might think proper. For a neutral may lawfully carry corn to an enemy, except in case of a siege or famine.

The states-general, by the third section of their edict of the 26th of *September*, 1590, prohibited the treating of neutrals, their vessels and goods, in a hostile manner, even though found in the enemy's territory, provided they were bound to the *United Provinces*, or thence to other places. Yet there are those who have written, as if the states-general on the 15th of *December* 1672, had decreed by a general law, that even neutral vessels, when coming from enemy's ports might be lawfully condemned. But no credit is to be given to those wretched scribblers; for the fact is that the edict of the 15th of *December* 1672, was a special one, and made merely by way of retaliation for the condemnation of the *Hamburg* ship, as I have before shewn in chapter 5.

† K

CHAPTER X.

Of Contraband.

IT was formerly a capital crime at *Rome* to sell arms to the barbarians;* that is to say, it was capital in the subjects of the empire, for whom alone the *Romans* made laws. And it is now certainly so in every country, for a subject to carry arms to an enemy. Nay, by the first section of the edict of the states-general against *England*, of the 5th of *December* 1652, not only every subject, but a foreigner who should carry any kind of merchandize to the *English*, is to be considered as an enemy. Which by the second section of the edict of the states-general against the *Portuguese*, of the 31st of *December* 1657, is justly restricted to contraband goods. By the 1st section of the edict of the states-general of the 14th of *August* 1672, and 11th of *April* 1673, against the *English* and *French*, and the 1st section of the edict of the 19th of *March* 1665, against the *English*, he is punished as an enemy to the state, who carries to the hostile nation any warlike ammunition, provisions, materials for the building of ships, or any other prohibited merchandize. It is the same with a foreigner who carries those goods to the enemy from this country.

But the states-general as well as every other prince may make what laws they please with respect to their subjects; not so with respect to foreigners. Hence it is properly asked what is lawful for us by the law of nations, to carry to the enemies of our friends, or, what is the same thing, what may our friends lawfully carry to our enemies? Whatever is not lawful to be carried, if the friend take it, he may lawfully con-

* Cod, quæ res export. non deb. l. 2.

fiscate, and by that confiscation alone, the whole penalty of the law is satisfied. *Grotius, de Jure B. ac P.* l. 3. c. 1. § 5. n. 1, 2, 3., being engaged in the consideration of this subject, distinguishes between those things that are useful for the purposes of war, those which are not so, and those which may be used indiscriminately in war and in peace. The first he prohibits neutrals from carrying to our enemies, the second he permits, the third he sometimes prohibits, and sometimes permits. If we adopt the principles which we have contended for in the preceding chapter, we cannot be much at a loss with regard to the first and second class of articles. As to the third class, *Grotius* distinguishes, and permits the intercepting of things of promiscuous use, but in case of necessity only, when otherwise we cannot protect our own, and then under the obligation of restitution. I shall only ask here who is to be the judge of that necessity, for it is very easy to allege it as a pretext. Shall it be I, who have taken the articles? Such, I think, is his opinion. But all laws prohibit my sitting as judge in my own cause, unless so far as custom, the prince of tyrants, admits, when treaties between sovereigns are to be interpreted. Nor have I been able to observe, that this distinction of *Grotius* is supported by the usage of nations; it rather confirms what he afterwards says, that it is not lawful to carry to besieged places, things of promiscuous use, because it would be assisting one party to the destruction of the other, as will be more fully explained in the next chapter. As to what he adds, in conclusion, that a distinction is to be made between the justice and injustice of the war, I think I have sufficiently proved in the preceding chapter, that it may be proper for *allies** in a certain case, but never for neutrals.

* Our author in the chapter to which he refers seems to consider *qualified neutrals* as *allies*, and indeed, as we have said, the line is often difficult to be drawn between a qualified neutrality and an alliance: but why should states be the judges of the justice of the war in one case more than in the other, and what has that to do with their engagements? Will they not in every case, as our author himself has before observed, decide for their own advantage? See notes p. 71, 72. *T.*

The law of nations on this subject is not to be drawn from any other source than reason and usage. Reason commands me to be equally friendly to two of my friends, who are enemies to each other, and hence it follows that I am not to prefer either in war. Usage is pointed out by the constant and as it were perpetual custom which sovereigns have been in of making treaties and laws upon this subject, for they have often made such regulations by treaties to be carried into effect in case of war, and by laws enacted after the war begun. I have said *by, as it were, a perpetual custom;* because one or perhaps two treaties, which vary from the general usage, do not alter the law of nations. It is agreed amongst almost all nations, that it is not lawful for a friend to carry arms to an enemy, or other things which come under the denomination of *contraband goods;* nevertheless, by the 10th section of the treaty of peace of *Westminster,* made in the year 1654, between the *English* and *Portuguese,* it was stipulated that it should be lawful for the *English* to carry those things to the enemies of the *Portuguese,* as is observed by *Zentgravius, De Orig. Verit. & Oblig. Jur. Gent.* art. 7. § 8. p. m. 296, 297. And the *Dutch* obtained the same privilege of the *Portuguese* by the 12th article of the treaty of peace between them of the 6th of *August* 1661. Otherwise the rule which is proved by an almost perpetual succession of treaties, is, that neutrals cannot carry contraband goods to enemies, and that if they do it and are taken in the act, the goods are forfeited; but with the exception of these, they may freely trade with either party, and carry any thing to them with impunity.

According to these principles it was free to the *Dutch,* by the 3d article of the marine treaty between *Spain* and the states-general of the 17th of *December* 1650, section 4, to trade with the *French* in any kind of merchandize, in the same manner that they could have done before the war between *France* and *Spain;* so however, that they should not carry from the *Spanish* dominions to the *French,* things that might be employed against *Spain;* but by section 5, the *Dutch* are prohibited from carrying contraband goods to the *other* enemies of *Spain,* and

by the 6th section those goods that are contraband are enumerated.

Again, by the 2d article of the abovementioned edict of the
states-general against the *English*, of the 5th of *December* 1652,
neutrals are prohibited from carrying to the *English* any ammunition of war, or any materials, serving to the equipment of
vessels. Provision is also made against carrying contraband
goods, by the 2d section of the edicts of 1665, 1672, and
1673, which I have already spoken of; there, after enumerating various species of contraband articles it is added, " and
all other articles manufactured and prepared for warlike
use." Nearly the same thing is found in the 27th and 28th articles of the commercial treaty between *France* and the states-
general of the 27th of *April*, 1662; in the 3d article of
the marine treaty between *Charles* II. king of *England* and
the states-general of the 1st of *December* 1674; the 3d
article of the treaty of commerce between the king of *Sweden*
and the states-general of the 26th of *November* 1675; the
15th article of the marine treaty between the same powers
of the 12th of *October* 1679; the 15th article of the treaty
of commerce between *France* and the states-general of *August*
1671; the 11th section of the edict of the states-general
de contrabandis, of the 28th of *July* 1705, and in several
other treaties between different nations, some of which are
enumerated by *Zentgravius*, l. 7. § 8.

From these I understand generally, that contraband articles
are such as are proper for war, and that it is of no consequence
whether or not they are of any use out of war. Very few are
the implements of war, which are not also of some use out of
war. We wear swords for the decoration of our persons, we
make use of the sword for the punishment of criminals; nay,
we even make use of gunpowder for our amusement and to
express public joy. And yet there is not any doubt but that
these come under the denomination of contraband articles.

Of those things which are of promiscuous use, it would be
endless to dispute, and it would be so if we were to follow
Grotius's opinion about necessity and the various distinctions
which he brings forward. If we examine the treaties made

between the different nations, which we have already mentioned, and also those which exist elsewhere, it will be found, that every thing is called contraband, which is of use to belligerent nations in making war; whether they be warlike instruments or materials *by themselves* fit to be used in war. For what the states-general on the 6th of *May* 1667, decreed against the *Swedes*, that even materials, *not of themselves* fit for war, but which might easily be adapted to warlike use, were to be considered as contraband, was founded on a special reason, to wit, the right of retaliation, as the states themselves express it in the said decree.

And hence you will judge whether the materials themselves out of which contraband goods are formed are themselves contraband? *Zouch, de Jure Fec.* part, 2. § 8. Q. 8., appears, if any thing, rather inclined to this opinion. For my part I am not, because reason and precedents incline me to the contrary. If all materials are prohibited out of which something may be made which is fit for war, the catalogue of contraband goods will be immense, for there is hardly any kind of material, out of which something at least, fit for war, may not be fabricated. The interdiction of these amounts to a total prohibition of commerce, and might as well be so expressed and understood. And the 4th article of the said treaty of the 1st of *December* 1674; the 4th of the said treaty of the 26th of *November* 1675, and the 10th article of the said treaty of the 12th of *October* 1679, which prohibit neutrals from carrying arms to enemies, permit the carrying of iron, brass, metals, materials for building ships, and in short every thing which is not already prepared for warlike use.

Sometimes, however, it happens, that materials for building ships are prohibited, if the enemy is in great need of them, and cannot well carry on the war without them. When the states-general by the 2d section of their edict against the *Portuguese*, of the 31st of *December* 1657, prohibited the supplying the *Portuguese* with those things which by the general usage of nations are considered as contraband of war, they specially added by the 3d section of the same edict, that as they feared nothing from the *Portuguese* except by sea, no one should carry to them even materials for building ships; thus openly distinguishing those materials from contraband articles, and prohibiting them only for a special reason expressly set forth. For the same reason, materials for ship building, are joined with instruments of war, in the 2d section of the edict against the *English* of the 5th of *December* 1652, and in the edict of the states-general against the *French* of the 9th of *March* 1689. But these are exceptions which confirm the general rule.

It is asked whether *scabbards* are to be considered as contraband? *Petrinus Bellus, de Re Militari*, part 9. n. 26, 27, 28., says that it has been so decided by the military judges, though he himself does not approve of that decision. *Zouch, De Jure Fec.* part 2. § 8. Q. 2., satisfied with giving out of *Bellus*, the arguments on both sides, decides nothing, according to his custom. For my part, I approve of the decision of the military judges, and I am opposed to the opinion of *Bellus*, because scabbards, although of promiscuous use, are however, instruments prepared for war. Without scabbards, swords cannot be used, and without swords there can be no war. Nay, *holsters, saddles* and *belts* are numbered among articles of contraband in the said 2d, 3d and 5th articles of the said edicts and treaties which I have above mentioned. Holsters, as to their use, do not differ in any thing from scabbards: the latter are cases for swords and the others for pistols. Certainly these might be excused, if they were in very small quantity; and the said third article of the treaty of the 26th of *November* 1675,* has also this exception: " unless those instruments should be in so small a quantity, that it might be inferred from thence that they were not designed for the use of war."

What shall we say of *sword hilts?* The same, I think, as of scabbards, for they are instruments fit and prepared for war, and are also included in the list of contraband goods, in some of the edicts and treaties which I have before cited. Of *saltpetre*, more doubt might be entertained, because it is not of itself an article fit to be used in war; and yet saltpetre is contained in all the lists of contraband articles which I have mentioned, for out of saltpetre gunpowder is made, which is now

---

* Between the states-general and *Sweden*, see p. 77.　　　　*T.*

the principal article used in war. Nay, I have observed that saltpetre is sometimes mentioned with the addition of gunpowder and sometimes without. Where gunpowder is omitted, saltpetre is mentioned in lieu of it; when both are mentioned, they are considered as synonymous words, unless saltpetre, on account of its important use in war, should have been excepted by nations out of those articles which of themselves are not fit for war.

Of tobacco, *Zouch* informs us, *De Jure Fec.* part 2. § 8. Q. 12. that there was a great contention between the *English* and the *Spaniards*, and that the latter considered it as contraband,* to the great indignation of the *English*, who went so far as to issue reprisals against them. What became afterwards of that controversy I know not; this I know, that I cannot concur in opinion with the *Spaniards*, because the fact is, that tobacco cannot be of any use in destroying the enemy. Nay, by the said 3d, 4th, 15th and 16th articles† it is lawful to carry tobacco to an enemy, for by the same articles, it is lawful to carry to the enemies of our friends all things which in the condition they are in are not fit for war, and tobacco is nominally included among lawful goods, by the 4th article of the said treaty of the 1st of *December* 1674.

It is clear by the l. 22. § 1. ff. *de Jure Fisc.* that if a pledge is forfeited, the *jus pignoris* is not thereby extinguished. Hence if neutrals had shipped contraband goods to our enemies and bound them for the freight, if the goods are taken in the course of the voyage, and condemned as contraband, the *Dutch* lawyers have given it as their opinion that the captain is entitled to his freight, as though the whole voyage had been performed. And it is related that it was thus decided by the court of admiralty of *North Holland*, on the 6th of *May* 1665, and of *Friesland*, on the 12th of *July* in the same year, on the principles that *res transit cum suo onere*, that the fisk yields to creditors, (*fiscus cedit creditoribus*‡) and others of the like

* The reason alleged was that tobacco might be used, as well as salt, to preserve provisions from corruption. *Zouch, ubi suprà.* T.

† See p. 77, 78.

‡ In this country, and in *England*, the opposite maxim prevails. The sovereign is entitled to a priority of payment, *et creditores cedunt fisco*. T.

kind. But the court of admiralty of *Amsterdam* decided differently on the 9th of *July* 1666; they refused to allow freight to the captured, without prejudice, however, to his rights against whomsoever else it might concern. And this is very correct; for the freight is not due unless the voyage is performed, and the enemy has lawfully prohibited its being performed. Then contraband goods are condemned, either *ex delicto*, when the captain and mariners are no less in fault than the owners of the goods, or *ex re*, for the very carriage of the goods themselves; for although we cannot prohibit neutrals from trading with our enemies, yet we may prohibit their assisting them in the war to our destruction. Therefore what is condemned, is condemned without regard to any man, and is to be considered as if it had perished by the act of God, whereby the *jus pignoris* is extinguished.* I am not, however, astonished at those lawyers having been of opinion, that the master of the vessel has a lien for the freight on contraband goods that are condemned, I rather wonder that they have not allowed it in preference to the owners of the merchandize; for they have *jus in re*, a right of property, which is the strongest of all.†

It is denied that the subject of an ally or confederate, trading with a common enemy, may be punished by us, or his property condemned; because it is said that every one is bound only to obey the laws of his own sovereign, and therefore that an ally can have no control over him. But reason, usage and public utility, are opposed to that decision. The reader may, if he pleases, turn to what *Aitzema* has written‡ upon that subject; for my part, I shall abstain from it. As I am now only treating of what contraband *is*, such a discussion cannot with propriety be introduced in this place.

* This doctrine is now adopted as to *contraband* goods, which are condemned *ex delicto;* but not as to *enemy's* goods, which are condemned only *ex re.* In the latter case, when the conduct of the captured is fair, freight is generally allowed. See *post*, c. 14. *in note.*   *T.*

† There seems to be no real difference here, for the master can only claim as agent for the owners, to whom the freight belongs.   *T.*

‡ Aitz. 1. 46.

† L

CHAPTER XI.

Of Trade with blockaded and besieged Places.

I HAVE said in a former chapter,* that by the usage of
nations, and according to the principles of natural reason,
it is not lawful to carry any thing to places that are blockaded
or besieged. *Grotius* is of the same opinion; for he reprobates
the carrying any thing to blockaded or besieged places, " if
it should impede the execution of the belligerent's lawful
designs; and if the carriers might have known of the siege or
blockade; as in the case of a town actually invested or a port
closely blockaded, and when a surrender or a peace is already
expected to take place."† Indeed, it is sufficient that there be
a siege or blockade to make it unlawful to carry any thing,
whether contraband or not, to a place thus circumstanced;
for those who are within may be compelled to surrender, not
merely by the direct application of force, but also by the want
of provisions and other necessaries. If, therefore, it should
be lawful to carry to them what they are in need of, the belligerent might thereby be compelled to raise the siege or

---

* Above, c. 4. p. 31.

† *Si juris mei executionem rerum subvectio impedierit, idque scire potuerit
qui advexit,* UT SI *oppidum obsessum tenebam, si portus clausos, & jam deditio
aut pax expectabatur, tenebitur ille mihi de damno culpâ dato, ut qui debitorem
carceri exemit, aut fugam ejus in meam fraudem instruxit; si damnum
nondùm dederit, sed dare voluerit, jus erit rèrum retentione eum cogere ut
de futuro caveat, obsidibus, pignoribus, aut alio modo.* If he (the carrier)
should by his supplies impede the execution of any lawful designs; *as
if* I kept a town besieged or a port closely blockaded, and I already
expected a surrender or a peace; he will be liable to me for the damage
occasioned by his fault, in like manner as he who should make my debtor
escape out of prison, or aid him in his flight to defraud me of my right;
and if he has not occasioned to me any actual damage, but has been
willing to do it, in that case, it will be lawful by the detention of his goods,
to compel him to give security for the future, by hostages, pledges or in
some other way. *Grot. de J. B. ac P.* l. 3. c. 1. § 5. n. 3.   *T.*

blockade, which would be doing him an injury, and therefore would be unjust. And because it cannot be known what articles the besieged may want, the law forbids in general terms carrying *any thing* to them; otherwise disputes and altercations would arise to which there would be no end.

Thus far my opinion coincides with that of *Grotius*, but ‚I cannot agree with him when he requires *an expectation of a surrender or a peace,** and when he says immediately afterwards that even under those circumstances, the carrier is only bound to *an indemnity for the damage occasioned by his fault*, and if no damage has been suffered, that he may only be compelled by the detention of his goods *to give security that he will not do the like in future.* I wish that *Grotius* had not laid down such principles, which are neither consonant to reason, nor to the sense of treaties. For on what principle am I to be the judge of the future surrender or peace? and if neither is expected, is it then lawful to carry any thing to the besieged? I think on the contrary, that during a siege, it is always unlawful. It is not acting a friendly part to ruin, or in any way impair, the cause of a friend, and if so, why shall he who carried supplies to my enemy not be bound farther than for the damage occasioned by his fault? Such conduct has always been considered as a capital crime in subjects, nay, in neutrals, when previously warned by a proclamation, and often without such warning. As they are generally private individuals, who, impelled by the thirst of gain, are in the habit of administering supplies to the besieged; suppose, for instance, that such a one has been the cause that a city has not been taken, I should hardly think in such a case that any individual could be rich enough to repair the damage thereby suffered. And if he should be intercepted on his way to the besieged town with

* Our author appears here to have mistaken the meaning of *Grotius*. That writer does not, in our opinion, require as a *necessary ingredient* in a strict blockade, that there should be an expectation of peace or of a surrender, but merely mentions that as an *example*, and by way of putting the strongest possible case. We have transcribed the passage in the original language, with a literal translation in the preceding note, in order that our readers may be enabled to judge for themselves of the correctness of this remark. *T.*

the supplies that he is carrying thither, shall we be content
with taking and retaining the articles, and that merely until
he gives security that he shall not commit the like in future?
I cannot subscribe to this opinion; being taught by the usage
of nations, that the least punishment in such a case is the forfeiture of the things taken; and that a corporal penalty at
least, if not a capital one, is often inflicted on the offender.*

Let us now turn to some treaties on this subject. By the 9th
article of the marine treaty between the king of *Spain* and the
states-general, of the 17th of *December* 1650, it is simply agreed,
" that it shall not be lawful to carry goods, even not contraband,
to places blockaded and besieged." The same clause is contained in a variety of other treaties† ‡ all of which, however,
merely stipulate that it is unlawful to carry any thing to
besieged or blockaded places, without affixing any penalty
to the offence. But, if the carrying of any thing to a besieged
town or place is illicit, it follows that every thing which is
carried thither is to be considered as *contraband;* for every

---

* This is a very severe doctrine, and which certainly is not conformable
to the usage of nations at the present day; but it must be observed that our
author, as well as *Grotius*, only meant to speak of a strict and actual siege or
blockade, where a town is actually invested with troops, or a port closely
blockaded by ships of war, *portus clausus*, as *Grotius* emphatically expresses
it; for at the time when those great men wrote, no idea was entertained of that enormous system of universal blockade, by means of edicts
and proclamations, the effects of which have desolated the world for the
last twenty years.   *T.*

† Treaty of commerce between the states-general and the king of *France*,
of the 27th of *April* 1662, art. 29.—Marine treaty between the king of
England and the states-general, of the 1st of *December* 1674, art. 4.—Treaty
of commerce between the king of *France* and the states-general, of the 10th
of *August* 1678, art. 16.—Treaty of commerce between the king of *Sweden*
and the states-general, of the 12th of *October* 1679, art. 16, and a great
number of other treaties.

‡ In our treaties with other nations, no other punishment is contemplated
for a breach of blockade, than a confiscation of the ships and goods. In our
treaty with *Great Britain* of the 19th of *November* 1794, art. 18, it is even
stipulated that that punishment shall not be inflicted, except in the case of
a vessel which shall, after being warned, attempt to enter a blockaded port.
2 *Laws U. S*. 484. A similar stipulation is contained in the 12th article of
our convention with *France*, of the 30th of *September* 1800. 6 *Laws U. S.*
Appendix xx.   *T.*

thing which is carried from one place to another contrary to law and *treaties** is *contraband*, and as such, is at least liable to forfeiture. Thus usage has established it, as will be more fully shewn in the sequel; it has also established that the offenders may be punished capitally, or with a milder punishment, according to the circumstances of the case.†

Not only towns or cities, but *camps* likewise may be surrounded with troops and as it were besieged. In such a case it is not more lawful to carry any thing to them, than to invested cities. But if they are not besieged, I see no reason why neutrals may not lawfully carry thither any thing which may be lawfully carried to towns, ports and places so circumstanced; that is to say, every thing which is not actually *contraband*. And yet, the counsellors of the states-general, in the name of the states, issued an edict on the 9th of *August* 1622, by which they decreed, that all who should carry any thing to the *Spanish* camp before *Bergen-op-Zoom*, should be considered as enemies. The same counsellors, on the 2d of *September* 1624, and on the 21st of *March* 1636, decreed the same thing against those who should carry any thing to the *Spanish* camp.

Those edicts are undoubtedly too unjust to be defended, if the camp to which they apply is not besieged, and the things

---

* Goods prohibited by treaty between the sovereigns of the captors and the captured, though otherwise they might not be considered as contraband, are condemned *ex delicto*, and no freight is allowed upon them. *The Neutralitæt*, 3 *Rob.* 240. *Am. edit.*   *T.*

† At this day, however, the only penalty which is inflicted for trading with a blockaded port is the forfeiture of the property detected in the pursuit of such trade. It is true, that on the strict principles of the law of nations, those who knowingly trade with blockaded ports, may justly be considered and treated as enemies, and so *Vattel* lays it down in his *Treatise on the Law of Nations*, l. 3. c. 7. § 117. But, in the manner that war is now carried on, such treatment cannot extend farther than the confiscation of the property, and perhaps, the imprisonment of the neutral captains and crews, which has sometimes, though rarely, taken place, and can only be justified (if at all) in very flagrant cases. *Vattel* does not mention any specific punishment to be inflicted in cases of this kind, though he relates the story of *Demetrius*, who hanged the captain and pilot of a ship carrying provisions to *Athens*, which he was besieging. But precedents are not now to be drawn from such barbarous times.   *T.*

are not carried through the neutral's territory. The two first, however, extended to the subjects of the *United Nether-lands*, to neutrals, and to the subjects of those states who were under the protection of the *Dutch*. But, although every sovereign has a right to enact with respect to his own subjects, what laws he may think proper, and no one can find fault with him for so doing; yet as far as they apply to neutrals, and the subjects of countries under the protection of the states, those edicts cannot be supported unless they are restricted to *con-traband* only. The third edict of the 21st *March* 1636, relates to neutrals who should carry provisions or implements of war to the *Spanish* fortresses; but that was done, as is expressly mentioned, by way of retaliation, because the *Spaniards* had treated as enemies those who had assisted the town of *Maes-tricht* with provisions and arms. *Retaliation,** therefore, re-moves the hardship of the edict as to provisions, which otherwise neutrals may lawfully carry, if there be no treaty to the contrary; but it is otherwise with arms and military stores, even though they be carried to a place not besieged, and so far this edict is perfectly just. As to other things, whether they were or not lawfully prohibited by the edicts of the *Spaniards* or of the states-general, depends entirely upon the circumstance of the places being besieged or not.

* It is but seldom that we are disposed to controvert the principles laid down by this excellent author, but we must here again refer the reader to what he says himself in chapter 4: *Retorsio non est nisi adversus eum, qui ipse damni quid dedit, ac deinde patitur, non verò adversùs communem amicum.* "Retaliation is only to be exercised on him who has inflicted the injury, and therefore justly suffers for it, but not on a common friend." *See above,* p. 33. How then can he maintain in the present instance, as well as in another (p. 61.) that an injury done to a neutral can be justified on the principle of retaliation upon the enemy? We would have supposed that national preju-dice (as in both the above cases the *Dutch* were the authors of the injury to neutrals) had made him overlook the very principle on which he had set out in the beginning of his work, were it not that he applies it there against a similar act of his own government, and freely reproves their conduct in several other instances. Whatever may have been his motive, we are com-pelled to say that he is here in direct contradiction with himself, and that on his own clear and luminous principle, his justification of the conduct of the *Dutch* in these two instances cannot be supported.   *T.*

The same law which obtains with respect to towns that are really besieged, and by a parity of reasoning has been applied to camps, as being, as it were, besieged, applies also to enemy's ports, which are blockaded by ships of war, and therefore are considered as in a state of siege. There is on this subject a remarkable decree of the states-general, of the 26th of *June* 1630, made with the advice and opinion of the court of admiralty of *Amsterdam*, and of other courts of admiralty, nay, it is probable, with the advice also of some private lawyers.* At that time, the states were blockading with ships of war the maritime coast of *Flanders;* it was then made a question whether neutrals might carry on trade with the ports of that country, and upon that the states made the decree in question, which we shall here lay before our readers and accompany it with a few remarks.

The first article provided " that the ships and goods of neutrals which should be found going in or coming out of the enemy's ports in *Flanders*, or being so near thereto, as to shew beyond a doubt that they were endeavouring to run into them, should be confiscated, because their high mightinesses kept the said ports continually blockaded with their ships of war, in order to prevent any commerce between them and the enemy;† as had been the custom many years before, *after the example of all other princes, who had claimed and enforced a similar right in like cases.*"

By the second article it was ordered that the ships and goods should be confiscated, " if from the charter-parties, or other documents on board, it should appear that the vessels were bound to the said *Flemish* ports, although they should be found at a distance from them, unless they, of their own accord, before coming in sight of or being chased by our country's ships, should repent their intention, while the thing was yet undone, and alter their course; in which case the matter should be decided according to conjectures and circumstances."

* Consil. Holland. vol. 5. Consil. 161.

† The *Spaniards*, whose king was at that time sovereign of the county of *Flanders*, and of the rest of the Catholic *Netherlands*.　　　　　　*T.*

The third article directs the confiscation of such ships with their cargoes, " as should come out of the said ports, not having been forced into them by stress of weather, although they should be taken at a distance from thence, unless they had after leaving the enemy's port performed a voyage to a port of their own country, or to some other neutral or free port, in which case they should not be condemned; but if in coming out of the said *Flemish* ports they should be pursued by our own ships, chased into another port, such as their *own* or that of their *destination*, and found on the high sea coming out of *such* port, in that case they might lawfully be captured and confiscated." There is also a fourth article, which I have recited and commented upon before,* and which I think it unnecessary to say any more upon. But the three first articles of this law appear to me to require some explanation.

As to the first article, inasmuch as it condemns vessels found actually going into or coming out of the enemy's ports, there is no reason for it, but that which is expressed in the edict itself. It goes however further, and confiscates those which shall be found *so near to the enemy's ports as to shew beyond a doubt that they intend running into them.* This is reasonable also; because if prohibited goods are found on the confines of the hostile territory, they are presumed to be carrying to the enemy, not only according to the most general opinion of the civilians,† but also according to the intent and meaning of the states-general, which is fully expressed in this law and in various other edicts,‡ unless, indeed, as is provided in all the said edicts, they should prove that they were driven in by stress of weather. The same exception is made in the second article of this decree.

But, not to leave the coast of *Flanders*, precisely the same thing was decreed on the same subject, in the infancy of our

---

* Above, c. 4. p. 30.

† *Zouch*, De Jure Fec. p. 2. § 8. Q. 10. quotes a number of authorities to this point.

‡ Edicts against the *English*, of the 5th *December* 1652, and 19th of *March* 1665, § 4.—Against the *English* and *French* of the 14th of *April* 1672, and 11th of *April* 1673, § 4.

republic; for by the edicts of the earl of *Leicester*,* by which
he prohibits as well to foreigners as to subjects all commerce
with the *Spaniards*, and by the edict of the states of *Holland*,
of the 27th *July* 1584, neutrals, trading with the *Flemish* ports,
are punished with the confiscation of their ships and goods,
and that edict expressly provides that those " who shall be
found on the coast of *Flanders*, or *near* " *to some of the prohibited ports*, shall be adjudged to have contravened this
ordinance, *except in cases of extreme and well proved necessity.*"
The opinion of *Cynus*, who writes that they are, even in such
a case, to be punished as going to the ports of the enemies,
when they have so far advanced on their way that they cannot
return, is therefore not admissible, although it has the approbation of *Albericus Gentilis.*†

Thus much I have thought proper to observe on the first
article of this law; the reasonableness of which applies equally
to the second article; for those things which are taken near to
besieged places, are not condemned for any other reason, than
that an intention of trading with the enemy is tacitly collected
from the internal evidence of the fact itself, and it amounts to
the same thing, as if that intention had clearly appeared from
the documents on board, and therefore there is no room for
any doubt. But what is added about repentance, I find some
difficulty to admit; if, however, there is sufficient proof of
the alteration of the voyage, I should not be far from acceding
to that opinion.

The third article properly distinguishes between vessels
which are *chased* or compelled to take refuge and those who
proceed *voluntarily* to the port of their *destination*. The latter
are excused, when found coming out of that port, their voyage
being considered as ended, and a new one begun, while the
former are condemned, as being taken in the very act of
violation of blockade. But on the subject of these, the edict
speaks in the disjunctive, and says, " if they are chased into
their own port OR *the port of their destination*," so that there
may be a doubt as to the sense of these words and the law

* Edict of the 4th of *April* 1586—of the 4th of *August* same year, § 9.
† De advocat. Hispan. l. 1. c. 20. p. m. 86.

† M

which results from them. Certainly there can be no doubt, if the same thing is meant by their *own port*, and the port of *their destination;* But if an *Englishman* who was bound to a port of *Denmark* is driven into a port of *England,* and coming out of it, and prosecuting his voyage, should be taken before he reached the *Danish* port, it appears to me that he would be taken in the course and in the very act of the illicit voyage, and that it would be of no consequence, whether it was his own port, or not, which he had entered into, if the voyage which he was engaged in had not been completely finished. Therefore, as disjunctives are frequently to be construed as conjunctives, I understand these words " *their own port,*" in the said article, to mean the port to which the vessel was bound, and where her voyage was to be ended.* I shall put a case, in order more fully to illustrate my meaning: Suppose that a vessel from *Zierikzee*† is taken by the *Dunkirkers*, who condemn and sell her, and she is purchased by a *Scotchman*. By the 4th article of the said decree which I have above recited at large‡ it is only lawful to capture and condemn her, if found coming out of an enemy's port before she had entered into her *own* or into some *other free port*, but not afterwards. This vessel now belonging to the *Scotchman*, and coming out of *Dunkirk*, is met with, but not taken. She runs into *Yarmouth*, where she was not bound to; and coming out of that port, is captured. It is asked whether she is to be considered as having entered into *her own* port within the meaning of the edict? I cannot say that she is, because she has not entered into the port to which she was *bound*. The states-general in a similar case, with the advice of the admiralty of *Zealand*, decreed on

---

* We cannot perceive how any difficulty can arise as to the construction of this part of the edict; since, whether the vessel was chased into the actual port of her destination or into any other port of her own country, she is equally to be condemned according to the letter of the law as it is given to us. So that the interpretation which our author contends for, appears to us to be not only unnecessary but dangerous, as it would make a merely *constructive* offence, of what the legislator expressly made a *positive* one.　　　　　　　　　　　　　　　　　　　　*T.*

† A port of *Zealand*, in the island of *Schouwen*, at the mouth of the *Scheldt*.　　　　　　　　　　　　　　　　　　　　*T.*

‡ C. 4. p. 30.

the 27th of *January* 1631, that the vessel should be condemned, as being within the edict of the 26th *June* 1630.* †
What is said, moreover, in this third article about a *free port*,
is explained by the fourth; for that cannot be understood to be
a free port, which is under the same king or government with
another which is not considered as such.‡

This decree of the 26th *June* 1630, was for some time not
carried into execution, and in the mean while a free commercial intercourse in 1642 carried on with *Flanders*. During
that period certain neutral vessels, trading thither were captured by our vessels, and carried into *Zealand*. The contraband goods, however, were alone detained and condemned,
and all the remainder was acquitted and released. It has been
asked by what law the contraband goods were condemned
under those circumstances, and there are those who deny the
legality of their condemnation.§ It is evident, however, that
while those coasts were guarded in a lax or remiss manner,
the law of blockade, by which all neutral goods going to or
coming from a blockaded port may be lawfully captured, might
also have been relaxed; but not so the general law of war,

* Aitz. l. 11.

† This decree appears to us to have been very correct, not because the
vessel had gone into a port of her own country, different from that of her
actual destination, which, if she had done *voluntarily*, would have been a
sufficient excuse, but because she had run into the port of *Yarmouth* to
avoid *pursuit*, and was captured coming from thence, in consequence of
which she was clearly within the letter of the third article of the edict. *T.*

‡ The 4th article provides, that ships coming out of enemy's ports shall
be condemned, if they are taken before they shall have been into *their own*
or *other free ports. (See above, p.* 30.*)* Our author impressed with the idea
that the words *their own* in the 3d article, only meant the ports of their
actual destination, and being embarrassed by the words *or other free ports*
in the 4th article, which clearly point to the opposite construction, thinks
to get rid of his embarrassment, by assuming that *other free ports* cannot
mean ports *of the same country*, that is to say, of the country to which the
neutral belongs; thus arguing in a circle to which his first mistake una-
voidably led him. We are loth to controvert the opinions of so great a
writer, in any case, particularly when he is construing *a law of his own
country;* but in the present instance the mistake is so obvious that we could
not avoid noticing it.   *T.*

§ Consil. Holland. vol. 2. Consil. 21.

by which contraband goods, when carried to an enemy's port, even though not blockaded, are liable to confiscation.

But although, as I have observed, the rigour of this decree of the 26th *June* 1630, may be sufficiently justified, it may however, be relaxed, if it shall be thought proper, and it has in fact often been relaxed. When admiral *Van Tromp*, in the year 1645, blockaded the ports of *Flanders*, with the fleet of the states-general, and asked of them, what he should do with neutral vessels, they decreed on the 1st of *July*, that neutrals should by all means be prevented from entering the ports of *Flanders*, but that their goods, *not being contraband*, should not be condemned.* The states, on that occasion, deviated from the principles which their predecessors had adopted in 1630. But when men change, what is there to prevent opinions from changing likewise?

If the principles which I have contended for in this and the two preceding chapters are correct, it will be easy with their help, to decide on the difference which took place between the *English* on one side, and the *Poles* and other nations on the other, of which *Zouch* gives us a particular account.† ‡

---

* Aitz. l. 4. Ibid. l. 25.

† De Jure Fec. p. 2. § 8. Q. 7.

‡ The difference to which our author alludes, is related by *Zouch*, substantially as follows: Queen *Elizabeth* being at war with *Spain*, had prohibited neutrals from carrying on any trade with that country. The ambassador of the king of *Poland*, in the name of his master, complained of it to the queen herself, in terms rather indecorous, to which she replied with becoming dignity, and defended her conduct by alleging, that the kings of *Poland* and *Sweden* had acted in the same manner some time before in a similar circumstance. The fact was, however, that those sovereigns in the year 1572, being at war with the czar of *Muscovy*, had merely prohibited the intercourse of neutrals with the ports of *Livonia*, which they blockaded with their ships, and which was at that time the theatre of the war by land, so that if *Zouch* is correct in his statement, the two cases were not parallel. But *Elizabeth* at that time was flushed with her victory over the *invincible armada* of *Spain*, and thought that there were no bounds to her maritime power.

To the *Hanse Towns*, *Selden* informs us, that she gave as a reason for the same proceeding, of which they also complained, that their ships could not go to *Spain* without passing through the *English seas*, which they had no right to do without her permission. Indeed, that author tells us that the measure

CHAPTER XII.

Of the mixture of lawful with contraband goods.

IF a neutral carries at the same time, lawful and unlawful goods to the enemy, and the vessel should be taken, it is asked, " whether the vessel itself and the lawful goods that are on board are to be condemned on account of those which are unlawful?" The same may be asked; if from any other cause, lawful and unlawful goods are mixed together. This was one of the several questions which were proposed in the year 1631, by the admiralty of *Amsterdam* to the states-general, for the interpretation of their edict of the 1st of *April* 1622. But, although the states gave their answer to the other questions which were propounded to them at the same time, *Aitzema* informs us[*] that they kept this under advisement. And I do not find that any decision has been given upon it, either at that time, or at any time since; the states-general, however, on the 6th of *May* 1667, gave public orders to their courts of admiralty, that they should not condemn lawful goods, or even the ship, on account of illicit merchandize. Thus much and no more, we are told by *Aitzema*,[†] and the states-general express themselves in the same general terms, in their several edicts of the 11th *September* 1665.[‡]

was not merely intended by *Elizabeth* to distress her enemies, but also to assert her claim to the *dominion of the seas (dominii maris causâ.)* From his relation, however, and that of other respectable writers, such as *Thuanus* and *Camden*, it would seem that the prohibition was not general, as *Zouch* represents it, but was restricted to *warlike stores* and *provisions*, which at that time were by many considered as contraband. See on this subject, *Zouch, ubi suprà.*—*Selden, Mare Claus.* l. 2. c. 20.—*Camden, Annal. sub anno* 1597.—*Thuan. Histor.* l. 96—*Marquard. De Jure Mercat.* p. 149.— *Koch, Hist. des Traités,* vol. 3. p. 19—28.　　　　　　　　*T.*

[*] L. 11.　　　　[†] L. 47.

[‡] Consil. Belg. vol. 4. Consil 206. Q. 2.

But I am of opinion with the authors quoted by *Zouch*, in his treatise on the Law of Nations,* that there is a wide distinction to be made between the case where both the lawful and unlawful goods belong to the same owner, and that in which they are the property of different persons. If they belong to the same owner, then the whole may be lawfully condemned, as a just punishment for the offence; but on the contrary, if they are the property of different shippers, then the act of one of them ought not to affect the others. This distinction was very properly taken by the *Dutch* lawyers, on the 31st of *July* 1692.† The *Digest*‡ also affords a strong argument in favour of this opinion, where, speaking of the owner of the vessel, *Paulus* distinguishes whether he knew or not that unlawful goods had been laden on board; if he knew of it, as if it was done in his presence, the law in that case declares that the ship also is forfeited; if on the contrary it had been done in his absence, and therefore he did not know of it, then the vessel is to be restored to him because he is not in fault. *Zouch*,§ however, without making any distinction, relates a case from *Petrinus Bellus*, by which it would seem that lawful goods had been condemned on account of others which were illicit, but on referring to that author,¶ it appears, that in that particular case, both the lawful and unlawful goods belonged to the same owner, who knew of the fraud, and therefore was properly punished with the confiscation of both: But of this we shall speak more at large presently.

In the meanwhile we shall turn our attention to the treaties and laws of our country, which have been made upon the subject. By the treaty of navigation between *Spain* and the states-general, of the 4th of *February* 1648, and the 12th article of the marine treaty between the same powers of the

* De Jure Fec. p. 2. § 8. Q. 13. In the original, the reference is by mistake to Q. 3.   *T.*

† Consil. Belg. vol. 4. Consil 210.

‡ ff de Public. & Vectigal. l. 1. § 2.

§ *Ubi suprà.*

¶ *Zouch* does not point out where the passage is to be found, but it is in *Bellus's Treatise De Re Militari*, part 9. 22. 26. 27. 28.

17th, 1650, it is simply agreed, " that it shall not be lawful for the subjects of either country to carry contraband goods to the enemy of the other, otherwise, that such goods shall be confiscated. The same stipulation is contained in the 24th and 36th articles of the treaty between *France* and the states-general of the 27th of *April* 1662, but without any particular provision as to goods not contraband. In like manner, the several edicts of the states-general against the *English* and against the *English* and *French** after enumerating a long series of contraband articles, direct the confiscation of these, without saying any thing as to lawful goods which may be found with them.

But by the 7th article of the marine treaty between *Charles* II. of *England* and the states-general, a distinction is clearly made between lawful and contraband goods, and the latter, but not the former, are declared liable to confiscation; nay, if the unlawful goods are immediately delivered up to the captors, the ship is to be instantly released, with the remainder of the cargo, and suffered to proceed on her destined voyage. A similar provision is made in a variety of other treaties† in which they differ from the edicts above mentioned, which direct the ships to be sent into port for legal adjudication, in all cases where contraband goods are found on board. By the 7th article of the treaty of commerce between the king of *Sweden* and the states-general of the 26th of *November* 1675, it is only stipulated that contraband goods shall be confiscated, but not the ship or lawful merchandize. No provision is made, as in the other treaties, for the immediate release of the vessel and of the innocent part of the cargo.‡

* Of the 19th of *March* 1655, 14th of *April* 1672, and 11th of *April* 1673.

† Marine treaty between the *Swedes* and the states-general of the 12th of *October* 1679, art. 21. 26.—Treaty of commerce between *France* and the states-general of the 10th of *August* 1678, art. 21. 26.—Treaty of commerce between the same, of the 20th *September* 1697, art. 26. 31.—and of the 11th of *April* 1713, art. 25. 30.

‡ In the treaties of the *United States* with other nations, the most liberal principle has been adopted in respect to the seizure of vessels having contraband goods on board going to the enemy. By the 17th article of our treaty with *Great Britain* of the 19th *November* 1794, it was stipulated

Such are the rules laid down by our own laws and treaties, and if we are to infer from them what the law of nations is, it will follow as a principle, that ships and lawful goods are never to be condemned on account of contraband merchandize carried on board of the same vessel. But it is not from thence that the law of nations is to be deduced. Reason, as we have said before, is the supreme law of nations, and she does not permit that we should understand these things altogether generally and without distinction. As to the *vessel*, I think that it ought to be distinguished, whether she belongs to the captain himself or to others. If to the captain, I should here again distinguish, whether he knew (as is most frequently the case) that contraband goods had been shipped on board of her, or whether he was ignorant of it; as if the mariners, in his absence, had concealed such goods on board. If he knew of it, he is himself guilty of the fraud, because he hired his ship for an unlawful purpose, and she ought therefore to be confiscated; but it is otherwise, if he did not know it, because in that case, the fraud cannot be laid to his charge. Such is the doctrine laid down by *Paulus*,* and it is evidently conformable to the dictates of sound reason and of common sense.†

"that in all cases where vessels should be captured or detained on just suspicion of having on board enemy's property, or of carrying to the enemy any of the articles which are contraband of war, the said vessel should be brought to the nearest and most convenient port; and if any property of an enemy should be found on board such vessel, that part only which belonged to the enemy should be made prize, and the vessel should be at liberty to proceed with the remainder, without any impediment.—2 *Laws U. S.* 483— and by our convention with *France* of the 30th *September* 1800, art. 20, it was agreed, that in case the vessels of either party should be captured for carrying contraband to the enemy, the contraband goods only should be condemned, "saving always the ship and the other goods which it should contain." 6 *Laws U. S.* append. xxxii.   *T.*

* ff. de Public. & Vectig. l. 11. § 2.

† At present, neutral ships are not confiscated for carrying contraband goods to the enemy, though with the master's knowledge. *The Neutralitet,* 3 Rob. 240. *The Mercurius,* 1 Rob. 242. *The Jonge Tobias,* 1 Rob. 277. *Am. edit.*   *T.*

The same is to be said if the vessel belongs to another person, for *Paulus* applies his principle to the master only. If,
therefore, the master has taken illicit goods on board, without
the knowledge of the owners, their ship shall not be confiscated; but the law will be otherwise, if they knew of their
being shipped, and thus have become parties to the unlawful
act. It would be unjust, that the owners should suffer for
the act of the master; but it is right and proper that they
should suffer for their own. This distinction between the
knowledge and ignorance of the captain is not so frequent at
this time as it was formerly, because, according to the present
usage, the master is in the habit of signing bills of lading of
the merchandize shipped on board of his vessel, by which he
promises that he will take good care of it for the shippers.
It may, however, still apply, if nevertheless, unlawful goods
should be privately conveyed on board of the vessel, without
the knowledge of the master. But as to owners of the ship,
others than the master, the rule may have even now a frequent
application.

As to the owners of the goods, I think, that for the same
reason, a distinction ought also to be made, as I have said
above, and it ought to be distinguished, whether all the goods
belong to one and the same person, or to several. If to one
and the same, I think that the whole may justly be confiscated,
exactly as by the *Roman* law in revenue cases, if any one
carries at the same time lawful and unlawful merchandize, and
declares the one and conceals the other, both are confiscated
on account of the fraud of the carrier, as the commentators on
the title of the Digest *De Publicanis & Vectigalibus** have
properly collected from the text of that law itself, and from
the third law of the code *De Nautico Fœnore*.† Others are
pleased with another distinction, to wit: whether the lawful
goods may be easily separated from the unlawful; if they cannot, then they are of opinion, that the whole is to be condemned, otherwise the contraband goods alone are to be
confiscated, and the remainder to be released without consi-

* L. 11. § 2.
† See that law translated in the *American Law Journal*, vol. 3. p. 155.   *T.*

dering whether it belongs to the same owner or not. But this distinction, as the separation can always be made, is neither founded on reason, nor on any authority of law. It is more reasonable, and at the same time more consonant to legal principles, to distinguish whether the lawful goods belong to another than the author of the fraud; then the principle properly applies, that one person should not be deprived of his goods for the fraud of another. This doctrine may be supported by a variety of authorities taken from the *Roman* law, in analogous cases; as if one of several co-heirs defrauds the revenue of the tax on dutiable property belonging to the estate of the deceased, the shares of the other heirs are not on that account to be confiscated.* In the same manner, if the farmer or servants of a landholder should manufacture iron on his estate, contrary to law,† if it should be done without the knowledge of the owner, he shall not suffer any penalty,‡ nor shall the bottomry or respondentia creditor suffer, if by the fraud of his debtor in shipping unlawful goods, the ship and cargo should be confiscated.§

But what if the owners of lawful goods should merely have known that others had laden unlawful merchandize on board of the same vessel? Shall this mere knowledge occasion also the confiscation of the lawful goods. Such appears to have been the opinion of a certain lawyer, which is recorded in the *Consilia Belgica:*¶ but I do not agree with him, nor do I find that he is supported by any authority; he might, perhaps, have appealed, (though he does not do it), to the abovementioned text of the Digest, where it is said, that the owner is not to suffer, if his farmer or servants have manufactured iron upon his estate without his knowledge: from whence he might have implied, that if the same thing is done with the knowledge of the owner, he ought to be punished, because it was

---

* ff de Public. et Vectigal. l. 8. § 1.

† By the *Roman* law, no individual was allowed to manufacture *arms* without the special permission of the government. Cod. l. 10. tit. 46. *Lex unica. Ut armorum usus inscio principe interdictus sit.*　　*T.*

‡ ff de Public. et Vect. l. 16. § 11.

§ Cod. de Naut. Fœn. l. 3.

¶ Vol. 4. Consil. 10.

his duty to forbid it, and to order his farmer and servants not to do any thing unlawful upon his estate. But, if several owners, as is often the case, ship their goods on board of the same vessel, they have no control over each other, nor over the master who receives the goods on freight. Therefore, the owner of the lawful goods ought not to suffer for what he cannot prohibit; he might, indeed, not have shipped his goods on board of that vessel, but if it was not convenient for him so to do, he cannot be made answerable for the act or fraud of another person.*

Such is my opinion, and I wish that the several treaties and edicts which I have cited, had spoken more explicitly upon the subject. It will be said, perhaps, that the distinctions which are not therein expressed, are to be tacitly understood, and that thus the treaties and edicts may be interpreted according to each particular case. I wish that I could be of that opinion; but I fear that it cannot be done, because of the too great generality of the expressions. What *Albericus Gentilis* has written on all these subjects, is full of obscurity and confusion.†

---

* By the law of *France*, if a vessel is captured with contraband on board going to the enemy, the contraband goods only are forfeited, but the vessel and the remainder of the cargo are to be released, unless the contraband articles amount to three-fourths of the cargo, in which case, the whole of the merchandize on board is to be condemned, as well as the ship. Ordin. of the 26th of *July* 1773, art. 1. 2. Code des Prises, 672, *edit.* 1784.

The rule in *England*, is to condemn only the contraband articles, and to restore the rest of the cargo and the ship, but without freight; provided, however, that they belong to a different owner from that of the illicit goods, who did not know of the illegality of the voyage, and was not by himself or his agent, concerned in any fraud or concealment, to impose upon the officers of the belligerent nation, by masking the real destination of the ship, covering enemy's property, or otherwise, and was not acting in violation of a treaty of his own country.—The *Mercurius, Meincke,* 1 Rob. 242.—The *Mercurius, Geddes,* ibid. 70.—The *Jonge Tobias,* ibid. 278.—The *Princesa,* 2 Rob. 42.—The *Rosalie & Betty,* ibid. 292.—The *Franklin,* 3 Rob. 183.—The *Neutralitæt,* 3 Rob. 240. Amer. edit.　　　　　　　　T.

† De Advoc. Hispan. l. 1. c. 20.

CHAPTER XIII.

Of Neutral Goods found on board of the ships of enemies.

IN the year 1602, after the conquest of *Portugal* by the *Spaniards*, several *Portuguese* ships were captured by the *Dutch*, who were then at war with *Spain*. *Grotius*, who relates the fact,* says, "that it was more difficult to decide whether the goods of the *Italians* which were found on board of the captured ships, were lawful prize," and he adds, "that the matter was decided by a *compromise between equity and the law of war*." That respectable writer, therefore, doubted whether neutral goods found on board the ships of enemies, were to be considered as enemy goods; but he entertained no such doubt in 1625, when he wrote his treatise *De Jure Belli ac Pacis;* for in that work he expressly says: "That nothing is acquired by the law of war, but what belongs to the enemy, and not the property of neutrals, although it be found on the enemy's territory;" and he infers from thence, that the vulgar saying, "that goods found on board of an enemy's ships are to be considered as belonging to the enemy," is not warranted by the law of nations, but that such are only to be *presumed* enemy goods, until the contrary is proved. He adds, that it was so decided in *Holland*, in full court, in the year 1338, while we were at war with the *Hanse Towns*, and that that decision has passed into a law.† He gives it his approbation in another place, where he treats of the same subject.‡

I must own, that I blush at my ignorance, for not having been able to find that decision of the year 1338, nor can I understand by what court it was pronounced; for it is a fact of public notoriety, that it was not until near a century after-

* Hist. Belg. l. 11. *sub anno* 1602.
† De Jure B. ac P. l. 3. c. 6. § 5.
‡ Not. ad l. 3. de J. B. ac P. c. 1. § 5.

wards, that the court of *Holland* was instituted by *Philip* of *Burgundy*. This, indeed, was corrected by *Grotius*, in a new edition of his book, in which he substituted the year 1438 instead of 1338.* But in the latest edition, published in 1632, in the octavo form, (which *Grotius* himself certifies to be entirely correct), the year 1338 is again mentioned, and this date has been followed by those who have quoted that passage out of his book.† Even my learned friend *Barbeyrac* has preserved the same year 1338, in his *French* translation of *Grotius*,‡ and attributes that decree to the *states-general*, although they never exercised judicial powers, nor ever were considered as a court of judicature; at any rate, the true date of it must be the year 1438, as *Grotius* alludes to the *Hanseatic* war, of which there is a book preserved among the archives of the court of *Holland*, entitled *Oosterlingen*.§

Although that decree of the year 1438, has escaped my diligent inquiry, I nevertheless believe *Grotius's* assertion, without requiring any other proof of the fact, and I can easily conceive how others have followed his opinion on the credit of his character alone, and without its being supported by any other authority. Thus *Loccenius*‖ speaks of the principle which *Grotius* lays down as being established law, and so do the six advocates whose opinions are recorded in *Consilia Belgica*.¶ I think, however, that they go too far when they seem to intimate that it would be otherwise if public notice

---

* In what we believe to be the last edition of *Grotius's* work, *Utrecht* 1773, the error appears to have been corrected. The decree there is said to have been pronounced in 1438.   T.

† *Zouch*, de Jure Fec. p. 2. § 8. Q. 25.—Consil. Belg. vol. 3. Consil 253.

‡ It is not so in the *Amsterdam* edition of *Barbeyrac's* translation, printed in 1724, which Mr. *Bynkershoek*, it seems, had not before him when he composed this work. The decree there is said to have been given in 1438.   T.

§ Or the *Easterlings;* by which name the inhabitants of the *Hanse Towns* were formerly known.   T.

‖ *Res in hostium navibus repertæ præsumuntur esse hostium, donec contrarium probetur.* Things found on board the enemy's ships are *presumed* to belong to the enemy, until the contrary is proved. *Loccen. De Jure Marit.* l. 2. c. 4. n. 11.   T

¶ *Ubi suprà.*

had been given that no neutral should ship his goods on board of an enemy's vessel, or if he who shipped them, was ignorant of the war.*

If by the general law of nations, it is lawful for a neutral to ship his goods on board of an enemy's vessel, I cannot conceive how it can be rendered otherwise by the proclamation of a belligerent sovereign. I am at liberty to carry on trade with two nations, who are in friendship with me, but at war with each other, unless I am prevented by express or tacit conventions, (as is almost always the case with respect to *contraband;*) what, then, if one of those nations, without the consent of the other, should prohibit altogether my trading with her enemy? Such an interdiction would be unjust as to all but the subjects of the prohibiting nation. *Grotius* appears to have been of this opinion,† otherwise he justly thinks that respect is due to the public proclamations of sovereigns, and that they are not to be disregarded with impunity.

As to the other point, what matters it, whether he who has shipped his goods on board of the enemy's ship, did or did not know of the war? Suppose that he did know of it, and that he also knew that the ship belonged to an enemy, the question will still recur, whether he has acted lawfully or unlawfully in shipping the goods? These fine spun niceties, although they may serve to make a display of legal ingenuity, cannot fail to be rejected by those who follow the rules of plain unsophisticated common sense.

Before I express my own opinion, I must first consult the treaties which have been made between different nations upon the subject. As far as I can understand, they nearly agree with the *French* law, which is laid down by *Mornac,*‡ *que la robe de l'ennemi confisque celle de l'ami.*§ *Grotius*‖ attempts

---

* The same opinion is given in Consil. Belg. vol. 4. Consil. 207.

† *Ubi suprà*, not. 4.

‡ Ad l. Penult. § 1. ff. *locati conducti.*

§ " That the goods of an enemy produce the confiscation of those of a friend." The word *robe* in the old *French* idiom signified *effects, goods, furniture, wearing apparel* and the like. *Roba* in *Italian, ropa* in *Spanish,* and *roupa* in *Portuguese,* at this day, mean the same thing.   *T.*

‖ In not. ad l. 3. de J. B. ac P. c. 6. § 6.

to explain away the rigour of this law, and understands it to mean, that if enemy goods are shipped on board of a neutral vessel, *with the consent of the owner of the ship*, then the ship herself, though neutral, is liable to confiscation.* But this is not the subject before us, and will be treated in the next chapter. If, however, the consent of the owner of the vessel is the cause of her confiscation, why do we not confiscate *neutral* goods, which, with their owner's consent, are shipped on board of an *enemy's* vessel? Of this, *Grotius* has said nothing, and yet the rule of reciprocity required that the same law should be applied to both cases.

But if, setting aside for a moment these considerations, we turn to the treaties themselves: we shall find that they all simply stipulate, that "neutral goods found on board of an enemy's vessel, are liable to confiscation."† In this they have adopted the principle of the old *French* law, which confiscates the goods of neutrals merely because they are found on board of the vessel of an enemy,‡ and therefore do not agree with what *Grotius* states to have been decided by the court of *Holland*,

* But *Valin* rebukes him strongly for entertaining this opinion. " *Grotius,*" says he, " pretends that our ordinances are to be understood with this restriction; it would, if it were admitted, furnish an excuse to the neutral master, with which he never would fail to elude the confiscation of his vessel and the remainder of his cargo." *Valin, Traité des Prises,* p. 64.

There is no doubt that such was the ancient law of *France,* and that it confiscated alike neutral goods found on board the enemy's ships, and neutral ships carrying enemy's goods; so true it is, that injustice has always followed power.   *T.*

† Marine treaty between *Spain* and the states-general of the 17th *December* 1650, art. 13.—Treaty of commerce between *France* and the states-general of the 27th of *April* 1662, art. 35.—Treaty between the same powers of the 10th of *August* 1678, art. 22.—Of the 20th of *September* 1697, art. 27.—11th of *April* 1713, art. 26.—Between *England* and the states-general, 1st of *December* 1674, art. 8.—*Sweden* and the states-general of the 26th of *November* 1675, art. —. And 12th of *October* 1679, art. 22.

‡ But by the same treaties, as will be seen in the next chapter, it was on the other hand stipulated that enemy's goods found on board of neutral ships should not be liable to confiscation, or in other words, that *free ships should make free goods;* so that if, in one respect, they were conformable to the old severe law of *France,* they established upon the whole, the more equitable principles of the *modern law of nations.*   *T.*

and to have obtained the force of a law. It is true, that the
treaties which I have related are subsequent, and that they
are of no force except between those who are parties to them.
But the rule which they establish cannot be defended on
rational principles: for why should I not be allowed to make
use of my friend's ship to carry my property, notwithstanding
his being at war with you? If treaties do not prohibit, I am at
liberty, as I have already said, to trade with your enemy; and
if so, I may likewise enter into any kind of contract with him,
buy, sell, let, hire, &c. Therefore, if I have engaged his vessel
and his labour, to carry my goods across the seas, I have done
that which was lawful on every principle. You, as his enemy,
may take and confiscate his ship, but by what law will you also
take and confiscate the goods that belong to me, who am your
friend? All that I am bound to do, is, to prove that they are
really mine; for here I agree with *Grotius*, that there is some
room for *presuming*, that goods found on board of an enemy's
vessels are the property of the enemy. .

But what shall we say, if the owners of the goods knew and
consented that they should be shipped on board of the vessel
of their friend, indeed, but of your enemy? I should think
that this knowledge and consent do not authorize a confiscation. The matter depends upon this only question, whether
the owners of the goods, in shipping them on board of an
enemy's vessel have acted lawfully or unlawfully! I have
contended for the former position, because, as I may lawfully
carry on any kind of trade with your enemy, I think that I
may therefore enter with him into any kind of contract, and
make use, for a valuable consideration, of his ship for my
own utility. Take, if you can, every thing which belongs to
your enemy, but restore to me what is my own, because I am
your friend, and in shipping my goods, I have not intended to
do you any injury.

With what I have said, nearly agrees what is laid down
in the *Consolato del Mare*, to wit: " that the enemy's ship
when taken, belongs to the captors, and the neutral goods to
the owners thereof, but that those owners may, if they are
present, compound for the purchase of the vessel, and thus be

enabled to prosecute their voyage.* If, however, a composition does not take place, the vessel may be carried into a port of the captor, but still the goods are to be restored to their owners, on paying the freight thereof, in the same manner as if the voyage had been performed." I approve of this general doctrine; but what is said there on the subject of freight, I cannot admit to be founded in law. I understand very well, that he who has taken the vessel, has also taken all the right arising out of it which belonged to her or to the master; but the freight was not due to the ship, nor to the captain, unless the goods had been carried to their destined port.† The question, however, is asked, whether, if a ship is taken in the course of her voyage, the owner of the goods on board is obliged to pay freight to the captor? I answer, that if the captor is ready to carry the ship with the goods to the place of their destination, I think that he is entitled to demand his freight, otherwise I am of opinion that he is not. The shipper is sufficiently punished for his imprudence, in putting his goods on board an enemy's vessel, when he is obliged to claim them at his own expense, and to carry them away at his own risk. I have shewn, in a former chapter,‡ that difficult questions will arise respecting this matter of *freight*, and that it requires a sound judgment to form a correct opinion upon them.

* *Consol. del Mar.* c. 273. This chapter has been elegantly translated into *English*, by the learned Dr. *Robinson*, and is bound together with his interesting collection, entitled, *Collectanea Maritima, London, Butterworth* 1801. The passage referred to by our author, is in that translation marked §§ 6 & 7. In M. *Boucher's French* translation, it is c. 276. §§ 1012, 1013, vol. ii. p. 511.

† This doctrine of our author is fully recognised in *England*, where the captor of an enemy's ship is not considered as entitled to freight on neutral goods, unless he has carried them to the port of their destination. The *Fortuna*, 4 *Rob.* 228. *Am. edit.* It is, however, allowed in certain cases, when the goods are brought to the claimant's own country. The *Diana*, 5 *Rob.* 64. *Am. edit.*

‡ C. 10. p. 80.

CHAPTER XIV.

Of Enemy's Goods found on board of neutral ships.

IF a neutral ship be taken, having enemy's property on board, two questions are to be considered: the one, whether the neutral ship itself, the other, whether the enemy's goods are liable to confiscation?

As to the first question, if we follow the ancient law of *France*, a neutral ship will be liable to confiscation for carrying enemy's goods. That such was the law of *France*, in ancient times, is clear, by the exemption from it granted to the *Hanse Towns*, in their treaty with that country of the 10th of *May* 1655. *Grotius*, in the passage mentioned in the preceding chapter, is of opinion, that the *French* law does not extend farther than to the case of a neutral ship, the owner of which *knowingly* receives enemy's goods on board,* relying on that law of the *Digest*† in which, as I have said above,‡ a distinction is made between the master's *knowing* and his being *ignorant* of unlawful goods being laden on board of his ship; in the first case, but not in the second, the law directs the ship to be confiscated. *Loccenius*§ also distinguishes the present case in the same manner.

---

* See the note * p. 103.

† *Dominus navis, si illicitè aliquid in nave, vel ipse, vel vectores imposuerint, navis quoque fisco vindicatur. Quod si absente Domino, à magistro vel gubernatore aut proretâ nautâve aliquod id factum sit: ipsi quidem capite puniuntur, commissis mercibus, navis autem Domino restituitur.* If the owner of the ship or any of the passengers shall put any thing unlawfully on board, the ship shall also be confiscated. If, however, it shall have been done in the absence of the owner, by the master, mate, or some of the mariners, they shall be capitally punished, and the goods shall be confiscated, but the ship shall be restored to the owners. *ff. de Public. & Vectig.* l. 11. § 2.

‡ C. 12. p. 94.

§ *Ubi suprà.*

This distinction of *Paulus** between the knowledge and ignorance of the master of the ship, is certainly very important, and has been very much attended to in the *Roman* law, but now is hardly of any force if the vessel belongs to the master himself; for it is generally he who receives the goods, and who attests their shipment by an instrument commonly called a *bill of lading*. It is of greater use, if the ship belongs to other owners than the captain, and he has received the goods without their knowledge, as I have already shewn in another place.† It may, however, be doubted, whether other owners, if they have given a special authority to the master to take goods on freight, and he has shipped unlawful merchandize, are not bound for his act? In general the rule is, that he who entrusts an unfit person with his business, is answerable for his faults and for the frauds that he commits; and if a distinction is made between the master and another owner of the vessel, the question will present itself in a pretty difficult point of view. But this is not the ground that I go upon. I am willing to admit, that the owners of the ship are bound for the act of the master, even without having given him a special authority; that the receiving of the goods was ordered by the owner himself, and that he knew in every case what goods were shipped on board of his vessel, and to whom they belonged; notwithstanding all that, I see no reason for confiscating the ship, merely for having enemy's property on board, whether or not the owner knew of or gave his consent to it.

I do not grant to *Grotius*, that the case which *Paulus* speaks of in the passage which he cites, extends to that which we are now contending about. Not because in those things which depend solely upon reason, the principles of the law of nations may not safely be sought for in the rules of *Roman* jurisprudence, but because the doctrine of *Paulus* has no application here. He only speaks of a master of a vessel, who, knowingly or unknowingly, carries goods in fraud of the revenue. In that case, it is true, that if the master acts with full knowledge of the circumstances, he employs his vessel and his labour for an

* The author of the abovementioned passage in the Digest.   *T.*
† Above, c. 12. p. 96.

unlawful purpose, and she is justly liable to confiscation; for he who conceals and knowingly carries on board of his vessel, goods which ought to be declared for the purpose of paying the duties thereon, commits a fraud upon the public. And therefore, at present, by the laws of almost every country, ships which are employed in defrauding the revenue, are confiscated, for no other reason than that they are employed in an illegal act.

I have myself adopted the same distinction of *Paulus*, with respect to contraband goods,* and have given it as my opinion, that if such goods were shipped on board of a neutral vessel, to be carried to the enemy, with the knowledge of the owners, the ship itself is also liable to be confiscated, unless there should be treaties to the contrary; because the owners in such a case are concerned in an act prohibited by law.

But now, let us pause and consider, whether he is guilty of any offence against the law of nations, who carries on board of his vessel the goods of his friend, although that friend is your enemy? By what right will you, who are my friend, capture my ship, merely because she carries your enemy's goods? I, who am a friend to both parties, shall serve them both, in those things that are not hurtful to either, and in the same manner both will serve me in things that are indifferent. On this principle, your enemy may with propriety hire his vessel out to me, and I am at liberty to hire mine out to him. Of those who act thus innocently and without fraud, I have treated more at large in the preceding chapter, and if what I have said there is correct, there is no need of saying any more upon this question, but it must be laid down as a principle, that a neutral vessel is not liable to be confiscated for having enemy's goods on board, whether the owner of the vessel knew of it, or not; because, in either case, he knew that he was engaged in a lawful trade; and in this his case differs from that of him who knowingly carries *contraband* goods to the enemy. Wherefore, on the present question, I do not admit the application of the distinction made by *Paulus;* but I approve of the

* Above, p. 96.

opinion which was given in general terms by the *Dutch* lawyers, and is recorded in the *Consilia Belgica,** that a neutral ship, although laden with enemy's goods, is not liable to confiscation.*

We will now proceed to consider the second question, whether the enemy's goods themselves, taken on board of a neutral vessel are liable to confiscation? Some will wonder, perhaps, that any doubt should be entertained about it, as it is clearly lawful for a belligerent to take the property of his enemy. And yet, in all the treaties which I have cited in the preceding chapter,† there is an express stipulation, that " enemy's goods found on board of neutral vessels, shall be free," or, (as we commonly express it), that *free ships shall make free goods,* except, however, contraband of war, when carrying to the enemy. And what will be thought more astonishing is, that among those treaties there are four to which *France* is a party, and according to them, even *enemy's goods* laden on board of neutral vessels are not liable to confiscation; much less, therefore, ought the *neutral vessel* to be confiscated, on board of which they are shipped. So that it must be said, either that the principle of the old *French* law which I have above mentioned, has been entirely abandoned, or, what is more probable, that those treaties are to be considered as exceptions to it. However this may be, we are bound, in the discussion of general principles, to attend more to reason than to treaties. And on rational grounds, I cannot see why it should not be lawful to take enemy's goods, although found on board of a neutral ship; for in that case, what the belligerent takes is still the property of his enemy, and by the laws of war, belongs to the captor.

It will be said, perhaps, that a belligerent may not lawfully take his enemy's goods on board of a neutral vessel, unless he should first take the neutral vessel itself; that he cannot do this without committing an act of violence upon his friend, in order to come at the property of his enemy, and that it is quite as unlawful as if he were to attack that enemy in a neutral port,

* Vol. 4. Consil 206. n. 2.
† Above, p. 103.

or to commit depredations in the *territory* of a friend.* But it ought to be observed, that it is lawful to detain a neutral vessel, in order to ascertain, not by the flag merely, which may be fraudulently assumed, but by the documents themselves which are on board, whether she is really neutral. If she appear to be such, then she is to be dismissed, otherwise, she may be captured. And if this is lawful, as on every principle it is, and as it is generally practised, it will be lawful also to examine the documents which concern the cargo, and from thence to learn, whether there are enemy's goods concealed on board, and if any should be found, why may they not be captured by the law of war? The *Dutch* lawyers, whose opinion I have already cited,† and the *Consolato del Mare*, in the chapter above referred to,‡ are equally clear upon this point. According to them, the neutral ship is to be released; but the enemy's goods are to be carried into a port of the captor, and there condemned.§

* It is worthy of observation, that our author, while he supports the belligerent principle, on the long agitated question, whether *free ships* " do or do not make *free goods,*" tacitly admits, that neutral vessels are entitled to be considered as *neutral territory,* a proposition which Mr. *Hubner* thought so self-evident, that he did not think it worth while (though he professedly wrote in favour of the neutral doctrine) to devote a single page of his work to its proof and development. *Hubn. de la Saisie &c.* vol. 1. p. 211. This principle being admitted, the question is reduced to the single point, " Whether the right of taking enemy's property on board of neutral vessels, *necessarily* follows as a consequence of the right of search, for the purpose of ascertaining their neutral character?" On this point alone, the whole of our author's argument turns, and he maintains the affirmative; but like *Hubner,* he takes his proposition for granted, without taking any pains to demonstrate it. On the whole, he must be considered as having made a very important concession in favour of neutrals, and having greatly narrowed for them the field of that celebrated controversy.   *T.*

† Consil. Belg. *ubi suprà.*

‡ C. 273. § 2. of Mr. *Robinson's* translation, and c. 276. § 1004. of that of M. *Boucher.*   *T.*

§ Above, p. 104. This opinion of our author is adopted, as we have shewn before, p. 105. in the case of neutral goods found on board of an enemy's vessel; but the contrary rule universally takes place in the case of enemy's goods taken on board of a neutral ship, in which case, as we have observed above, p. 81, the owner of the vessel is entitled to his freight, though he has not carried the goods to the place of their destination. Such is the opinion of

Those authorities say further, that the captor must pay the freight to the master of the vessel, but I do not think that opinion reasonable, because freight is not due, unless the goods have been carried to their port of destination. It may, indeed, be said, and with great truth, that it was not the fault of the master, that he did not carry them; but it must be said also, that when he took enemy's goods on board of his ship, he did it at his own peril, as he must have known that they might be taken, and thus be carried into a port of the captor. Therefore, he has no cause to complain, if his ship be merely dismissed without paying him any freight; unless it should be agreed between him and the captor, that he should carry the enemy's goods to the place of their destination, and thus have hired his vessel out to the captor himself. I have argued on this same principle in the preceding chapter, but in a case directly opposite; being that of neutral goods and an enemy's vessel.*

I shall not now turn to the particular cases in which this subject has been discussed. The reader, if he approves of the principles which I have laid down, will be able to form a correct judgment of what is said by *Albericus Gentilis*,† and *Zouch*,‡ on the same question, and of the controversy, which, as the latter relates, was once agitated with so much warmth between the *English* and the *Zealanders*.§ *Zouch*, himself, is

Vattel, which is at this day generally considered as law." *Si l'on trouve sur un vaisseau neutre des effets appartenants aux ennemis, on s'en saisit par le droit de la guerre: mais naturellement on doit payer le fret au maître du vaisseau, qui ne peut souffrir de cette saisie.* If on board of a neutral vessel, goods are found belonging to the enemy, they are seized by the law of war: but naturally, the freight is to be paid to the master of the vessel, who cannot suffer from that seizure." *Vatt.* L. of N. 1. 3. c. 7. § 115. Such is also the rule in *England*, though very much restricted, and rendered almost illusory in practice. The *Atlas*, 3 *Rob.* 243. *Am. edit. in not.* The *Emanuel*, 1 *Rob.* 249. The *Rebecca*, 2 *Rob.* 84. The *Immanuel*, *ibid.* 172. *Am. ed.*

The reason of this rule is very plain, *enemy's goods* are not, like *contraband*, seized and confiscated, *ex delicto*, but merely *ex re;* for, he who carries enemy's property, is not guilty of any *offence* against the law of nations, as our author himself has ably demonstrated, above p. 108. *T.*

Above, p. 105.

† De Advoc. Hispan. l. 1. c. 28.——‡ De Jure Fec. p. 2. § 8. Q. 6.

§ It is related by *Zouch*, that in the year 1576, the merchants of the *Spanish Netherlands*, being in the habit of carrying on their commerce with

of opinion, that the neutral vessel ought to be released, and the enemy's goods confiscated; but, he thinks that freight ought to be paid to the master, in which he agrees with the *Consolato del Mare*, but not with me. He is, however, for allowing such freight only *pro ratâ itineris peracti.** If his doctrine were correct, as in my opinion it is not, it would be very difficult to explain this restriction, on satisfactory principles.†

After writing thus much, the works of the learned *Heineccius* have come to my hands, and among them his dissertation " *On the confiscation of ships for carrying prohibited goods,*"‡ in which§ he briefly considers the two questions which are the subject of this and the preceding chapter. The perusal of that treatise has not induced me in the least to alter my opinion; I am, on the contrary, confirmed in it by the authority of so great a man. If the reader will take the trouble to compare what has been said by each of us on the same subject, he will be satisfied of the reason why I have not thought it necessary to make any alteration in this chapter, nor in that which immediately precedes it.

Spain, then at war with the *United Provinces*, under cover of the *English* flag, the privateers of *Zealand* captured several *English* vessels engaged in that trade, and had them condemned as prize in their court of admiralty. He adds, that the *English* complained of it, and by way of retaliation, detained the ships of the *Zealanders* which they found in the ports of *England*, and imprisoned their commanders. But the prince of *Orange* prevailed upon the queen to accept of a compromise, by which the property taken was restored on both sides. *Zouch, ubi suprà.*   T.

* In proportion to the voyage performed.   T.

† We have shewn in former notes, p. 81. 110. that contrary to the opinion of our author, freight is generally allowed to the neutral master in the prize-courts of *Europe*. And it is not only paid to him, as *Zouch* would have it, *pro ratâ itineris*, but *in toto*, and as if the whole voyage had been performed. The reason given for it, which appears founded on very sound principles, is, " that the captor represents his enemy, by possessing himself of his goods, *jure belli;* and that, although the whole freight has not been earned by the completion of the voyage, yet, as the captor, by his act of seizure, has prevented its completion, his seizure shall operate to the same effect as an actual delivery of the goods to the consignee, and shall subject him to the payment of the full freight." The *Copenhagen*, 1 Rob. 245. *Amer. edit.* T.

‡ *De navibus ob vecturam vetitarum mercium commissis.*——§ C. 2. § 9.

CHAPTER XV.

Of the Right of Postliminy on neutral territory.

IT has been questioned whether this right extends to persons or things, which, after being taken by an enemy, are carried by him into the territory of a neutral. It might be supposed that this question is settled by that passage from the *Digest*, in which *Pomponius* says, " that one of our people who has been taken by the enemy, is understood to be returned among us, if he arrives among our friends or upon our territory;"* and as the same law which, on the subject of postliminy, applies to persons, applies also to things, there does not appear to be any further room for controversy; for it seems, that under the general denomination of *friends*, *Pomponius* has meant to include *neutrals*, who are certainly entitled to that appellation. But *Grotius* construes it in a different manner;† he thinks, and in my opinion justly, that by the word *friends* are not generally to be understood, all those who are at peace with us, but only those who are engaged with us *in the same war*. He gives the same interpretation to what is said by *Paulus*, that " those are considered as having returned to us by right of *postliminy*, not only who have actually entered our territory, but who have arrived within the dominions of a *friend* or *ally;* because there they begin to be under the safeguard of the public faith."‡

If we take the words " OR an *ally*" *conjunctively*, (which we may, perhaps, do, in the same manner that we frequently construe a *conjunctive* into a *disjunctive*), *Paulus's* opinion will support the interpretation of *Grotius;* for an *ally* certainly

---

* ff. de Capt. & Postlim. Revers. l. 5. § 1.
† De J. B. ac P. l. 3. c. 9. § 2. n. 1 and 2.
‡ ff. *ut suprà*, l. 19. § 3.

comes within the description of the word *friend*. If, however, we take it in the *disjunctive* sense, it will be sufficient that it be a *neutral* or *friendly*, though not an *allied* nation. Of this opinion is *Albericus Gentilis;*[*] but he is clearly in the wrong; because the reason which *Paulus* gives, that the person who was taken begins, when on a friend's territory, to be under the safeguard of the public faith, applies as well and rather more to an *ally* than to a *mere friend*.

Of the same opinion with *Grotius*, and before him, was *Antonio de Gama*,[†] whom *Gentilis* on that account undertook to refute. *Zouch*,[‡] according to his custom, contents himself with relating the different opinions of others, and gives none himself, though he rather appears to incline to that of *Gentilis*. As to *Grotius*, he supports what he says merely by the authority of precedents, without adding a single argument of his own. " Among those," says he, " who are friends, but not allies, prisoners of war do not change their condition, unless it be so specially agreed by treaty," and by way of example, he immediately quotes the second treaty between the *Carthaginians* and *Romans;*[§] but *Zouch* very properly observes, that it does not sufficiently appear whether what the two nations agreed upon together is to be considered as a declaration of the law of nations, or as an exception to it. In various treaties, among the most ancient as well as the most modern, this is a question which it is often difficult to decide; and it is always dangerous to infer the law of nations merely from treaties, without also consulting reason. *Grotius* adds, in his notes, that it appears from *Thuanus*, that the king of *Fez* and *Morocco* was of the same opinion with him; but no one will be willing to be instructed by such masters in the law of nations.

* De Advoc. Hisp. l. 1. c. 1.
† Decisiones Lusitanicæ, 384.
‡ De Jure Fec. p. 2. § 8. Q. 2.
§ It was stipulated by that treaty, that if the prisoners made by the *Carthaginians* on some nation in friendship with the *Romans*, should come into the countries under the *Roman* dominion, they might be reclaimed, and should again become free; and that the friends of the *Carthaginians* should have the same right within the *Punic* dominions. *Grot. ubi suprà.*

As to other writers, *Huberus** is of the same opinion with *Grotius*, when he understands by the word *returned*, one who is come back into the territory of an *ally*. *Hertius†* agrees also with him, and considers the right of postliminy as not being founded on the law of nations, but on municipal law. He decides on the question so often discussed among nations, " whether a prisoner of war, or captured property, which is brought into a neutral country, are entitled to their liberty by the right of postliminy?" He maintains that they are not; " because," says he, " neutrals are bound ' to take the *fact* for the *law*,' and therefore cannot say that the capture was illegally made."‡

But, indeed, if we chuse to consider this subject by the mere light of reason, this question appears to me so idle, that I wonder that it has exercised the minds of so many writers. He who returns among the allies of his sovereign, is entitled to the right of postliminy, because he is considered as having returned to his own country, for allies are considered as making but one state with ourselves.§ Certainly they are not to be considered as separate nations in respect to the war in which they unite their forces and mutual assistance. Therefore, by the word *friends*, which *Pomponius‖* makes use of, I would understand those who are such in the highest degree, that is to say, who are in alliance with us against the same enemy; and by *Paulus's* expression,¶ " a *friend* or *ally*,"

* De Jure Civitatis, l. 3. § 4. c. 5. n. 11.

† Adnot. ad Puffend. De Jure N. and G. l. 8, c. 6. n. 25.

‡ Such is also the opinion of all the modern writers, and particularly of *Vattel. Le droit de postliminie n'a point lieu chez les peuples neutres; car quiconque veut demeurer neutre dans une guerre est obligé de la considérer quant à ses effets, comme également juste de part & d'autre, & par conséquent de regarder comme bien acquis tout ce qui est pris par l'un ou l'autre parti.* The right of postliminy does not take place among neutral nations; for whoever will remain neutral in a war, is obliged to look upon it, as to its effects, as being equally just on both sides, and consequently to consider as a lawful acquisition whatever is captured by either party. Law of Nat. l. 3. c. 14. § 208.

§ *Unam constituunt Civitatem.* See the *Henrick* and *Maria*, 4 Rob. 49. *Amer. edit.*

‖ Above, p. 113.——¶ *Ibid.*

I would understand him, who is at the same time in *friend-ship* and in *alliance* with us; for otherwise, it would have been sufficient to have made use of the word *friend.** With such alone, because of the alliance, the right of postliminy

---

* The doctrine of *postliminy*, among the ancient *Romans*, applied principally to *persons*, it being the practice at the time when that country flourished, to make *slaves* of prisoners taken in war. To such, *Pomponius* and *Paulus* particularly meant to apply their principles on this subject, and therefore, it is not easy to refer them to the case of ships and goods taken at sea in a modern maritime war. Nor does it sufficiently appear whether those authors meant to speak of prisoners who made their *escape* into a friendly or allied country, as well as of those who came thither in the *possession* of their masters who had purchased them from the captors. It is possible, that a different rule might have obtained in each of these different cases. The civilians take too much pains to apply the principles of the *Roman* law to every case that presents itself; not considering, that the difference between ancient and modern manners renders them, in many instances, little susceptible of a direct application.

There would be, in our opinion, little difficulty in settling this question of *postliminy on neutral territory*, if a proper attention were paid to the distinction which the law has established between *military* and *civil* rights. We call *military* rights those which belligerents acquire in war, by capture or conquest, to the property of their enemies, and *civil rights*, those which are acquired out of war by contract or otherwise. These different rights receive a different kind of proof. *Military* rights are evidenced by *possession*, and *civil* rights by the ordinary proofs of *title*. A prize, therefore, which is brought into a neutral territory, *in the possession* of the captors or of their agents, does not return to its former owner, by the law of postliminy, because neutrals are bound to take notice of the military right which the *possession* evidences. But they are not bound to receive any other proof of it than the possession itself; for with the *mere right of property* of the captor they have nothing to do; the *right of possession* is the only thing that they cannot controvert, and in that, as *Hertius* says, they are bound to take the *fact* for the *law*. If, therefore, a vessel, after capture, should escape, or be brought into a neutral territory by others than the captor, his agents, or those who otherwise lawfully claim under him, as there is no longer any legal *evidence* of the military right, no *fact* which is to be taken for *law*, the civil right of the former owner revives, and the property returns to him by the law of postliminy. We do not mean to speak here of property regularly condemned in the tribunals of the captor; such a condemnation converts the *military* into a *civil* right, of which the sentence is the legal evidence.

For want of attending to these distinctions, the broad and unqualified propositions of our author have led many into an error.   *T.*

takes place, but with those who are merely friends to both parties, the state or condition of our citizens, or of our property, does not change, because there is no reason for it. Wherefore, I wonder that *Gentilis* and others have been of opinion, that every thing which is brought into the dominions of a neutral country, returns by postliminy, and as a conse-quence thereof, that prisoners carried into the territory of a friend, become free.*

This doctrine, as to prisoners, is roundly asserted by *Joannes de Immola*,† and *Petrinus Bellus*,‡ with whom *Zouch* appears to concur in sentiment.§ But the contrary is so plain, that even sceptics have never seriously entertained a doubt of it; for all unanimously agree, that a right of property is ac-quired by capture in war, and that that right continues in the country of a friend. And if it be true, that the prizes which I have taken, and the prisoners that I have made, remain my property, by what right shall a prince, who is my friend, take from me those things which belong to me, *pleno jure*, and give

---

* By the law of nations, as at present understood, the right of postliminy takes place with respect to *persons*, even in a *neutral* country. For the mo-ment that a prisoner sets his foot on *neutral territory*, no force whatever of the belligerent can protect him. " A privateer," says *Vattel*, " carries his prize into a neutral port, and there freely sells it; but he would not be allowed to put his prisoners ashore, in order to confine them; *for to keep or detain prisoners of war, in order to confine them, is a continuation of hostilities.*" Law of Nat. l. 3. c. 7. § 132. True, the captor may confine them on board of his ship, even though in the neutral's port, or within his jurisdiction; because a ship is considered as it were a part of the territory of the sovereign to whom it belongs. (See above, p. 109, 110.), but beyond that, no force can lawfully be exercised by a belligerent on *persons* in a neutral country.

If, however, a passage should be granted to a body of land troops through a neutral territory, there is no doubt that they might keep under confine-ment the prisoners that they had with them. For this power would be incident to the right of passage, which otherwise would not be effectually granted. And an *army* (as well as a *fleet*) is considered, *wherever it may be*, in many respects, as a *præsidium* of the nation to whom it belongs. See above, p. 29.   *T*.

† Consil. 50.

‡ De Re Militari, p. 2. tit. 18. n. 12.

§ De Jure Fec. p. 2. § 9. Q. 8.

them up to another, though he be equally his friend? It is sufficiently clear, that he cannot do it without injuring me. Nor
can he do it by his courts of justice, for he cannot lawfully
judge between me and my enemy, without the agreement of
both.* As therefore, what is taken in war remains the property of the captor, though in a neutral country, the *Swedish*
ambassador was wrong, when, in the year 1657, he claimed
certain letters of his, which had been intercepted by the *Danes*,
with whom his sovereign was at war, and delivered to the
states-general, who were his friends; contending that, by that
delivery they had again become his own.†

Treaties, however, are sometimes made between sovereigns
on a different principle, as was the case formerly between the
Romans and *Carthaginians*, by the second treaty which *Grotius*
quotes from *Polybius*. And thus, by the 20th article of the
treaty of peace between the king of *Portugal* and the states-
general of the 6th of *August* 1661, it was stipulated, that
" what should be taken by the enemy of either, and carried
into the port of the other, if demanded within a certain time,
should be restored." But such conventions cannot be made
without injury to him who carries his prizes into the territory
of his friend as into a safe place. Therefore, they effect no
change in the principles of reason, or of the law of nations.
For more upon this subject, see *Cunæus's* dissertation *De
Causâ Postliminii*, and *Loccenius*, *De Jure Maritimo*,‡ where
the arguments of *Cunæus* are briefly stated.||

* As between the belligerents, the neutral is bound to see *right* wherever
he sees *possession:* of a right unaccompanied with possession, he cannot
take notice. We mean to speak only of rights acquired by or founded on
the law of war, for of other rights he may judge as if no war existed.   *T.*

† Aitz. l. 37. Because the possession of the captor continued in the
hands of his *donee;* and because such things as letters and the like, when
taken in war, do not require a sentence of condemnation to divest the right
of property of the first owner. *Statim capientium fiunt.*   *T.*

‡ L. 2. c. 4. n. 6. 10.

|| *Ut enim victor intrâ propria præsidia tutus est, itâ si amici fidem elegerit,
& in sua præsidia se et sua contulerit, etiam illic publico nomine tutus est.—
Serum est atque inutile, hostem tentare in alieno territorio vi suum alteri
adimere; aut cum communi amico agere, ut sibi restituat. Nihil enim hostile aut*

This, however, is true only as to captures made in a just war, for if any thing has been taken by pirates, it is by all means to be restored to the former owners; and so it has been stipulated in various treaties between different nations.* And it is a rule generally adopted among all the nations of Europe, that a capture by pirates does not change the property, which subject has been treated more at large by others, as I shall shew hereafter.†

Agreeably to these principles, if my property, captured by enemies, comes into the territory of an ally, it returns to my use, and hence it is considered as if it had been delivered by my ally from the common enemy. And yet, the French in a similar case, formerly acted on a different principle, in consequence of which, the states-general, on the 4th and 5th of *December* 1637, decreed, that the same should be done with respect to them.‡ §

violentum vel ipse molietur, vel alterum agitare in suos fines contra alterum patietur, quem FIDE PUBLICA *in portum suum admisit.* The same safety that the conqueror finds in his own fortresses, he will find in the dominions of his friend; if relying upon his honour, he has put himself and what belongs to him into his power, the public faith will protect him there. In vain shall his enemy endeavour to retake by force what was taken from him, or to prevail upon the neutral sovereign to restore it to him. The neutral sovereign will not commit an act of hostility against his friend, whom he has admitted into his country under the protection of the public faith; nor will he suffer any other person to hurt him within his territory. *Loccen. ubi suprà, in Scriptor. de Jure Nautico & Marit. Fascicul.* vol. ii. p. 976. We have thought that our readers would not be displeased with our transcribing this beautiful passage out of the writings of one of those *Northern professors,* against whom sir *James Marriott* has so unjustly and so illiberally vented his spleen. Vide *his decree in the case of the ship* Columbus, *in the first volume of* Collectanea Juridica.   *T.*

  * Treaty between the emperor of *Morocco* and the states-general, of the 24th of *September* 1610, art. 4.—Treaty of peace between the *United Provinces* and *Portugal*, of the 6th of *August* 1661, art. 20.—Treaty of commerce between *France* and the states-general, of the 27th of *April* 1662, art. 45.— Treaty of peace between *England* and the states-general, of the 14th of *September* 1662, art. 11.

  † *Post,* c. 17.

  ‡ Aitz. l. 21. 24.

  § *Aitzema* relates, that France being in alliance with *Holland,* and both being at war with *Spain,* the *French* had refused to restore to the *Dutch*

It is more doubtful, whether a captor may in a neutral territory, sell the thing which he has taken from his enemy, and recover the price of the sale? By the 12th article of the treaty of peace between the *United Provinces* and *England*, of the 4th of *September* 1662, it was provided, that in such a case, if the consideration of the sale had not been paid to the captor, the property should return to its former owner, which article, in a particular case, that happened afterwards, the states-general ordered to be carried into execution.* But I would wish to know on what principle this stipulation was founded? And how, if the sale of the prize by the captor is lawful, his enemy can be made to derive an advantage from it? It will be difficult to account satisfactorily for this; for it is an established principle, that we may lawfully assist our friends, although enemies to each other, provided we do not supply them with implements of war, and do not shew more favour to one than to the other. It cannot, therefore, be required, that we should shut our ports against them, or prohibit all commercial intercourse between them and our citizens. I am of opinion, that this 12th article is to be classed among special treaties, the reason of which is often concealed from us; for in general, we are free to exercise the rights of

their property which they had recaptured from the *Spanish* privateers; whereupon, the *Dutch*, by way of retaliation, issued the edict which our author mentions, by which they ordered that no part of the *French* property which their vessels of war should retake from the *Spaniards* should be restored to the *French*, until they should pursue a different line of conduct with respect to them. 2 Aitz. p. 752. *fol. ed.*   *T.*

* Aitz. l. 44. It is difficult to understand how prohibiting the sale of prizes in a neutral country is tantamount with interdicting all trade with the country of the captors; but this strong language of our author, shews how much he was in favour of the right of the belligerents to sell their prizes in neutral countries; and that this right exists, is not only the opinion of *Bynkershoek*, but of almost all the writers on the law of nations, and particularly of *Vattel* in the passage last above cited. The same right, however, should be granted to both parties alike, otherwise, the one to whom it is refused, will have a just right to complain. But neutral governments generally find it inconvenient to permit the privateers of contending nations to frequent their ports with their prizes at the same time, and therefore the right is either only granted to one of the parties, by virtue of a special treaty, or denied to both.   *T.*

ownership over our property in a neutral country, whether we have acquired it by the law of nations, or by the municipal law.

Although it be lawful, on rational principles, to carry a prize into a neutral territory, and there to sell it if the captor thinks proper, laws have, nevertheless, more than once, been made to the contrary. The states-general, on the 9th of *August* 1658, issued an edict, by which they ordered, that no foreign captor who might be compelled by stress of weather, or some other reasonable cause, to bring his prize into the ports of this country, should presume to sell any part of it, or even to break bulk, but that he should inform the bailiff of the place of his arrival, who, having placed a guard on board of the ship, should keep a strict watch over her, until her departure, inflicting, moreover, a discretionary penalty, and a fine of one thousand florins, on any one that should assist in unlading, or purchase any thing out of her. To which edict, the said states-general, on the 7th of *November* in the same year, enacted a supplement, by which it was ordered that no prize-ship should be brought into the port itself, but merely into the outer roads, where she might be sheltered from danger, and that nothing should be unladen or sold out of her; and if any one should act to the contrary, the prize should be restored to the former owner, as though it had never been taken, and the captor himself should be detained, and his own vessel seized and confiscated. The remainder of the edict merely confirms that of the ninth of *August* above mentioned. Whether those edicts were extorted from the states-general, by fear or by any other cause, I do not know; but lest they should hereafter militate against rational principles, we must declare that we rather believe them to have been temporary than perpetual laws.

†Q

CHAPTER XVI.

Of the Right of Postliminy as applied to cities and states. *

IT has been very properly said by *Grotius*,† that " the right
of *postliminy* is applicable to a *whole people*, as well as to
an *individual*, and that a political body, which was free before,
recovers its freedom when its allies, by force of arms, deliver
it from the yoke of the enemy." *Hotoman* is of the same
opinion, but there is some doubt whether this principle has
been always and every where observed in the *United Netherlands*. In the case of *Groningen*, there is no doubt that it was
attended to, as that city and province was admitted into the
confederation, after we had reconquered it from the *Spaniards*,
though it is to this day doubtful, whether they had ever before
formally signed the articles of *Utrecht*, and they had certainly
renounced them while under the *Spanish* dominion. Those
articles had, however, been signed by the district of *Ommelan-
den*, which constitutes much the largest part of that province.

The inhabitants of the district of *Drenthe* were, on the 11th
of *April* 1580, admitted into the confederation of *Utrecht*, but
their country was afterwards invaded and occupied by the
Spaniards. After the enemy had withdrawn and evacuated
their territory, it seems clear, that they had recovered all their
former rights, by virtue of the law of postliminy. Nevertheless, although they several times petitioned the states-general,
to be readmitted into the union, no order has yet been taken
upon any of their petitions; and once, in the year 1650, when,
after having received a summons, which, it is said, the presi-

---

* We have taken the liberty to abridge several parts of this chapter,
which, in the original, contains a variety of details, altogether uninteresting
to us, and which do not at all elucidate the author's principles.   *T.*

† De J. B. ac P. l. 3. c. 9. § 9. n. 1.

dent of the states-general had signed by mistake, their de-
puties attended at a meeting of the states, they were refused
admittance. This certainly appears to be an act of injustice,
particularly as neither the states-general nor the provincial
states* have ever given any reason for their refusal to admit
them, in which they persist to this day. It may, perhaps, be
alleged, that the *Drenthers* did not renounce their allegiance
to the king of *Spain*, as the other confederates did on the 26th
of *July* 1581; consequently, that they remained under the
dominion of the *Spaniards*, and are to be treated as a conquered country. But I would not exclude them on that
account, as I am not clear that they forfeited the privileges of
the *Dutch* union, merely because they did not renounce the
king of *Spain*, nor do I find that this has ever been objected
to them. Therefore, I see no reason why the *Drenthers*
should not enjoy the benefit of the law of *postliminy*.†

The inhabitants of those parts of *Brabant*, which were
under the dominion of the king of *Spain*, but were afterwards
taken by the *United Dutch*,‡ also petitioned the states-general,
in 1648, to be admitted into the confederation of *Utrecht;* but
they were not even permitted to manage their own internal
government. Some of the provincial states, however, gave
power to their delegates to decide upon that business, but
nothing was done in it. The *Brabanters* again petitioned on
the 22d of *March* 1651, but to no purpose. Their case does
not appear to come properly within the principle of the law of
postliminy, for none of their cities, except *Breda*, had ever
been admitted into the confederation of *Utrecht*. But as to
the inhabitants of *Breda*, I entertain the same opinion which
I have already expressed with regard to those of the district
of *Drenthe*.

---

* Of *Over-Yssel*, within which the territory of *Drenthe* was included.   *T.*

† They were not, however, admitted to that benefit, and they were
still a dependent territory at the time of the invasion of *Holland* by the
French.   *T.*

‡ The districts of *Maesland, Kuyck*, and *Kempenland*, with the cities of
Boisleduc, Breda, Bergen-op-Zoom and their territories, which constituted
what was formerly called *Dutch Brabant*.   *T.*

The case of *Guelderland, Utrecht,* and *Over-Yssel,* three out
of the seven united provinces, comes much more properly
within the law of *postliminy.* In the year 1672, they were
taken by the *French,** and afterwards recovered by us. While
they were in the power of the enemy, they certainly were not
entitled to their former rights as confederates, and on that account their delegates were very properly ordered not to attend
any longer at the meetings of the states-general; but when
those provinces again came into our possession, they were
with equal propriety, considered as being restored to their
former rights, by virtue of the law of postliminy. Indeed, the
states-general decreed, on the 20th of *April* 1674, that those
provinces should be restored to their former municipal and
confederate rights, as they enjoyed them before their capture,
except, however, that they deprived *Guelderland* of one vote in
the assembly of the states, and several other conditions were,
in fact, imposed upon them before they were readmittted into
the union; for, they were informed, that they should swear
anew to the articles of confederation, as if they were admitted
for the first time. But if, by the operation of the law of postliminy, every thing is to be restored as if the captivity had not
taken place, as it is every where understood, and is conformable to the usage of nations, every thing ought to have
been restored to those provinces, which they possessed before
their capture. They were, in my opinion, fully entitled to the
benefit of the law of postliminy, and if so, why was a part of
their rights retained? If, on the contrary, they were not, why
was any thing granted to them?

It has been objected, I know, that the decrees of the states-
general, on the subject of postliminy, speak of our *subjects*
only, and that no mention is made in them of our *allies* and
confederates; but that was not the question at the time when
those decrees were made. Nay, even if the point were to be
decided by those decrees, those should certainly be considered
as *subjects* of this state or republic, who constitute so large a
part of it. Others are more properly of opinion, that on the
subject of postliminy, there ought to be no difference between

ourselves and our allies and confederates. Hence the decree
of the states-general, of the 23d of *October* 1676, which I have
mentioned above,* grants the benefit of that law, not only to
those things which have been taken on board of our vessels,
and afterwards recaptured, but also to those which are taken
by the enemy, on board of the vessels of allies and of neutrals,
and afterwards recaptured by us. I have also herein before
shewn, that such was formerly the doctrine adopted by the
states-general, and that they blamed the *French* for having
followed a different principle.†

While the kingdom of *Portugal* was in the possession of
the *Spaniards*, with whom we were at war, the states-general
conquered a considerable part of the colony of *Brazil*, and
several others of the *Portuguese* dominions in different parts
of the world. After *Portugal* had recovered her independence,
a truce of ten years was signed between that country and the
states-general, in 1640.‡ But our government would not permit that the *Portuguese* should claim by virtue of the law of
postliminy, any part of the dominions which once had belonged to them, and which we had taken from the *Spaniards*.
In 1657, the truce being expired, but before any notice given
of the renewal of hostilities, the *Portuguese* retook some of
those places, and on the states-general complaining of it, they
refused to restore them, but offered to pay a sum of money by
way of compensation, which our government not being disposed to accept, they declared war against *Portugal*, on the
22d of *October* 1657. At last this controversy was settled by
the treaty of peace which was made on the 6th of *August*
1661.

The *Portuguese* were undoubtedly in the right, to claim the
dominions which the states-general had taken from them, be-

---

* C. 5.——† Above, p. 119.

‡ Shortly after the restoration of the house of *Braganza* to the throne of
Portugal, the states-general made a treaty of alliance with that kingdom
against *Spain*, notwithstanding which the two allies remained at war with
each other, and although they united their forces against the common
enemy, their mutual hostilities were only suspended by a truce of ten years,
which was not very religiously observed. *Cerisier, Hist. Gen. des Prov. Un.*
vol. vi. p. 148.—*Raynal, Hist. Philos. & Polit.* 1. 9.

cause the states themselves asserted, that the kingdom of *Portugal* did not belong to *Spain*. In addition to this, the *Portuguese* had been in alliance with the states-general in the war against *Spain*, so that the places belonging to them which had come into the possession of the *Dutch*, their allies, were clearly to return to their former sovereign, by virtue of the law of postliminy. It is true, that at the very time when those places came into the power of the *Dutch*, there was no king of *Portugal*, but when afterwards, that country was restored to its independency, the *Portuguese* were entitled to resume the possession of the territories that had been conquered by their allies from the enemies, saving the claim of the states-general for the expenses which they had incurred in taking them.

CHAPTER XVII.

Of Pirates.

IT is a principle consonant to reason and sanctioned by the rules of positive law, that things taken by *pirates* or *robbers*, do not thereby undergo a change of property, nor require the operation of the law of *postliminy* to return to their former owners. The authority of the *Digest* is in point,* and I have shewn in a former chapter,† that this rule has been adopted by several nations in their treaties with each other. I need not, therefore, bring forward the additional authorities of *Grotius*,‡ *Gentilis*,§ and *Zouch*,‖ and of a number of other writers. But I shall proceed to examine who are the persons to whom we may properly apply the denomination of *pirates* and *robbers*.

We call *pirates* and *plunderers*, *(prædones)* those, who, without the authorization of any sovereign, commit depredations by sea or land.¶ Hence, by the law of this country, they

---

* ff. De Capt. & Postlim. Revers. l. 19. § 2. Ibid. l. 24. 27.

† C. 15.

‡ De J. B. ac P. l. 3. c. 9. §. 16.

§ De Jure Belli, l. 1. c. 4.

‖ De Jure Feo. P. 2. § 8. Q. 15.

¶ Our author's definition seems to be intended to apply equally to *pirates* and *land-robbers;* whereas it might have been expected that he would have given one to be applied exclusively to the former description of men. We have not been able to find one in the books altogether satisfactory, that given by Mr. *Hawkins* seems deficient, inasmuch as it might possibly be applied to those who sail *with*, as well as to those who sail *without* a commission from a sovereign. He defines a pirate, " one who to enrich himself, either by surprise or open force, sets upon merchants or others, trading by sea, to spoil them of their goods and treasure." 1 *Hawk.* P. C. 267. Independent of the objection which we have made, there appears to be in this definition a great deal of unnecessary redundancy.

Were

are punished as pirates, who sail out for the purpose of making depredations on the enemy, without a commission from the admiral, and without having complied with the requisites of

Were we to presume to offer a definition of our own, we would say, that a pirate is "he, who sailing without being authorized by any sovereign to make captures, (or with commissions from different sovereigns at war with each other), commits depredations at sea or on shore." We say, " *or on shore*," because it appears to us, that on the principle of the celebrated case of *Lindo* v. *Rodney, Doug.* 591. (which, we think, may be extended thus far without straining its analogy), if the crew of an unlicensed cruiser should land on a defenceless coast, there commit depredations and carry off the booty on board of their ship, the act would be *piracy;* and to be tried in a court having admiralty jurisdiction. This doctrine (if correct) may find its application in case such pirates should be brought or found in a country different from that in which the depredations were committed. There, unless they could be tried as *pirates*, they could not be tried at all.

We mean to speak here of *piracy* by the *law of nations* only, not of that offence as it is considered at the *common law.* The definition above quoted from *Hawkins*, was clearly meant by him to apply merely to piracy by the law of nations, for, in the very next page he gives us the common law definition of the same crime, which is very different from the former one. " A pirate," says he, " *at the common law*, is a person who commits any of those acts of robbery and depredation on the high seas, which, if committed at land, would have amounted to felony." 1 *Hawk.* P. C. 268. On the same principle, the law of the *United States* defines piracy *in general*, the commission at sea, or in a river, haven, bason or bay, out of the jurisdiction of any particular state, of murder, robbery, or any other offence, which, *if committed within the body of a county*, would, by the law of the *United States*, be punishable with death. *Act of the 30th of April* 1790. § 8.—1 *Laws U. S.* 102. Several other offences are made *piracy* by the same statute, which come within the proper scope of municipal legislation.

Here, then, appear to be two different and distinct species of offences; one against the *general law of nations*, and the other against the *municipal law of the land.* The laws which constitute the latter kind of crime, are in some respects more *extensive*, and in others more *restricted* than that which defines the former. They are more *extensive*, in as much as they make *piracy* of an act of felony committed by an individual at sea, even on board of a commissioned vessel of his own nation, and more *restricted*, because they require, in order to constitute a piratical act, the commission at sea of a *common or statute law felony*, whereas the law of nations in its definitions of crimes, does not take notice of the technical rules of the common or any other municipal law.

An important question here occurs: " Whether an act of piracy, clearly considered as such by the law of nations, may be inquired of, and punished by the courts of *England* or the *United States* possessing admiralty jurisdiction in criminal cases, although it should not be *piracy* at the *common*

the law, on the subject of privateering. If an inhabitant of the *United Netherlands* should sail out under a commission from any foreign prince, or, without the consent of the states-general, should take a foreign commission in addition to one from our own government, he is to be punished by the forfeiture of life and goods, and of the security given on receiving his commission here.* By another law† it is decreed, that those who shall act thus are to be considered as *pirates*,‡ which is very reasonable, because they might thus commit depredations on the subjects of nations in amity with us, and involve their own sovereign into a war.§ Probably this last law was made on

law, nor be expressly provided for by statute? The learned *Wooddeson* is in favour of the affirmative. " Whether," says he, " a charge amounts to piracy or not, *must still depend on the* LAW OF NATIONS, except where, in the case of *British* subjects, express acts of parliament have declared, that the crimes therein specified shall be adjudged *piracy*, or shall be liable to the same mode of trial and degree of punishment." 1 *Wooddes.* 140.   *T.*

* Edicts of the 27th of *July* 1627, and 26th of *April* 1653.

† Edict of the 29th of *January* 1658.

‡ By the law of the *United States*, " any *citizen* accepting or exercising within the *American* territory, a commission from a foreign prince, shall be fined not exceeding two thousand dollars, and imprisoned not exceeding three years; and any *person* who, in the *United States*, shall fit or attempt to fit out or be concerned in a privateer, with intent to commit hostilities against a foreign state, with whom the *United States* are at peace, or shall deliver a (foreign) commission for any ship or vessel to be employed as aforesaid, shall be fined not exceeding five thousand dollars, imprisoned not exceeding three years, and the vessel with all her materials shall be forfeited." *Act of the 5th of June* 1794.—3 *Laws U. S.* 89. And by a subsequent act, " if any citizen of the *United States* shall, *without* the limits of the same, fit out or procure to be fitted out, or knowingly be concerned in the fitting out of a privateer for the purpose of cruising against the subjects of a nation in amity with us, or shall take the command, or serve on board of such privateer, or purchase any interest in her, he shall be adjudged guilty of a high misdemeanor, and be punished by a fine not exceeding ten thousand dollars, and imprisonment not exceeding ten years." *Act of the 4th of June* 1797.—4 *Laws U. S.* 3.   *T.*

§ Sir *Leoline Jenkins* considers those who commit depredations under several commissions from different sovereigns, as pirates *in the highest degree*. " The law," says he, " distinguishes between a pirate who is a highwayman, and sets up for robbing, either having no commission at all, or else hath two or three, and a lawful man of war that exceeds his commis-

† R

account of those who, in the month of *November* 1657, committed depredations under double commissions from *France* and *Portugal*,* of whom I have read in the newspapers of that time.

But what shall we say of those who make use of double passports or sea-letters, as is frequently done by masters of vessels, in order to carry on a contraband trade, or to commit other frauds with greater safety? They, indeed, are not equally guilty with pirates; yet, the states-general, by their edicts of the 31st of *December* 1657, have ordered the confiscation of their ships and goods. Certain sophistical lawyers† have pretended to argue, that such an act does no injury to us, if it is not done in fraud of *our own laws;* but this is a weak and silly argument, for it is important to the world at large,

sion. 2 *L. Jenk.* 714. There may be a difference, however, if the commissions are from sovereigns *in alliance* with each other; but although in such a case it might not amount to the crime of piracy, still it would be irregular and illegal, because the two belligerents might have adopted different rules of conduct with respect to neutrals, or may be separately bound by engagements unknown to the party. Regularly, no one ought to accept of a commission from a foreign prince, without the permission of his own sovereign.

On this subject, we know, that there have been various opinions. The chevalier *de Abreu,* (a *Spaniard*), in his *Treatise on Captures,* first published at *Cadiz,* in 1756, and lately at *Paris,* in a *French* translation, in 1802—thinks, that there can be no inconvenience in taking several commissions from different sovereigns *allied in the same war,* because they all tend to the same end, the destruction of the common enemy. *Abreu, part* 2. c. 1. § 7.—but we cannot agree with him on this point, because we think, that it does not belong to an individual to judge of the relations that may exist between different sovereigns, and on his single responsibility to run the risk of involving his own country into a war. *Louis* XIV. in his *Ordonnance de la Marine* of 1681, expressly forbids his subjects and all persons residing in *France,* to take commissions from other sovereigns, without distinguishing whether his allies or not, under the penalty of being punished as *pirates. Ord. tit. des Prises,* art. 3. *Valin,* for various excellent reasons, thinks, that independent of positive law, the taking of several commissions even from allied sovereigns, cannot be justified, and strongly combats the opinion of the chevalier *de Abreu.* 2 *Val. Comment.* 236.   *T.*

* *France* and the *United Netherlands* were at that time in alliance together against *Spain,* and the *United Netherlands* were engaged in a separate war against *Portugal.*   *T.*

† Consil. Belg. vol. 4. Cons. 203.

that good faith should be preserved between sovereigns and their subjects, and that the latter should not be permitted to injure the former, by their fraudulent conduct.*

There are also others, who, although they are not properly called *pirates*, yet on account of the atrocity of their crimes, are punished as such. It is so with those hostile ships who come too near our shores, in violation of the prohibition of the sovereign. On the 24th of *February* 1696, the states-general issued an edict, by which it was enacted, " that all *French* privateers which should come *close to the land, within the buoys*, a fleet not being at hand to protect them, should be capitally punished, and this law was actually carried into execution, at *Groningen*, on the 14th of *March* of the same year. By what right such things are done, I have discussed in a former chapter.† Those also by our laws are punished as pirates, who commit frauds in matters of insurance,‡ and likewise those who cut the nets which are spread out for the herring fishery.§

Albericus Gentilis,‖ and several other writers are of opinion, that those nations of *Africa*, whom we call *Barbarians*, are to be considered as pirates, and that captures made by them, work no change of property; but that opinion cannot be defended on any rational principle. The *Algerines*, *Tripolitans*, *Tunisians*, and those of *Salee*, are not pirates, but regularly organized societies, who have a fixed territory and an estab-

---

* In *England* and in the *United States*, the rule is, that the courts take no notice of the revenue laws of other countries; and therefore, insurances made on goods or voyages prohibited abroad are supported when not contrary to the stipulations of the parties. *Planché* v. *Fletcher*, Dougl. 238. This principle, however, has been much contested by writers on both sides of the question; of which controversy see an account in *Park* on *Insur.* 341. 6th *edit.*   T.

† Above, c. 3. p. 19.

‡ Edict of *Philip* the 2d on Insurance, of the 26th of *January* 1550. § 22. We have not been able to ascertain the precise extent of this law. It is not mentioned in the *Curia Philipica*, nor inserted with the other maritime ordinances of the same sovereign, in *Les Us & Coutumes de la Mer*, nor in *Adriaan Verwer's* collection of *Spanish* and *Dutch* maritime laws, entitled " *Over de Zee-Rechten.*"   T.

§ Edict of *Philip* the 2d. of the 9th of *March* 1580. § 23.

‖ De Advoc. Hispan. l. 1. c. 15.

lished government, with whom we are now at peace and now at war, as with other nations, and who, therefore, are entitled to the same rights as other independent states. The sovereigns of *Europe* often enter into treaties with them, and the states-general have done it in several instances.* *Cicero* defines a regular enemy "one who hath a commonwealth, a court of justice, a treasury, the consent and agreement of the citizens, and who pays some regard to treaties of peace and alliance.† All these things are to be found among the *Barbarians* of *Africa*, for they pay the same regard to treaties of peace and alliance that other nations do, who generally attend more to their convenience than to their engagements. And if they should not observe the faith of treaties with *the most scrupulous respect*, it cannot be well required of them; for, it would be required in vain of other sovereigns. Nay, if they should even act with more injustice than other nations do, they should not on that account, as *Huberus*‡ very properly observes, lose the rights and privileges of sovereign states.

Indeed, as the *Algerines* constitute a republic, ambassadors are sent to them by other princes, and those who are made prisoners by them, change their condition and become slaves.§ Perhaps the *Spaniards* do not reckon those *Barbarians* among the number of regular enemies; but, although it may be correct, as to them, the principle will not bear to be extended beyond *Spain*. The *Dutch*, it is true, are in the habit of carrying their *Algerine* prisoners into *Spain*, and there by the *lex talionis*, to sell them into slavery, but this is conformable to the law of war, which may be carried into execution against

---

* Particularly on the 30th of *April* 1679, and 1st of *May* 1680, and often afterwards.

† *Qui haberet Rempublicam, curiam, ærarium, consensum & concordiam civium, rationem aliquam, si res ità tulisset, pacis & fœderis.* Cic. Philip. 4. C. 14.

‡ De Jure Civitat. l. 3. c. 5. § 4. n. ult.

§ Hence, those who are taken by the *Algerines* are not only privately, but sometimes publicly, redeemed. The states-general, on the 25th of *September* 1681, ordained, that the bailiffs of towns should report to the magistrates those of their inhabitants who should be taken by the *Algerines*, and that the magistrates should report to the counsellors of the states of *Holland*, that they might take measures to effect the redemption of the captives.

an enemy, if one thinks proper, under such circumstances as I have above discussed in the third chapter.

There has been a case, however, in which those *Africans* have been considered to a certain degree as pirates, so far, at least, that their capture was not thought to have worked any change of property. On the 15th of *July* 1664, the admiralty of *Amsterdam* restored, *without salvage*, a vessel which the *Algerines* had taken from the *English*, and which the *Dutch* admiral had recaptured from the *Algerines*, and the said vessel was so restored, as *Aitzema* relates,* at the request of the *English* ambassador, in hopes that the *English* would do the same by us in similar cases. But lest this case should be drawn into a precedent, it ought to be known, that the *Algerines* had taken that vessel in the midst of a peace which had been lately concluded by them with the *English* and *Dutch*, and for that reason alone it had been considered that their capture under such circumstances, had worked no change of property. Such, according to *Aitzema*, was the reason given by the *English* ambassador; whether it was sufficient or not, I shall not now consider, being satisfied with observing, that this ought to be, and in fact it was considered by both parties at the time, as a singular case.

What is the proper *forum* or jurisdiction for the trial of pirates may be and has often been questioned?† If such a one, although a foreigner, should commit depredations upon our citizens,‡ and be taken, I have no doubt but that he may

---

* Aitz. l. 44.

† In the original, there is in this place, a long dissertation on the subject of the respective jurisdictions of the *Dutch* admiralty courts and their ordinary tribunals, which we have left out, as uninteresting and useless.   *T.*

‡ As the law of nations is at present understood, it is of no importance, for the purpose of giving jurisdiction, on *whom* or *where* the piratical offence has been committed. A pirate is considered as an enemy of the human race, *(hostis humani generis;)* and therefore, may be tried, convicted and punished in any country where he may be found. "Every man," says sir *Leoline Jenkins*, "by the usage of our *European* nations, is *justiciable* in the place where the crime is committed; so are *pirates:* being reputed out of the protection of all laws and privileges, and to be tried *in what ports soever they may be taken.* 2 L. *Jenk.* 714.   *T.*

properly be tried and punished by our own tribunals, not only
if he is taken in the fact and brought into our country, but
also if he should be found and taken among us on any other
occasion. This must be admitted, if he has committed depredations upon us without any commission from his sovereign,
but if he had a commission, and it is only alleged that he
exceeded it, then the question becomes more susceptible of
doubt.

In the year 1667, this subject was agitated between the
*English** and the states-general, concerning those who had
obtained letters of reprisal while there were differences sub-

* The *English*, however, a few years afterwards, unjustly, in our opinion,
claimed and exercised the right of trying and punishing *a regularly commissioned privateer* for having exceeded the bounds of his commission.
The case is related by sir *Leoline Jenkins,* whose advice was taken and
followed on the occasion. In the year 1675, one *Cheline,* the commander of
a *French* privateer, having committed several unwarrantable depredations
at sea, and among other things, plundered several *English* vessels of their
provisions, (*England* being at that time in amity with *France*), went with his
ship into the port of *Kinsale,* in *Ireland,* where his crew having informed
against him, sir *Leoline Jenkins* was consulted by the king on his case, and
gave it as his opinion, that he was liable to be punished with death as a
pirate, and that his goods and vessel should be confiscated. *Cheline,*
however, having had wind of the intended prosecution, escaped from
Ireland, but his vessel and goods were seized, proceeded against in the
court of admiralty and confiscated. In vain the king of *France,* whose commission he bore, demanded that the cause should be remitted to him for
trial, sir *Leoline* answered, that this matter of *renvoy* (remitting of causes
to foreign sovereigns for trial) was quite disused among princes; and as to
Cheline's commission, he said, that it had only been given to him to cruise
against the enemies of the *most christian king,* and did not give him the
right of pillaging the king's friends. 2 *L. Jenk.* 714. 754.—Mr. *Wooddeson*
is mistaken, when he says, that *Cheline* was held not to be punishable for
piracy, *because he had a commission from the king of France.* 2 *Wooddes.* 425.
He was actually punished as a pirate as far as the confiscation of his ship
and goods, and if his person had been laid hold of, would have been hanged
as such, for plundering the *English* vessels at sea. It is true, that among
the charges exhibited against him, there was one for attacking and taking
a *Dutch* ship, near the port of *Dublin,* and that on this particular charge,
sir *L. Jenkins* gave it as his opinion, that he could not be capitally
convicted; but it was not on the ground of his being bearer of a *French*
commission, but because the statute had provided a different punishment.
2 *L. Jenk.* 754.   T.

sisting between the two nations, and who committed depredations even after the peace. The *English* contended, that
they were to be tried by the courts of the sovereign who had
granted the letters of reprisal. The ambassadors of the states-
general insisted, that those who committed hostilities without
a lawful authority from their sovereign, were to be considered
as pirates, that such was the general law of nations, and that
offenders of that description might be punished by any sovereign into whose dominions they might be brought, of which
there was a great number of examples. The *French* ambassadors at that time were of the same opinion in which the
English and the states-general then concurred.*

But whether one be a pirate or not, depends upon the fact,
whether he has or not, a commission to cruise; and if it should
be alleged that he exceeded the authority which that commission gave him, I would not, on that account, hold him to be a
pirate. Generally, the sovereigns who grant the commissions,
decide on the captures that are made by virtue thereof, because
the prizes are brought within their dominions;† but I would
have no objection to such decision being made by the sovereign
whose subjects complain of depredation, if the perpetrators
should be brought or apprehended within his territory.‡ By

* Aitz. 1. 47.

† Professor *Rutherforth,* in his Institutes of Natural Law, gives a different
reason for allowing to the sovereign of the captors, the exclusive right of
adjudicating prizes made under his authority. " It is not," says he,
" because the prize has been brought into the territory of that sovereign,
that he is entitled to an exclusive jurisdiction in such cases; for, the
controversy arose upon the main ocean, which is out of his territory, and
as he had no jurisdiction in the first instance, the subsequent act of bringing
the prize into his territory will not give him any. But the reason is, that
the state to which the captors belong has a right to inspect into their behaviour; both because they are members of it, and because it is answerable
to all other states for what they do in war." 2 *Ruth.* 595, 596. *Cambridge*
edit.   *T.*

‡ Several plausible schemes have been proposed for establishing a more
impartial jurisdiction for the trial of neutral property taken in war, but
none of them has yet obtained the general assent of mankind, or has even
been adopted by a single nation. *Hubner* is for a mixed tribunal, to consist
of commissioners respectively appointed by the sovereigns of the captors
and the captured, with the addition, when the prize is carried into a neutral
port, of one or more judges appointed by the sovereign of the neutral ter-

the 22d article of the treaty of peace between the king of *France* and the states-general, of the 27th of *April* 1662, it is stipulated, " that vessels which shall be taken by ships of war or commissioned privateers, shall be tried in the dominions of the sovereign by whom the commission shall have been granted, and not elsewhere."

It is more difficult to decide, whether a foreigner who has committed depredations on other foreigners, may, if he should be found among us, be tried by our tribunals? In the year 1661, doubts were entertained upon this subject, in the case of a *Portuguese* privateer who had committed depredations on the subjects of a nation in amity with us and not at war with *Portugal*, but the spoliator having died in the meanwhile, nothing was decided upon it.[*] In the year 1668, the king of *England*, on the representation of the ambassadors of the states-general, ordered an *Ostend* ship, cruising under a com-

ritory. 2 *Hubn.* 44.—*Galiani* is for vesting that jurisdiction, in some cases, in the tribunals of the captor, and in others in those of the captured. *De' doveri, &c.* l. 1. c. 9. § 8., but the ancient practice has continued and still continues to be followed.

It is true, however, that when prizes are brought into a neutral port, the neutral sovereign will restore the property of its subjects or citizens, if it has been illegally captured. That this doctrine is not new, appears clearly from the 15th article of the marine ordinance of *Louis* the XIV. title *des Prises*, which contains this express clause: " If on board of the prizes which shall be brought into our ports by foreign armed vessels, there shall be found goods belonging to our subjects or allies, those of our subjects shall be restored to them," and this right, says *Valin*, " is exercised by way of compensation for the asylum, granted to the captor and his prize." 2 *Valin's Comment.* 274.

The same right has been exercised by the courts of the *United States*, in various instances, during the last war between *Great-Britain* and *France*. *Glass & Gibbs* v. *The Betsy.* 2 *Dallas's Reports* 6.—*Hollingsworth* v. *The Betsy.* 2 *Peters's Admiralty Reports*, 330.

In like manner, prizes taken by foreign privateers fitted out in the *United States*, in violation of our neutrality, and brought into our ports, have been invariably restored. *Talbot* v. *Jansen.* 2 *Dallas*, 133. and by an act of congress of the 5th of *June* 1794, the district courts are authorized " to take cognizance of complaints, by whomsoever instituted, in case of captures made within the waters of the *United States*, or within a marine league of the coasts or shores thereof." 3 *Laws U. S.* 91.   *T.*

* Aitz. l. 41.

mission from the king of *Spain*, which had taken a *Dutch* vessel, to be detained, and the laws to be executed upon the captain.*

It is clear, that if the law of the neutral country (like the two edicts which I have mentioned above)† forbid the selling of prizes on the neutral territory, unless they have been carried into the port where the privateer was fitted out, and there legally condemned, it will appear unjust to give an action against the captor, either to the government for the punishment of the offence, or to the owners of the captured property for the damage suffered. The condition of both foreigners ought to be alike; if the spoliated party is permitted to bring his action against the captor, the latter ought to be allowed to justify himself, by shewing that his prize was legally captured. And yet, it would be hard and unexampled, to deny to the owner of the captured ship and goods, the right of claiming satisfaction from a foreigner whom he finds here, and who may be immediately going nobody knows whither. For this reason, I am not satisfied with the two edicts above mentioned.

---

* The fact, as related by *Aitzema*, (1. 48.) is as follows: The *Dutch* ambassadors complained to his majesty of the intolerable insolence of the *Ostend* privateers, and expressed their opinion of the manner in which it should be proceeded against them; they spoke in particular of the ship *Jupiter* of *Amsterdam*, which those corsairs had shot at for a long time, (making them believe that they were *Turks*), and had frightened them so much, that the crew of the *Jupiter* had forsaken her, and made their escape to the shore, and the privateer had run in with the ship into the *Isle of Wight*.

The king was pleased to answer, that he had heard great complaints on all sides of the conduct of the *Ostend* privateers; that they were, in fact, mere pirates, but that he would put a stop to it; that if any of his subjects should be found on board of such privateers, they should be *hanged*, and that he would make strong representations to the court of *Brussels*, that they should inflict the severest penalties upon such robbers; that with regard to the ship *Jupiter*, the ambassadors should present a memorial to the council of state, who would take order upon the subject. " The memorial," continues *Aitzema*, " was accordingly presented, on which his majesty was pleased to resolve, that the captain of the privateer and his ship should be arrested, and proceeded against according to law." 6 *Aitz.* 395, *fol. edit.* What was afterwards done with them, does not appear.   *T.*

† C. 15. p. 121.

The common punishment of pirates is the forfeiture of their lives and goods, which is sufficiently pointed out by all the edicts which I have above related, made on the subject of those, who, from the atrocity of their crimes, are to be considered as such. But there is a special edict of the states-general, of the 25th of *August* 1611, against *pirates*, properly so called, their aiders and abettors, by which they are punished with the forfeiture of life and goods, one third of the goods being given to the informer. The penalty, therefore, is capital, and it is not in the power of the judges to mitigate the punishment: They do, however, execute the law with more or less rigour, on account of the frequency of piracies and other offences of the like nature. And, indeed, provided death is inflicted, the remainder may be left to the discretion of the judge, as is the case with almost all other crimes, for which the law in general terms directs a capital punishment.*

---

* If we have not mistaken the meaning of this passage, it seems that the *mode* of inflicting the punishment of death, when the law had not expressly provided it, was formerly left, in *Holland,* to the discretion of the judges. We wish that we may have misunderstood it.   *T.*

CHAPTER XVIII.

Of Privateers.

THIS subject also properly belongs to the law of nations, not only because privateering cannot be lawfully carried on without an authorization from the government, but because the controversies which arise out of it, often create disturbance within the state, and set sovereigns at variance with each other.

It was formerly held at *Rome*, that one who was not regularly enrolled as a soldier, could not lawfully kill an enemy of the *Roman* people. Such was the opinion of *Cato*, as we are informed by *Cicero** and *Plutarch*.† But it appears from the *Digest*,‡ that the law of *Solon*,§ by which individuals were permitted to form associations for the purpose of plunder, was afterwards introduced into the *Roman* system of laws, and made a part of their code.‖

---

* De Offic. c. 11. The reference in the original is by mistake to c. 36, 37.   *T.*

† Quæst. Rom. 39.

‡ ff. de Colleg. & Corpor. l. 4.

§ Among the ancient *Greeks* and *Romans*, down to the time of *Tarquin*, it was considered as glorious, to plunder foreigners at sea, with whom there were no treaties of peace or alliance, even though there was no public or open war against them. Grot. De *Jure B. ac P.* l. 2. c. 15. § 5.—*Justin.* l. 43. c. 3. It seems, that the manners of those nations at that time were very similar in this respect to those of the barbarians of *Africa* at the present day, who plunder indiscriminately all those with whom they have not, by an express treaty, agreed to remain at peace.   *T.*

‖ But in the *Latin* translation which is subjoined in the *Digest* to the *Greek* text of *Solon*, the words of the original ἐπὶ λίαν οἰχόμενοι, (*those who go out for plunder*) are not translated, and the compilers have inserted in lieu thereof, *sodales qui multum simul habitantes sunt*, (*associates who live a great deal together.*) This difference has very much exercised the ingenuity of the doctors of the civil law, to whose works we shall refer those of our

It is now, indeed, a long time since sovereigns have begun to make use of the aid of individuals against their enemies, as auxiliary to the public force. Formerly, in the *United Netherlands*, there were no vessels of war but such as were owned by private persons, to whom, besides bounties out of the captured and recaptured property, the state paid a certain sum, by way of indemnity from the public treasury, proportioned to the expense which they were at, and to the time which they employed in hostile expeditions. A great use was made of those private armed vessels (which were then called *cruisers*) by the states-general, in their war with *Spain*. Several edicts were made respecting them, which it is needless to relate.

At present, as well as formerly, when war takes place, vessels are fitted out, manned and armed by private adventurers at their own expense, with which they attack the enemy's vessels at sea, with no other inducement than that of the captures which they expect to make. These have been called *capers* and *freebooters*, but now by a more decent appellation are denominated *privateers*. It is not possible to ascertain whether they were the same description of men, who, in the *Digest*, are called *latrunculi*.* For my part, I do not believe it, nor do I think that *Albericus Gentilis* is right in giving them the name of *pirates*, which he does throughout his work *De Advocatione Hispanicâ*, whenever he has occasion to speak of them, and even when he treats of the laws and usages by which their conduct is regulated. This is so very absurd, that it does not deserve a serious refutation; for, after all, what those men do, is done under the sanction of public authority. In this country they are not allowed to sail without a commission from the states-general or the admiral, countersigned by the lieutenant of the admiralty of their particular district, nor without having first made oath and given satisfactory security that they will not do any injury to neutrals. These and other regulations are to be found in the *Formæ Admiralitatum*,† and

readers whose curiosity may lead them to investigate the subject. Our author has written a dissertation upon it, in his *Observ. Jur. Rom.* l. 1. c. 16.   *T.*

* ff. de Capt. & Postlim. Revers. l. 6.

† Instructions or regulations for privateers.   *T*

in various edicts, which have been made on the subject of privateers whenever foreign powers have complained of their depredations. But as those edicts are in every body's hands, I think it unnecessary to give here a more particular account of the regulations which they contain.

I think it more worth while to inquire whether the captains of privateer ships, who are not themselves the owners of the vessels, may enter into a partnership with each other for sharing in the prizes which they may each separately take? If they are sent out merely to cruise and make captures, and have no further authority, it is certain that they cannot form such partnerships without the consent of their owners, otherwise, the agreements which they make with each other are to be considered as null and void.

Let it not be objected,* that by the law of *Solon* above-mentioned, the partnership contracts of those *who go out to plunder* are declared valid, for it is sufficiently clear, that the legislator only meant to speak of those who are their own masters, and go out to plunder on their own account. So, if the *owners* of privateers should enter into partnerships with each other, and agree that their prizes should be equally divided among themselves, such agreements as well as every other which they might make, would undoubtedly be valid; because every one may dispose of his own property as he thinks fit: but such a power can never be exercised by captains of private armed ships, unless they are also the owners of them, which is hardly ever the case.

We are speaking here only of those captains of privateers who have received an authority from their owners merely to cruise, and who exceed it by entering into particular agreements with each other. There was once a cause of very great moment decided upon this question, and which was even carried to the court of revision. Two privateers, one belonging to *A* and the other to *B* took a vessel together, and after-

---

* It ought to be remembered, that in *Holland*, at the time when our author wrote, the imperial law of *Rome* was the common law of the land. This will sufficiently account for the constant application which he endeavours to make of its rules and principles. *T.*

wards (as *B* alleged) the two captains agreed together, that
any future prize that they should make, should be divided
between them. Afterwards they separated, and *A*'s vessel
alone took another prize, which *B* insisted should be divided
between them, by virtue of their agreement. *A* denied that
the agreement extended to prizes separately made, and if
it did, he contended, that it was illegal and void. And so it
was determined by the inferior court at *Flushing*. But *B*
having appealed to the supreme court, the cause was decided
in his favour, on the 3d of *March* 1696, and that judgment
was affirmed by the court of review on the 4th of *October*
1697. To the same effect is the opinion of several advocates
in *Consilia Belgica*,* and a similar decision was given by the
court of admiralty of *Amsterdam*, in 1665.

But all these decisions, except that of the court of *Flushing*,
appear to me to have been erroneous, and I think that the
cause ought to have been determined in favour of *A*. I have
read with astonishment in the acts of the supreme court, in
which the opinions of several judges of that tribunal and of
the court of review are inserted, that in the particular case
that I have spoken of, the only question that was agitated was,
whether there had actually been an agreement between the
two captains, that the prizes which they should separately
take should be common between them, or whether it contemplated merely those which they should take in company; but
the question of the legality of the agreement, which was the
first that suggested itself to me, does not appear to have been
even thought of.

Admitting that it had been expressly agreed between the
two captains, that all the prizes which they or either of them
should take, whether jointly or separately, should be equally
or proportionably divided between them, still I do not think
that *A* was at all bound by that agreement. He had sent
out his vessel at his own risk, for the sole purpose of cruising
and making captures; he had given no other instructions
to his captain, and had in no manner authorized him to

* Vol. 4. Consil 204.

enter into partnership with others, which he might have done himself, if he had thought proper. His captain, therefore, had no authority for what he did, and in that case, his unauthorized act could not bind his owner. I know, that if *B*'s vessel had alone made a prize, it would not have been difficult to persuade *A* to receive his proportion of it; but neither would it have been difficult to persuade *B* to contend for the same principle, which *A* in the case before us, insisted upon. The first vessel which was taken by the two armed ships together, and by means of their joint force, was a prize common to them both, by an implied partnership arising out of the circumstances of the case; but it was not so with the second, which *A*'s vessel took alone, and which he ought to have kept exclusively to himself, if, agreeably to my opinion, he was not bound by the agreement of his captain. Therefore, on legal principles, setting aside the question of fact, I prefer the decision of the court of *Flushing* to all the others that have been given on the same subject.

I proceed to a question, which, in my opinion, deserves the most serious consideration; it is, " Whether, if one or more armed ships take a prize, others being *present*, but not fighting, it is to be divided between them?" As far as relates to ships of war, this question is settled by positive law; for, there is a decree of the states-general, of the 28th of *January* 1631, by which it is enacted, " That if a ship of war shall attack an enemy, another ship of war being present, may join in the fight, but not if the one who attacked first, shall call out that he has no need of assistance." But it appears to me, that this law was made *specially* for vessels of war, otherwise, there is nothing to hinder one armed vessel from joining another, in attacking and capturing a common enemy who is not yet subdued.

For the same reason I consider as a special ordinance, the sixth section of the *Forma* or regulation of the 15th of *July* 1633, expressly made for the privateers commissioned to cruise against the *Spaniards* in *America*, by which it was ordered, " that a privateer who should take a prize jointly with a vessel of the *West-India Company*, should not be en-

titled to a share thereof, unless he had been expressly called
to the assistance of the company's ship." The same may be
said of the seventh section, which enjoins upon all privateers,
on pain of forfeiture of ship and goods, " not to meddle or
interfere with the captures which the ships of the company
may wish to make." If, however, the aid of a privateer ship
should be called for, and she should take a prize, jointly with
a vessel of the *West-India Company*, there is no doubt but that
it should be distributed between them, in proportion to their
respective size and force, as is provided by the sixth section
of the said *Forma:* and if their force is equal, then the prize
is to be equally divided between them; otherwise, it is best to
observe what is called a *geometrical proportion.*

What shall we say, if one or more ships pursue an enemy's
vessel, and one of them perishes? or if more, perhaps, are
present, but one alone takes the prize, while the others
are merely spectators, and take no part in the action? The
decree of the 28th of *January* 1631, which I have mentioned
above, directs, that in such a case, " the prize is to be divided
between all the *vessels of war* which have pursued her, but
that she which has actually made the capture is to have the provisions, small-arms and *plunderage.*"* But this again only
concerns *ships of war*, of whose captures the states-general
dispose at their discretion; for otherwise, if the case concerned
privateers only, I would rather adjudge the whole prize to him
who has fought and conquered the enemy's vessel, how many
others soever might have pursued her, or been spectators of
the contest.†

---

* The precise expression used in the original: it probably means every
thing susceptible of being made booty of war, which is not a part of the
vessel or of her cargo, (properly so called.)   *T.*

† This opinion of our author accords with that of the modern writers
who have treated of this particular subject. " Excepting," says professor
Martens, " the case of an association among privateers, it is requisite, in
order to have a share in the prize, to prove the having contributed in some
manner to the taking of it, *and it is not sufficient to have been found in
sight. Martens on Captures,* § 32. *in fin.* p. 91. *Engl. transl.* It appears also
to be, as far as we know, generally carried into practice among the nations

There are those, I know, who are for admitting all who were merely present, or even in sight, though at a distance; but this cannot be admitted. It is true, that the mere presence

of *Europe*, with respect to privateers, though in the case of vessels of war, governments have been induced, from motives of policy, to adopt a different rule.

The ordinances of *France* provide, that with regard to vessels of war, " those shall be considered as *joint captors* who shall have found them-selves together *and in sight of the capture* at the time of its being made. Ord. of the 15th of *June* 1757, art. 10. 1 *Code des Prises*, (edit. 1784) p. 512. —*Valin, Traité des Prises, Append.* 199. Thus, the mere circumstance of being in sight at the time of the capture, entitles a *ship of war*, by virtue of this ordinance, to a share of the prize.

But, in the case of privateers, another ordinance prescribes the opposite rule. It enacts, " that none shall be entitled to a share in a prize taken from the enemy, who have not contributed to the taking of the vessel;" which the next article explains, can only be done " by fighting, or by making such an effort as may have compelled the enemy to surrender, by intimi-dating him or cutting off his retreat." Ord. of the 27th *January* 1706, art. 1 and 2. 1 *Code des Prises*, 282. (same edition.)—*Valin, ubi suprà*, p. 102.

In *England*, the same distinction appears to be adopted. *Ships of war* are entitled to share in a prize from the mere circumstance of having been *in sight* at the time of the capture, the ancient general rule having been re-laxed or modified in their favour. " Formerly," says sir *William Scott*, "*joint capture* was confined to cases of *actual co-operation*, and when, in con-sequence of frequent litigations, it was extended to *constructive assistance*, for the purpose of *preserving harmony and good understanding among the navy*, the being *in sight* became the principal *criterion. The Vryheid*, 2 *Rob.* 14. *Am. edit.*—In a later case, the same judge determined, in a contest between a *king's ship* and a *privateer*, that the mere being in sight was sufficient in the *former* to support the *animus capiendi*, and entitle her to a share of the prize. *The Flore*, 5 *Rob.* 239. *Am. edit.*

But, on the contrary, when a similar controversy arose between similar parties, and the *privateer* claimed a share of the *king's ship's* prize, because he had been *present* at the capture, sir *William Scott* decided, " that the mere being *in sight* was not sufficient, with respect to *privateers*, to raise the presumption of co-operation in the capture: they clothe themselves, said he, with commissions of war from views of private advantage only; they are not bound to put their commissions in use on every discovery of an enemy, and therefore, the law does not presume in *their* favour, from the mere circumstance of being *in sight*, that they were there with a design of contributing assistance and engaging in the contest." *L'Amitié*, 6 *Rob.* 264. *Am. edit.*

We have not been able to find a single case in any of Dr. *Robinson's* Reports, in which the naked question has been agitated exclusively

of others may have been the cause that the enemy has either surrendered sooner or been more easily subdued; but we are not to consider for what reason the vessel was taken or surrendered, but who took her. In the same manner, we should not admit the fort,* town or fleet in whose presence a capture was made, to a participation in the prize, even though it might be said to have been induced to surrender, by the fear which their presence excited. On the other hand, it is clear, that if another vessel has joined the captor in fighting the enemy, an accidental partnership must be considered as having taken place between them, and the reason of the thing requires, that what has been taken by their joint efforts, should be divided among them in proportion to their respective strength. Nor are we to discriminate in such a case between the different degrees of exertion; for that would be too difficult in practice; but we only consider whether the vessel which was present at the capture, did actually fight, and by her assistance, contribute to the victory.

Analogous to this principle is the doctrine which the civil law lays down on the subject of animals *feræ naturæ*, which do not become the property of those who pursue, but of those who actually take them.†

☞ *The remainder of this chapter is so entirely and exclusively local, that we have not thought it worth while to translate it.*

between *privateers.* In one case, indeed, a share in a prize was allowed to one of that description in competition with another, from the circumstance of his being *in sight* at the time of the capture, coupled with that of having *sailed in company* with the principal captor, and the capture was that of a defenceless neutral vessel, in which no fighting was required: *The William & Mary*, 4 Rob. 312. *Am. edit.* But we have not discovered one in which the question turned *singly* on the circumstance of being in sight, at the time of the capture; therefore, we presume, that the principles established in *L'Amitié*, would prevail in such a case. *T.*

* In *England*, land forces are not considered as entitled to share in a capture, unless they have actually assisted and co-operated in it. *The Dordrecht*, 2 Rob. 53. *Am. edit.* *T.*

† Inst. De Rer. Divis. § 13.

CHAPTER XIX.

Of the Responsibility of owners of Privateers.

BY the laws of our country, contained in the *Formæ Admiralitatum* and several edicts of the states-general, privateers are not permitted to sail from our ports, without giving security to answer for their good behaviour, that they will do no injury to neutrals, and that they will bring their prizes to legal adjudication, by the court of admiralty of the place where the security is given.*

The amount of this security has varied. It was at first required to be in ten thousand florins, the ship and the cargo at the same time remaining answerable for the consequences of the privateer's unlawful conduct. Afterwards it was ordered, that the owner should give security in twelve thousand, and the captain in ten thousand florins, the owner's bond to be resorted to in the first instance, and if it should not prove sufficient, then recourse might be had to that given by the captain.† But by the last edict which has been made upon this subject,‡ it is merely provided, that security shall be given in the sum of *thirty thousand* florins,§ and the law does not

---

* *Formæ Admiral.* of the 13th of *August* 1597. §§ 5. 69.—of the 15th of *July* 1634. § 5.

† Edicts of the 1st of *April* 1622.—9th of *August* 1624, and 22d of *October* 1627.

‡ *Forma* of 28th of *July* 1765. § 3.

§ About $12,000.—In *England*, the security given by a privateer is £ 3000 ($13,320) which is reduced to one half if the vessel carries less than 150 men. *Horne's Compendium of Admiralty Laws*, p. 9.—In *France*, by a decree of the 2d *Prairial*, 11th year, (22d of *May* 1803), the amount of such security is fixed at 74,000 francs (about $14,095) reduced in the same manner to one half, if the privateer is navigated by less than 150 men. *Dict. Univ. de Commerce*, verbo COURSE. By an act of congress, made during the partial hostilities between the *United States* and *France*, priva-

specify, whether by the captain or by the owners. It appears to me, however, that the captain is the person who is to give the security, because it is he who is to bring the prize into the port from whence the vessel has sailed. I might mention here several treaties between the states-general and other powers, by which it has been stipulated, that captains and owners of privateers should give security not to do any thing in violation of existing treaties, but as they do not enter into further details, I think that I may safely pass them over.

Thus much being premised, I shall proceed to inquire, whether, if a privateer has made an illegal capture, the damage suffered in consequence thereof is to be repaired by the captain, his securities, or the owners of the capturing vessel, and if to the latter, then to what extent they are liable? On this question, the *Dutch* lawyers have answered,* " that if the captain of a privateer ship has wrongfully taken a neutral vessel, and she should be lost in consequence of his having put an ignorant prizemaster on board of her, the party injured may sue, at his pleasure, the owner of the privateer, the captain, his securities and every one of them, until he recovers the whole amount of the damage, even though it should by far exceed the value of the vessel that made the capture." Let us now consider this subject in detail.

A doubt cannot be entertained of the liability of the *captain* to the whole extent of the damage suffered in consequence of his unlawful capture. He was employed for the purpose of capturing enemies, not neutrals; if, therefore, he has made prize of the latter, he has exceeded his authority, and is consequently liable for all the damage which the neutral has suffered. This principle is clearly sanctioned by the edict of the states-general, of the 1st of *April* 1622; for, after

teers were directed to give security in $14,000, if the vessel carried more than 150 men, and in half that sum if she carried less. *Act of the 9th of July* 1798, § 4.—4 *Laws U. S.* 165.

In *Spain*, however, according to their prize ordinances of 1779 and 1796, (we have not seen that which was probably made at the beginning of the present war), security is only required from all privateers, without distinction, in 3000 rials de vellon, equal to $1500.   T.

* Consil. Belg. vol. 4. Consil 205.

directing that security shall be given by the captains of privateers, in the sum of ten thousand florins, that they shall bring
their prizes into the port from which they shall have sailed,
the law proceeds and says: " reserving, nevertheless, to those
who shall have suffered damage by any unlawful act committed by the captain beyond the extent of his commission,
their personal action against the said captain and others who
shall have occasioned the said damage."

As to the *securities*, the advocates who subscribed the
opinion above mentioned, appear to me to have been mistaken; for, those securities cannot, I think, be made responsible for the whole damage suffered, unless they have bound
themselves to that extent; but if they have merely stipulated
in a certain fixed sum, as is usual in such cases, they cannot
be made liable beyond its amount, nor can they be called upon
to answer for any other acts than those for which they have
expressly made themselves responsible; as for instance, if they
have become bound for the carrying of the prizes into a particular port, and the prizes have been actually carried thither, I
conceive that they are discharged, and that it is nothing to
them, whether the captures have been lawfully or unlawfully
made, unless they have bound themselves for that likewise.
But because captains of privateers are in general so poor, that
they are not able to make good the damage which they have
occasioned, and because the securities are not in general
bound beyond a certain sum, which, after being compelled
to pay, they may recover back by an action against the owners,
it is upon the *owners* that the whole burthen falls in the end.
Let us, therefore, as to them, inquire in the first place, whether
they are liable for the whole of the damage suffered, or whether, as in the *actio de pauperie* and *actio noxalis*,* they are

* The first of these actions was given by the *Roman* law against the
owner of a quadruped, which had done an injury to some person, by kick-
ing, biting, &c. which was called *pauperiem facere*. See on this subject, the
title of the *Digest, si quadrupes pauperiem fecisse dicatur*. Dig. 1. 9. tit. 1.

The *actio noxalis* lay against the master of a slave for a theft or other
injury done or committed by him. Dig. 1. 9. tit. 4. *De noxalibus actionibus.*

In both these cases, the owner or master was discharged by delivering
up the *quadruped* or the *slave*.   T.

only bound to the amount of the value of the privateer and her appurtenances?

A question of this kind was formerly brought before the supreme court of *Holland*. Five *Dutch* privateers had unlawfully taken a *Venetian* ship. The owners of the captured vessel at first instituted a suit against the captains of the privateers, and obtained a judgment, by which they were condemned to restore the vessel only, without damages. But as the sentence was not complied with, they then brought an action against the five owners, contending, that they should jointly and severally be condemned not only to restore the vessel, but also to pay damages. The court, by their decree of the 31st of *July* 1603, condemned the owners jointly and severally, to restore the vessel and her cargo, and if that could not be done, then to pay their appraised value; but the sentence contained an express clause, that execution of it should be made only on the five ships which had made the capture, and that the owners should not be bound beyond their proceeds.

On the strength of this precedent, respectable lawyers have given their opinion to the same effect,* but I cannot concur with them, because I think, that when the owners of a privateer ship put a captain on board of her to make captures, they are bound for the whole of the damage that he may occasion. The master who captures, in consequence of an authority that he has received, is appointed for that particular purpose, and he who appointed him, is by that alone, responsible for every thing, good or bad, that he may do in the execution of his trust. Thus we give the *actio institoria*† against the proprietor of an inn, who has appointed an innkeeper; if the innkeeper makes any contract, we do not distinguish in what manner or with what intent he did it; and thus also we give the *actio exercitoria*‡ against the owner of a vessel for the act of the

---

* Consil. Holland. vol. 3. Consil 221.

† See the Digest, l. 14. tit. 3. *De institoriâ actione.*

‡ Dig. l. 14. tit. 1. *De exercitoriâ actione.* This title will be found translated into *English*, in the *American Law Journal*, vol. ii. p. 462.　　*T.*

master, provided the latter acted in the course of his employment as such; if otherwise, the owner is not bound, as *Ulpian*
fully demonstrates.* The appointment is the sole cause why
the proprietor of the inn and the owner of the vessel are responsible, if what has been done belonged to the business for
which the authority was given, and not to some other one,
different from it. He who appointed the captain of a privateer
must have known, that his business was to make captures, and
that if he should execute it improperly, it would be imputed
to the owner for having appointed a dishonest or an unskilful
captain. If the master having borrowed money for the repairs
of his vessel, applies it to his own use, *Ofilius* tells us very
properly, " that the owner is liable and must impute it to
himself that he employed such a person."† Wherewith agrees,
what the states-general say at the close of their decree of the
22d of *October* 1627, " *that the owners must take care that
they employ proper captains.*"

If the proprietor of an inn is liable for the acts of the innkeeper, and the owner of the vessel for those of the master,
it clearly follows, that they are so to the amount of their whole
property, and that they are not discharged by delivering up
the inn or the vessel. I do not remember to have seen this
doctrine contradicted any where, nor could it be contradicted
with any appearance of reason, for nothing is clearer, than
that those who are responsible for the acts of others are so to
the whole extent of the damage which they may occasion, and
therefore the owners of a privateer are bound to make good
in toto, the damage suffered by the illegal spoliations of their
captain.

The laws which I have already mentioned, afford strong
arguments in favour of this principle. The owners of privateer ships are bound to give security, formerly in twelve
thousand, now in thirty thousand florins, that no injury shall
be done to an ally or neutral. Now, if they are not personally
bound to a farther extent than the value of the vessel, why is

* ff. de exercit. act. l. 1. §. 12.
† Ibid, § 9.

a specific sum required which may, in many instances, greatly exceed that value? If the law had meant that the value of the ship should fix the extent of their responsibility, it should have directed her to be valued, and ordered security to be taken in the precise amount of the valuation. A still stronger argument may be drawn from the *Forma* of the 28th of *July* 1705; for, by that law the owners themselves are declared to be liable for the damage which may be suffered by the wrongful acts of the privateer ship, and every thing belonging to her equipment is made subject to a special lien or tacit hypothecation to answer for that damage. Away, then, with the doctrines which are drawn from the *Roman* laws, on the subject of the *actio de pauperie* and *actio noxalis*. These do not apply to the present question, and are founded on quite different principles.

We must therefore conclude, that the supreme court, in the case above mentioned, gave an erroneous sentence; for, if the owners of the privateer ships had appointed the captains who took the *Venetian* vessels, and had authorized them to make captures, they were bound for the whole, in the same manner as they would have been if they had appointed those captains for mercantile purposes, and had given them authority to make commercial contracts. Perhaps, however, it will be said, that the report does not expressly state, that those five vessels were *privateers;* but if they were not such, it cannot be said, that the owners gave authority to their captains to make captures, and in that case, I would wish to know, why the court condemned the owners to the restitution of the *Venetian* ship and cargo, and awarded execution even against the vessels of those owners, and thus condemned them for an act which was not within the authority committed to their captains, which is evidently contrary to the most familiar principles of law. In such a case, therefore, the owners of a vessel cannot be made in any manner liable; for they, indeed, have put the master in their place and stead, but merely as to the business which they have ordered him to transact, and if in the course of that business, the master had committed a fault, or has been guilty of fraud, they are bound to answer for him, otherwise not. If I give to a carpenter a vessel to repair, and he gives it to his apprentice, who, with one of his master's own tools, happens to kill somebody, the master will not be at all answerable for it. Therefore, the action against owners of ships cannot be assimilated to the action *de pauperie*, except so far as it makes the owner of a horse or mule liable, if by the fault of his driver, the animal has done some damage, but the analogy of that law does not reach farther.

Agreeably to the doctrines which I have contended for, owners of vessels will clearly not be liable, if they have not appointed the master for the purpose of making captures, otherwise they will be responsible, not merely to the amount of the value of their vessels, but to that of their stipulations, which formerly were of 12,000 and now are of 30,000 florins. In addition to that, those who have suffered the damage, may, by virtue of the decree of the 22d of *October* 1627, sue the security of 10,000 florins, which the captain is obliged to give, that he will bring his prizes into the port from whence he sailed, for so the decree expressly provides. I think, however, that such a demand would be unjust, unless it had been made known to the securities, at the time of their entering into the stipulation, that they would be exposed to that liability, and had agreed to it; for if they had simply engaged, as is almost always the case, that the captain should return with his prizes to the port from whence he sailed, I cannot express how unjust it appears to me, to make them liable on that security for any other cause; as I have already hinted, when speaking on the subject of securities.* But if all that I have mentioned is not sufficient to repair the damage, what shall we say in such a case? Are the owners to be held further? I think that they are, until they shall have made good the whole damage; for, it is clear, that a pledge or security does not liberate a debtor, unless it is fully sufficient to discharge the debt.†

* Above, p. 149.
† ff. de Distract. Pign. 1. 9. § 1.

† U

Moreover, if the vessel, which we are speaking of, be not a privateer, that is to say, if she has no commission, but nevertheless makes captures by order of the owners, I think that the same thing is to be said as if she really were a privateer; for, the right arises out of the authority and the appointment, and it is nothing to those who have suffered the damage, whether they are injured by a real privateer or by a vessel not provided with a commission.

CHAPTER XX.

Of Captures made by vessels not commissioned.

IT is properly made a subject of inquiry, whether, if a ship not commissioned to make captures is attacked by an enemy, and in her defence, or from some other justifiable cause, takes an enemy's vessel, to whom in such case the prize is to belong? Three contending parties appear, who seem to have an equal claim to it, and in favour of each of whom many ingenious arguments may be adduced; they are the *owner of the ship*, the *captain and mariners*, and the *shipper* who may have taken her to freight.

On behalf of the *owner of the ship*, it may be said, that he is entitled to the prize, because it was taken with his own ship and guns, and because the captain and men who effected the capture were in his employ, and bound to labour for his benefit: it ought not to be given to the captain nor to the mariners, because they are not entitled in law to any thing besides their wages, nor to the freighter, because he only hired the vessel for the transportation of his merchandize, and for nothing else.

The *master* and *mariners*, however, may plead that the capture was achieved by their prowess and with the danger of their lives, and therefore, that they are justly entitled to the benefit resulting from it: that with respect to the owner of the ship and the freighter, they cannot in justice claim the prize, because they had not hired him to make captures, and the contract which they had made together, was for purposes of a quite different nature.

And lastly, on the part of the *freighter*, it may be argued, that he had hired the ship, the guns, the master, the mariners, and the right to their labour, not only for the transportation of his merchandize, but also for the defence of the ship for the sake of the goods that it contained, which defence is to be taken with every thing incident to it, and involves the right not merely of repelling, but even of capturing the enemy, to prevent his doing any injury. That on these grounds, he is justly entitled to retain the prize, and it ought by no means to be given to the owner of the ship, his captain or mariners, who all ought to be satisfied with the stipulated reward for the hire of the vessel and their labours.

Such are the arguments which may be made use of in support of each of the above opinions. Before I proceed to state my own, I must premise, that there exists a decree of the board of directors of the *West-India* company, by which it is provided, " that fifty per cent. of the proceeds of every prize which shall be taken by a vessel hired out on freight, shall be paid to the company." This decree has been sanctioned by the states-general, and inserted in the instructions of the 15th of *July* 1633, for privateers cruising in the *American* seas.

It is clear, that the directors, when they made that decree, attended only to the interest of their company, nor had the states-general any thing else in view when they gave it their sanction; for, they made no rule whatever in this respect for other privateers than those above mentioned. It must, therefore, be considered as a special law, made with a view to particular persons and circumstances, and which is not to prejudice other cases to which it is not directly applicable.

As I have never seen a general law upon this subject, nor do I believe that any exists, the question is to be decided by the light of reason alone. On equitable principles, I think that the prize ought to be adjudged to the captain of the capturing vessel and his crew, and not to the owners or freighters. The latter, indeed, are the last who will be thought of. The owner of the ship appears better entitled, but still I would prefer to him the captain and crew. Others, however, have been of a different opinion.*

---

* In a case of salvage, which bears the strongest analogy to a case of unauthorized capture, (on the supposition that any persons, others than the sovereign of the captor, may be considered as entitled to the prize,) the late

In the year 1667, a ship sailing under a license from the *French* and *Dutch West-India* company, which had been granted to the freighters, captured an *English* vessel within the company's limits. The captors determined to keep the prize with them, though she was a worse sailer than their own vessel, because on consulting together, they agreed, that it was most advisable for the interest of the *owners and freighters*, as well as their own, that she should be carried into one of the *West-India* islands, where it was expected she would sell to better advantage. The question then occurred, to whom that prize was to be adjudged? The lawyers who were consulted on that question, decided, that the mariners, because they had been hired at a fixed salary by the month, and had not engaged themselves for shares of prize-money, should only have *one tenth* of the proceeds, and that the remainder should be equally divided between the *owners and freighters.*

I do not know upon what principle those gentlemen allowed one tenth to the mariners, nor perhaps did they know themselves. It seems, that they had no difficulty as to the one half of the remainder, which they gave to the owners of the ship; and therefore, they pass it over without assigning any reason for it; but they endeavour to justify, by argument, the allowing of the other half to the freighters. They contend, that it was by virtue of the license which the shippers had obtained from the *West-India* company, that the vessel was permitted to navigate to the *West-Indies,* that therefore they contributed, in a considerable degree, to the capture, and ought not to be placed in a worse situation than the owners of the ship. They say, that the mariners did not take the prize for the benefit of the owners of the ship only, but also for that of the owners

judge *Winchester,* district judge of *Maryland,* allowed *one ninth* part of the neat salvage to the *owners* and *freighters* of the salvor-ship, in proportion to their respective interests, in consideration of the risk to which their *property* had been exposed. The supreme court of the *United States,* before whom the cause was ultimately carried by appeal, increased the allowance to *one third.* The remainder was distributed among those who had been *personally* instrumental in the salvage. *The Blaireau,* 2 *Cranch's Reports,* 240.   *T.*

of the merchandize, and that they declared it themselves, in
the resolution which they took, as above mentioned, to carry
the prize into one of the *West-India* islands, *for the best advantage of the owners and freighters.* To these they add, a
variety of other trifling and frivolous arguments; as for instance, that the possession of things is not acquired merely by
ourselves, but also by those persons who are employed by us;
that the owners of the ship were not present any more than
the freighters, when the capture was made, and that if the
ship, instead of capturing, had been captured, the owners of
the goods on board would have suffered a considerable loss.

But I am not at all convinced by such arguments as these,
nor by those which I have mentioned above, in favour of the
owners of the capturing ship; for, it is clear, that a prize by
whomsoever taken, belongs solely to the captors, unless they
acted by the command or under the appointment of another
person. The only question, therefore, is, *who took the prize?*
and it is manifest, in this case, that it was the master and
mariners, and that they did not do it by the command or
direction of another. Their services were, indeed, hired, but
for the mere purpose of carrying goods, and for nothing else:
Whatever advantage, therefore, may arise from the carrying
of the goods, ought to be for the benefit of those who have
made use of the agency of others for that purpose; but neither
they, nor the owners of the ship are entitled to any share of
the prize, because the mariners were not employed to make
that capture, but, while they were attending to a business of a
quite different nature, to the mere navigation of the vessel,
fortune threw something else in their way, *fortuna aliud dedit,*
as *Tryphonius* elegantly argues, in an analogous case.* For
the same reason, in the case of a labourer, who, digging the
ground, had found a treasure, I gave it as my opinion, that
he was entitled to it.† The condition of the labourer in that,
and, for the same reason, of the mariner in the present case,
does not extend farther than the business for which they
were hired. Whatever is out of it, that is to say, whatever is

* ff. de Adquir. Rer. Dom. l. 63. § 3.
† Obs. Jur. Rom. l. 2. c. 4.

foreign to the subject of their contract, they are alone to suffer or enjoy, whether it be profit or loss.

This case clearly comes within the general doctrine of *principal and agent*. Now, the agent shall certainly not impute to his principal, that he was robbed by highwaymen, lost his property by shipwreck, or that he or his family being taken sick, he had spent a sum of money which had been put into his hands for a particular purpose; for, such occurrences are more properly to be imputed to accident than to the agency, as *Paulus* justly observes.* Such losses as these follow the person of the agent; while on the other hand, it is natural, as *Paulus* also very correctly says, that " those gains and advantages which happen by occasion of the agency, should follow it."† If *A* has sent *B* to carry something to *C*, and *B*, in the way, has found a sum of money, or has extorted something from a highwayman who attempted to rob him, no one, certainly, whose mind is not very weak, shall think that the money which *B* has so extorted, belongs to *A*, although the things which he was sending to *C* might have been endangered by it. He did not order *B* to find money, nor to extort any thing from highwaymen, but to carry some articles, which he did carry, and his agency being thus fulfilled, *A* has nothing more to ask of him.

The arguments of the advocates on the subject of the present question are really trifling. The *license* which the freighters had obtained from the *West-India* company could not avail them to make prizes, but only to navigate in the *American* seas. Nor are we to cavil about the words of the resolution of the mariners above mentioned, when they are susceptible of so many different interpretations. I think that they had no other object in view than to retain the prize with them, to whomsoever it might belong, whether to the owners, the freighters or themselves, or that the words rather signified, that they meant to divide it into three parts, and to give one to each of the said parties. Or perhaps (saving the decree of the board of directors) they might have believed that the

---

* ff. Mandat. l. 26. § 6.
† ff. De Reg. Jur. l. 10.

prize belonged to them alone; as if the vessel was laden with provisions or other necessaries of life, which they themselves were in need of, and thus might be useful to the owners of the ship and goods, by enabling them to prosecute the voyage, or they might have had various other motives of the same kind. And who will dare to suppose, that those mariners weighed and considered so particularly the words of their resolution, and that if the prize did belong to them, they wished to abandon their claim to the whole of it? Nay, if they had even believed that it did not belong to them, but to the owners and freighters, who would not excuse their simple honesty? He, who, thinking, that what is his own property belongs to another, gives it up to him, is not to suffer by it. Let not an error in point of law, be objected to those good mariners, since, as well from the resolution itself as from other circumstances, it appears that they made no final determination, and it is sufficiently clear, that they never had an intention to give up any right to which they might be entitled. It is true, however, that if they had fought more than was necessary for their defence, and the ship or goods had suffered by it, they would have been bound to an indemnity by the terms of their contract.

On these principles, a cause was formerly decided by the court of *Brussels*, which I think, bears a strong analogy to the present case. A person had lent a horse to the commandant of a corps of cavalry, to fight with; the court were of opinion, that the lender of the horse was not entitled to a share of the booty which the officer took with it. I fully approve of the legality of this sentence, though it has been doubted by some, and *Zouch** refers us to a contrary opinion, given by *Petrinus Bellus;*† there was, however, in that case, much more equity in favour of awarding a part of the booty to the officer, as it was nothing to him, whether the person to whom he lent his horse, should fight or not. And yet, he had no more right to the prize, than one who lends his net to another, has a right to the fish that he takes with it.

* De Jure Fec. p. 2. § 8. Q. 17.
† De Re Milit. P. 4. tit. 8. n. 8.

It will be said, perhaps, that I am wasting words on an idle and useless question, as it is unlawful to make captures without a commission from the states-general, or the admiral, and so far from the one who takes a prize without such a commission, being entitled to it, he is rather to be considered as a pirate, agreeably to the principles which I have above contended for. But this does not follow in every case. *Grotius* very properly says,* that " a private capture is acquired to a private captor, and there can be no doubt, that a prize taken under circumstances of necessity, by non-commissioned vessels, belongs to those who have taken it." I know, that the authority of *Puffendorff*† is adduced to the contrary, but he does not contradict this doctrine; for he speaks of those, who, without any authority, go out for the *express purpose* of making captures, not of those, who, being attacked by an enemy, turn upon him *in their own defence,* and these are the persons that I am speaking of. If, in such a case, it is denied, that it is lawful to take the enemy's property, it must be denied also, that it is lawful to despoil him, who otherwise will despoil us, and there must be an end to the right of self-defence. And yet, every declaration of war not only permits, but expressly orders all good and loyal subjects, to injure the enemy by every possible means, that is to say, not only to avert the danger with which the enemy threatens you, but to capture‡ and strip him of all his property. The case is different with those who sail out on cruises, without a commission, and without complying with the previous requisites of the law, because they are prohibited from doing so by various edicts of the states-general. But how can he be expected to have a commission, who, sailing merely for the sake of trade, meets an enemy who attacks him, and captures him in his own defence? If *Grotius* and *Puffendorff* had explained themselves in this

* De Jure B. ac P. l. 3. c. 6. § 10.
† De Jure N. and G. l. 8. c. 6. § 21.
‡ We have not meant to include such justifiable captures by non-commissioned vessels, in our definition of piracy, above, p. 128. We have, therefore, used in it the word *depredations,* as implying illegality, *ex vi termini.*   *T.*

† X

manner, those who now find fault with both, would have had no occasion to do it.*

* In *France* and *Great-Britain*, prizes taken by non-commissioned vessels belong to the lord high admiral, as a *droit* of his office. 1 *Valin's Comment.* 79.—*British order in council, of the 6th of March* 1665-6, *in a note to the case of the Rebecca*, 1. *Rob.* 193. *Amer. edit.* No distinction is made, whether the captor did or not make the capture in his own defence, or from some other justifiable motive. But, as in *Great-Britain* the office of high admiral is vested in the king, and has for a long time been executed by commission, suitable rewards are given, at the discretion of the government, in meritorious cases. And we presume, that the government of *France* is not backward in displaying its liberality on similar occasions.   *T.*

CHAPTER XXI.

Of Insuring enemy's property.

NEXT to the contracts of purchase, sale and hire,* there
is none, at present, in more frequent use, in commercial
countries, than that of *insurance.* It was, however, so entirely unknown to the ancients, that no trace of it is to be
found in the volumes of *Roman* jurisprudence. The reason
probably is, that commerce was not at that time carried on to
the same extent that it is at this day. Perhaps, also, the fleets
of the *Romans* secured their merchant vessels from depredations at sea, or the vast extent of their empire, bordering on
all the seas which their navigators were in the habit of fre-
quenting, dispelled all fears of enemies. Nor was there so
much to be feared as there is at present from the dangers
of the ocean, as their vessels generally sailed coastwise, pru-
dently keeping within a small distance from the shore, and
did not venture out to sea in the winter months,† whereas
our ships at present sail out to any distance, and we trust them
at all times and in all seasons to the treacherous element,
without knowing whither the fates may carry them.

I have read, however, in *Suetonius's* life of the emperor
Claudius, that during a time of great scarcity, when the people
abused him, and shewed him, by way of reproach, fragments
of stale bread, he not only gave great encouragement to the

---

* *Locatio, hiring or letting to hire.* At the civil law, the signification of this
word is very extensive; *locatio operum,* is when a man hires out or engages
his *labour* to another for a specific reward; *locatio rerum,* is the hiring or
letting to hire or farm (as we call it) of property of any kind, whether real,
personal or mixed.   *T.*

† *Ex die tertio Iduum Novembris, usque ad diem sextum Iduum Martii
maria clauduntur.* The seas are closed from the eleventh of *November*, to
the second of *March. Veget. de Re Milit.* l. 4. *Justinian's* code permits navigation from the first of *April* to the first of *October. Cod. de Naufrag.* l. 3. *T.*

building of ships, but proposed certain profits to the merchants, taking upon himself the risk of any loss that might be occasioned by the violence of the winds and seas. This was a species of insurance, which is nothing else than an engagement for the safety of another's property, by which the owner is liberated from the risk, which is assumed by the insurer, in consideration of a certain præmium.* *Claudius*, indeed, assumed upon himself the dangers of the sea, but he did it gratuitously and not for the consideration of a *præmium* or reward; nor did he undertake to bear the losses which might be suffered from pirates; therefore, I say that it was only a *species* of insurance.†

I have premised a definition of the contract of insurance, in order to make it appear, that the reason of war absolutely requires the prohibition of insurance on the ships, merchandize or other property of enemies. For, what else is assuming the risk to which their property may be exposed, than promoting their maritime commerce? The object of insurance is, that maritime trade may be carried on with the greatest possible profit, and the least possible loss. Hence, the states-general, on the 1st of *April* 1622, while we were at war with the *Spaniards*, issued an edict, annulling all insurances made and to be made by *Dutch* subjects on *Spanish* property, and laying a fine of one hundred pounds, *Flemish*, on all who should act

* The definition, which our author gives of the contract of insurance, is very similar to that which had been given, long before him, by *Roccus*, which is still the most logical and comprehensive of all that have ever been offered. " Insurance," says that able writer, in the excellent translation of his two treatises, *(on ships and freight and on insurance)*, lately published at *Philadelphia*, by Mr. *J. R. Ingersoll*, " is a contract by which a person assumes upon himself the risk to which the property of another may be exposed, and binds himself, in consideration of a certain præmium, to indemnify him in case of loss." *Ingersoll's Roccus*, p. 85.   T.

† For a full and complete view of all that is to be found in the works of the ancients which may be considered as having any relation to the subject of insurance, see Mr. *Park's* introduction to his *System of the Law of Marine Insurances*, which is fraught with a great deal of information on this particular subject, from whence Mr. *Park* justly concludes with our author, that the contract of insurance, as at present understood, was not known to the ancient *Greeks* and *Romans*.   T.

to the contrary. This was extremely proper, because, in all declarations of war, the subjects are ordered to do as much harm as they can to the enemy, and therefore, it follows, that they are prohibited from doing them any good. Such are the rules prescribed by the general law of war, and the states-general did no more than declare that law during the war with *Spain*, by their edict of the 2d of *April* 1559.

It may, perhaps, be said, that such insurances are productive of more profit than loss to the insurers, and therefore, that they are more advantageous to us than to the enemy. But this may prove a very fallacious reasoning, for the result of insurances on enemy's property, is, in a national point of view, very uncertain, nor does experience sufficiently enable us to judge of their effects upon the nation at large; while on the other hand, it is very certain that the enemy thereby acquires the means of extending his maritime commerce. It therefore, follows, that what is certainly useful to our enemy, and almost as certainly threatens our own destruction, is, on every principle, to be prohibited.*

* Trading with enemies, and insurances on enemy's property have been prohibited, from the earliest times, in almost every country of *Europe*. *England* and *Holland* are the only ones that are known to have pursued, for a while, a different policy. The ordinance of *Barcelona*, made in 1484, expressly forbids such insurances to be made, directly or indirectly, *no puxen esser aseguradas directamen o indirectamen. Cleirac, Us & Coutumes de la Mer*, p. 118.—*Consol. del Mar. (Boucher's Fr. transl.)* vol. ii. p. 717. § 1540. *Le Guidon*, a very old treatise on maritime law, declares it to be unlawful to trade with enemies, and to make insurance on enemy's property, c. 2. art. 5. in *Cleirac*, p. 117. Mr. *Valin* mentions several ancient ordinances of *France* to the same effect, which shew, that the law was always so understood in that country. But he observes that the *English*, during the seven year's war, were in the habit of insuring the property of the *French*, *even when bound from a French port to a French colony, or from one French port to another.* " By this means," says he, " one part of the nation restored to us, by the effects of the contract of insurance, what the other took from us by the law of war." 2 *Valin's Comm.* p. 32.

It is certain, that in *England*, not only during that war, but during that which immediately preceded, and that which immediately followed it, that is to say, during a period of near half a century, trading with enemies, and insurances on enemy's property were carried on to a great extent, and were sanctioned by the decisions of the tribunals of that country. In the

This reason alone would have been sufficient to justify the said edict of the 1st of *April* 1622, but it also adverts to a consequence that would follow, if those insurances should be

year 1749, lord *Hardwicke* considered an insurance as legal, which had been made on an *English* vessel that had been sent to *Ostend*, to be neutralized, and from thence to trade with the enemy, under cover of the neutral flag. He said, that "it had never been determined, that insurance on enemy's ships, during the war, was unlawful; and that it might be going too far to say, that *all trading* with enemies was prohibited by law, for the general doctrine would go a great way, even when *English* goods were exported, and none of the enemy's imported, which might be very beneficial." *Henkle* v. *Royal Exch. Ass. Comp.* 1 *Ves.* 317.

During the *American* war, insurances of this description were neither less frequent nor less favoured by the *English* tribunals. *Planché* v. *Fletcher,* was the case of a *Swedish* ship, laden for *French* account, and bound directly from *London* to *Nantz*, with a simulated destination for the neutral port of *Ostend.* Doug. 251.—*Thellusson* v. *Ferguson,* was an insurance on a *French* ship, which had sailed under *French* convoy from a *French* colony to a port in *France.* Ib. 361. In both these cases, the property insured had been condemned by the *English* court of admiralty, but the insurances were, nevertheless, held valid; and thus, the courts of *common law* sanctioned and encouraged the same acts which the courts of *admiralty* punished. In the former case, it was objected, that in time of war, the exportation of enemy's property, even in neutral bottoms, was illegal, and that an insurance upon such goods was void; but, lord *Mansfield* overruled the objection. "It does not appear," said he, "that the goods were *French* property; an *Englishman* might be sending his goods in a neutral ship. But it is indifferent whether they were *English* or *French;* the risk insured, extends to *all* captures." Doug. 363, 363. It is but justice, however, to observe, that sir *William Scott* has expressed doubts of the correctness of the report of this decision. *The Hoop,* 1 *Rob.* 182. *Am. ed.* But, in a subsequent case, *Gist* v. *Mason,* which was decided on by the court of king's bench, in the year 1786, lord *Mansfield* appears to have been even *astute,* to establish his favourite doctrines, and to give, as much as possible, a legal sanction to the trade of *British* subjects with enemies, and to their insurances on enemy's property.

This was not a case of insurance on property belonging to *enemies,* but on *English* property shipped on board of a *neutral* vessel, employed in the trade between *Ireland* and the enemy's *colonies.* The report does not state, whether the insurance was on the ship and goods, or on the vessel only, but it could not have made any material difference; because, if it was unlawful for *British* subjects to ship their merchandize to the *French* colonies, the *means* could not be legal, when the *end* was prohibited.

In this case, lord *Mansfield* is reported to have said: "This, on the face of it, is the case of a *neutral vessel.* It is no where laid down, that policies on

considered as lawful. The very property taken by our own subjects from the enemy, might be claimed by the underwriters.
And why should it not, if their contract was legal? It is well

neutral property, though bound to an enemy's port, are void. And, indeed, I
know of no cases, (except two, both of which are short notes,) that prohibit
a subject trading with the enemy. By the maritime law, trading with an
enemy, is cause of confiscation in a subject, provided he is taken in the
act, but this does not extend to *neutral vessels*." 1 *Term Rep.* 85. Lord
Mansfield here appears to have, as much as possible, kept the *cargo* out of
view, and to have endeavoured to palliate the illegality of its destination,
by holding up the *neutrality of the vessel*.

As to the *expediency* of permitting such insurances, he expressed himself
in a clear and decided manner. " It is," said he, " for the benefit of the
country, to permit these contracts, upon two accounts; the one, because you
hold the box, and are sure of getting the premiums, at least, as a certain
profit—the other, because it is a certain mode of obtaining intelligence of
the enemy's designs." *Park on Ins.* 316. 6th edit.

But, during the last war, the tribunals of *England* entirely discarded their
former ill judged policy, and restored, to all appearance, on a firm basis,
the ancient principle of the law of nations. In the year 1794, a death blow
was given to insurances on enemy's property, in the cases of *Brandon* v.
Nesbitt, and *Bristow* v. *Towers.* 6 *Term Rep.* 23. 35. Nothing, however, was
finally decided, as to the legality of trading with an enemy, until sir
William Scott, in the year 1799, gave his able and luminous judgment, in
the case of the *Hoop*, *Cornelis*, 1 *Rob.* 165. *Am. ed.* which was soon followed
by that of the court of king's bench, in *Potts* v. *Bell.* 8 *Term Rep.* 548, in
which it was held to be illegal, on general principles, for a subject to trade
with an enemy. We observe with pleasure, that these decisions were
principally founded on the authority of the irresistible arguments of our
author in the present chapter; it is not the only instance in which he has had
the honour of giving the law to the tribunals of the great nations of *Europe*.

That lord *Mansfield* made the well known principles of the law of nations
yield to his favourite policy, is at present too well authenticated to be
denied. " On the *legality* of these insurances," says Mr. *Justice Buller*, " I
never could get him to reason. He never went beyond the ground of *expediency*." *Bell* v. *Gilson.* 1 *Bos. & Pul.* 354. " He always," says lord *Alvanley*,
" entertained doubts upon the law, and endeavoured to keep out of sight, a
question which might oblige him to decide against what he thought for the
benefit of the country." *Furtado* v. *Rogers.* 3 *Bos. & Pul.* 197.

From this and other instances which might be adduced, it is evident, that
the law in *England* is made to subserve the great political interests of the
nation, and varies with the notions of policy that are entertained at different
times. It behoves us, therefore, to consider how far we are bound implicitly
to adopt the rules laid down by *English judges*, in cases which may affect
their political concerns, on the mistaken supposition that they are founded
on the principles of the *ancient common* law. The situation and interests of

known, that property insured, belongs in a certain manner to the insurers, and they are, in a great degree, identified with the owners, as appears by the printed policies that are in every body's hands. If, then, the underwriters could thus claim 'enemy's property, after it had been lawfully captured, it would not only occasion a considerable loss to the captors, but it would, (as the edict justly observes,) deter them from fitting out vessels to cruise against the enemies of the state. Surely, there can be nothing more directly in opposition to the law of war.*

America and Great-Britain are known to differ in many essential points, and therefore, the rules by which the one is led to prosperity, may prove greatly injurious to the other. We have had frequent occasion to observe, that many of their belligerent principles are entirely unsuited to our neutral situation, and this is so true, that the state legislatures have been obliged to make laws to counteract the effects of the application of British doctrines, as has lately been done in Pennsylvania, with respect to the conclusiveness of the sentences of foreign prize courts. But, we observe also, with regret, that in some of the states they have gone so far as to prohibit the reading or citing, in courts of justice, of British adjudications of a date posterior to the American revolution. It is paying a poor compliment to the patriotism and intelligence of the judges who grace the benches of our superior tribunals, and a degrading tribute to the presumed superiority of British jurists, to suppose, that their opinions would obtain an undue influence or ascendency over those of our own countrymen. To the sound discriminating minds of our enlightened judges, (aided from time to time by special legislative acts,) it might safely have been left to decide how far the principles adopted by the tribunals of Great-Britain are consonant with our own national policy, which undoubtedly is as much a part of our law, as that of the English is a part of theirs.   T.

* It does not seem to follow, because the loss suffered by the capture of enemy's property may be recovered from the underwriters, that the property itself may be recovered by the insurers from the captors; but the effect of such insurances is certainly, as Valin happily expresses it, that the nation which permits them, restores with one hand what it takes with the other.

We cannot help adverting here to what might be considered as another striking instance of injudicious policy, if we were not assured from high authority, that it originated in misapprehension and mistake. We mean to speak of the doctrine of conclusiveness, as applied to the sentences of foreign prize courts, which has so often frustrated, to the great loss of the parties insured, the insurances made in England upon neutral property. The ships and cargoes of neutrals are insured there for high war præmiums, against capture and its attendant confiscation by the enemies of Great-Britain; but, as the law is understood in that country, (and surely the unfortunate neutral is not aware

So far, no fault can be found with the said edict of the 1st of *April* 1622. But I have discovered a supplement to it, of the 13th of *May* in the same year, by which it was declared, that the edict should only operate on those insurances which were or should be made after its publication; as if this was a proper subject for the application of the rules of the *Roman* code, on the subject of *ex post facto* laws.* It would seem,

of it, otherwise he would not subscribe to such an unequal contract), if *condemnation* takes place, the sentence is in most cases considered as *conclusive* evidence of the property insured being *enemy's property*, and the innocent neutral being thus convicted of *fraud*, the insurer is allowed to *retain the præmium and to pay no loss*. In this manner, præmiums to an immense amount, have been earned by *English* underwriters, without risk, and neutrals have paid their money without being compensated for their losses. Such are the effects of the celebrated doctrine of *conclusiveness of foreign sentences*, so justly reprobated by two of the greatest law characters of our age, lords *Thurlow* and *Ellenborough; Donaldson* v. *Thompson*, 1 *Campb.* N. P. *Rep.* 429. These consequences were not contemplated, we are sure, by the respectable judges of *England;* but they, nevertheless, certainly followed, and at last it was found necessary to tolerate the evasion of that law by a special clause annexed to policies of insurance; (*Lothian* v. *Henderson*, 3 *Bos. & Pul.* 499.) otherwise, the *British* insurance offices would have been entirely deserted by neutrals. And yet it is supposed to be founded on a principle of the *law and comity of nations*, which, we would presume, it does not belong to *individuals* to dispense with.

It is much to be wished, that this fatal doctrine may be exploded throughout the *United States*, as it is in *Pennsylvania* and *New-York*. While our property is more than ever exposed to the captures of belligerent cruisers, and to the unjust condemnations of foreign tribunals, the effects of such a principle must be to deprive our citizens of the benefit of insurance in such cases, and thus to further the views of those powers who may wish to check our commercial career. *We* do not receive immense sums in præmiums from *foreigners; American* property, principally, is insured in *our* offices, and those insurances ought to be made as effectual as possible, that the risk and the loss may be divided among many, instead of falling upon a few. It is true, that we, also, can evade the doctrine in question, by a *special clause;* but a law which requires to be evaded is a snare to the unwary, and is *necessarily a bad law*.

We beg leave to refer the reader on this subject to the able and conclusive opinion of the honourable judge *Cooper*, of *Pennsylvania*, delivered in the high court of errors and appeals of this state, in the case of *Dempsey* v. *The Insurance Company of Pennsylvania*, and published with an excellent introduction, by Mr. *Dallas; Philadelphia, Byrne*, 1810.   *T.*

* *Leges & constitutiones futuris certum est dare formam negotiis, non ad facta præterita revocari: nisi nominatim & de præterito tempore, & adhuc pendentibus*

that the states-general considered that the insurance of enemy's property was legal, unless it was prohibited by an express
law, otherwise, there was no reason for not annulling those
insurances which were made before the publication of the
edict, as well as those which were made afterwards. The
edict had been very properly expressed in general terms, and
had made no such exception; and, as it did not enact a new
law, but was merely declaratory of the law of war, the supplement is rather to be considered as an oversight of the legislature, than as a law actually binding. So much of the edict,
indeed, as inflicts a penalty, may very properly have been restricted to future cases; but not so the prohibition itself: unless,
perhaps, we should say, that the insurance of enemy's property had before prevailed to such a considerable extent, that
it had acquired the force of an ancient custom or usage.
Nevertheless, even if there should be a great many instances
of insurances of that description, I would not take it to be
such an usage as is considered to have the force of law,
unless it should be confirmed by an uninterrupted series of
judicial decisions.

The states-general, therefore, acted in conformity to the
law of nations, when, on the 31st of *December* 1657, they
made an edict, prohibiting the insurance of the goods of the
Portuguese, with whom we were then at war; but I cannot say
the same thing of a clause which they added to it, by which
they extended the prohibition to the insurance of *any merchandize whatever*, going to or coming from the *Portuguese*
dominions: for, if those goods belonged to subjects of the
states-general, or to allies or neutrals, there was no reason to
prohibit their being insured, as the trade with *Portugal* was
not prohibited, except as far as related to contraband of war.
To these, therefore, the prohibition ought to have been restricted; in other respects, the freedom of insurance ought to
have been co-extensive with the freedom of trade. The states-

---

negotiis cautum sit. The laws are only to affect future and not past transactions, unless made with an express reference to them. *Cod. de Legib.* l. 7.

T.

general, however, on the 9th of *March* 1665, being at war with *England*, issued a similar edict, by which they prohibited the insuring of any merchandize going to or coming from the *English* dominions. They did the same thing on the 9th of *March* 1689, during the war with *France*, and thus interrupted the lawful commerce, not only of our own subjects, but of foreigners.* It is thus, that edict-makers content themselves with transcribing those of a prior date, and when once an error (though ever so contrary to the law of nations) has crept into one of them, it is copied, without reflection, into every new law that is made on the same subject, and no one troubles himself about rectifying it.

Upon the whole, it appears, even from subsequent edicts of the states-general, that it is not lawful to make insurance on *enemy's property;* and because the thing is of daily occurrence, I wish the prohibition had been inserted in all the general and special laws which the states-general have enacted from time to time, respecting that species of contract. I wish also, that *Straccha, Santerna,* and other *semi-barbarians,*† who have written on the subject of *insurance,* had left this question entirely untouched, and had contented themselves with observing, that unlawful merchandize, as for instance, *contra-*

---

* It would seem, however, that although it is not lawful for a belligerent nation to obstruct the commerce of neutrals with their enemies, yet they may lawfully prohibit insurances on such trade within their own dominions, and that such a prohibition is no more than the lawful exercise of the right of *municipal* legislation.   *T.*

† Our author is much too severe on those ancient writers, to whom we are indebted for the first methodical treatises on *commercial* and *maritime law.* Nor has he spared that venerable work, the *Consolato,* (above, p. 44), which has been the foundation of almost every subsequent maritime code. Far from joining in his opinion, we wish that those books were more frequently read and consulted than they are; they would be found to contain many excellent principles, which, in our modern times, have been unfortunately too much lost sight of. See the excellent decree of judge *Davis,* (district judge of *Massachusetts*), on an important question, respecting *mariner's wages,* the solution of which has been afforded him by a text of the *Consolato.* 2 *Amer. Law Journ.* 359. *Il Consol.* c. 127. and in M. *Boucher's* translation, c. 130. vol. ii. p. 195. § 321.   *T.*

band of war, could not be insured. For my part, I shall express in a few words, what I conceive to be the law upon this subject. I think, that it is not lawful to insure any ships or goods which are liable to capture by the law of war; but as to those which cannot be made lawful prize, I see no reason why they should not be insured.

I shall conclude with adverting to what some of our writers have said on the subject of insuring goods which are liable to condemnation. *Grotius** is of opinion, that he who has insured contraband goods, not knowing them to be such, is not bound to pay the loss. Others have said,† that he who has subscribed a policy in general terms, is released from his engagement, if the owner of the goods insured turns out afterwards to have been an enemy; for, enemy's property is never considered as being included in a general description, but must be expressly declared and made known to be such, to the underwriter.‡

---

* Consil. Holland. vol. 3. Cons. 175.

† Ibid. vol. 2. Consil. 322.

‡ A very correct general rule has lately been introduced in *England,* upon this subject. " Whenever," says *Park,* " an insurance is made on a voyage expressly prohibited by the *common, statute* or *maritime law* of the country, the policy is of no effect. *Park on Ins.* 307. 6th ed. Even though the insurance be made in general terms, a clause or proviso, excluding the prohibited risk, is always considered as ingrafted in the policy. *Furtado* v. *Rogers,* 3 *Bos. & Pul.* 191. *Kellner* v. *Le Mesurier; Brandan* v. *Curling, 4 East,* 206. 110.

According to the above decisions, the capture of *neutral* vessels by the cruisers of *Great-Britain* or her *co-belligerents,* is considered as a prohibited risk, " because," says lord *Ellenborough,* " *it is repugnant to the interest of the state,* and has a tendency to render the *British* operations by sea ineffectual." *Kellner* v. *Le Mesurier,* 4 *East,* 402. This is certainly correct, on the ground of *state policy;* but, another reason, founded on the broad basis of the law of nations, is afforded by our own judge *Johnson,* (one of the judges of the supreme court of the United States, and presiding judge of the courts which compose the sixth federal circuit:) " a neutral," says he, " who is captured for having violated his neutrality, is considered by the belligerent as an *enemy* waging an *individual war* against his nation, and is abandoned by his own government as such." *Rose* v. *Himely, Bee's Admiralty Reports,* 322. It follows, from this principle, that all risks of capture, by the armed vessels of the nation to which the insurer belongs, may be properly classed within the general prohibition against insuring

But, I think, that even though it be expressly mentioned and designated in the policy, yet, when enemy's property or contraband goods are insured, the insurance is void, and it depends on the will of the parties to fulfil or not, the contract which they have entered into; but no judicial recovery can be had thereon.

enemy's property. And, indeed, according to the *formula* which is used at present by the courts of admiralty of *Great-Britain*, whatever may be, in point of fact, the specific ground of condemnation of a *neutral* vessel or cargo, no other reason is assigned in the decree, but that it belonged, at the time of capture, to the *enemies* of that country. *Horne's Compend.* 148.

T.

CHAPTER XXII.

Of enlisting Men in foreign countries, and, incidentally, of
Expatriation.

I ENTER upon the discussion of a question which has been, and is still, the cause of much disturbance in many of the kingdoms and states of *Europe:* Whether it is lawful to enlist men in the territory of a friendly sovereign? Let it not be imagined, that I mean to contend, that it is lawful to entice away soldiers, by bribes or solicitations, from the service of another prince, in order to enlist them into our own. I know too well, that those who promote desertion, are not less guilty, and do not deserve a less punishment than the deserters themselves;* and, indeed, among some nations, that crime has even been construed into high treason. The question which I am about to investigate, is of a quite different nature. It is, whether a prince may, in the territory of a friendly sovereign, enlist private individuals who are not soldiers, and make use of them in war against his own enemies? It is certain, that if a prince prohibits his subjects from transferring their

---

* The important question respecting the delivering up, or as it is called, the *extradition* of deserters from one country to another, has been the subject of much controversy in *America* as well as in *Europe*, and is not yet at rest. It has been but slightly touched upon by some of the writers on the law of nations, and by others not at all. *Vattel* says nothing upon it. *Hubner* lays it down as a general principle, that " a neutral sovereign may receive in his dominions, and even among the number of his subjects, deserters from either of the belligerent armies, unless he is obliged to deliver them up by a special convention, called a *cartel*." 1 *Hubn. De la Saisie, &c.* p. 39. But *Galiani* distinguishes and contends, that if the army from which the soldiers desert is on the neutral territory at the time when the desertion takes place, as for instance, if it has been allowed the right of passage, the neutral sovereign is bound to deliver up those who have deserted their colours within his dominions; otherwise, it will be considered as a violation of the laws of hospitality. *Galiani, De' doveri, &c.* l. 1. c. 8. § 4.   *T.*

allegiance and entering into the army or navy of another sovereign, such sovereign cannot, with propriety, enlist them into his service; but, where no such prohibition exists, (as is the case in most of the countries of *Europe*), it is lawful, in my opinion, for the subject to abandon his country, migrate into another, and there serve his new sovereign in a military capacity.

It is lawful, I repeat it, if there is no law that prohibits it, for a subject to change his condition, and transfer his allegiance from one sovereign to another. The writers on public law are all of this opinion; nor does *Grotius* dissent from them, but he adds, that expatriation is not lawful among the *Muscovites;* and we know, that it is unlawful also among the *English* and *Chinese.* We know likewise, that *Louis* XIV. king of *France*,* declared by an edict of the 13th of *August* 1669, that those of his subjects who should, without the permission of the government, emigrate from his dominions, with the intention never to return, should be punished with the forfeiture of life and goods. Before that period, it was lawful to emigrate from *France*, and it is so wherever the country is not a prison.† And if it is lawful for a subject

---

* This edict was made with a view to the *Protestants.* It was in the same year that *Louis* the XIV. began to violate the *edict of Nantz*, by abolishing the *chambres mi-parties*, tribunals consisting of judges of both religions, which that edict had established. *Hénault, Abregé de l'Hist. de Fr. sub anno* 1669. He foresaw the immense emigration which its final repeal would produce, and thus vainly endeavoured to prevent it.   *T.*

† By the first constitution of *Pennsylvania*, made on the 28th of *September* 1776, it was declared, (c. 1. § 15.), " that all men have a natural inherent right to emigrate from one state to another that will receive them." 1 *Dallas's Laws of Penn. append.* p. 54. The present constitution merely provides, (art. 9 § 25), " That emigration from the state shall not be prohibited." 3 *Dallas's Laws of Penn.* p. xxii.

The question, " whether it is lawful for a citizen to expatriate himself," has been brought several times, and in various shapes, before the supreme court of the *United States.* It was made a point, incidentally, in the case of *Talbot* v. *Jansen*, mentioned above, p. 136. In that case, it appeared to be the opinion of the court, that expatriation is lawful, provided it is effected at such time, in such manner, and under such circumstances as not to endanger the peace or safety of the *United States.* " The cause of removal," said judge *Patterson,* "must be lawful, otherwise, the emigrant acts contrary to

to pass under the dominion of another prince, it must be so
likewise for him to seek the means of procuring an honest

his duty, and is justly charged with a crime. Can that emigration be legal
and justifiable, which commits or endangers the *neutrality*, *peace* or *safety*
of the nation of which the emigrant is a member?" 3 *Dallas's Reports*, 153.—
" That a man," said judge *Iredell*, " ought not to be a slave; that he should
not be confined against his will to a particular spot, because he happened
to draw his first breath upon it; that he should not be compelled to continue
in a society to which he is accidentally attached, when he can better his
situation elsewhere; much less where he must starve in one country, and
may live comfortably in another, are positions which I hold as strongly as
any man, and they are such as most nations of the world appear clearly to
recognize. The only difference of opinion is, as to the proper manner of exercising this right." *Ibid*. 162. Judge *Cushing* concurred in the general principle, that expatriation is lawful, and approved of the doctrine laid down
on this subject by *Heineccius, Elem. Jur. Nat.* and *Gent.* 1. 2. c. 10. " But,"
said he, " the act of expatriation should be *bonâ fide*, and manifested at
least by the emigrant's actual removal, with his family and effects, into
another country." *Ibid*. 169. In the case then before the court, no such
removal had taken place.

In that of *Murray* v. *The Charming Betsy*, it was decided, that a citizen
of the *United States* who has *bonâ fide* expatriated himself, is to be considered as an *alien* for *commercial purposes*. One *Shattuck*, a natural born
citizen of the *United States*, had for many years, resided with his family,
and had been naturalized in the *Danish* island of *St. Thomas*. It was objected to him, that he had traded from that island with the *French colonies*,
in fraud of an act of congress, by which all trade was interdicted to the
citizens of the *United States*, with the dominions of *France*. But, the court
were of opinion, " that an *American* citizen may acquire, in a foreign
country, the commercial privileges attached to his domicile, and be exempted from the operation of the general prohibitory laws of his native
country." The court did not, however, determine, whether a citizen of
the *United States* can divest himself absolutely of that character, otherwise
than in such manner as may be prescribed by *our own laws*, nor whether
his expatriation would be sufficient to rescue him from punishment, for
a crime committed against the *United States*. 2 *Cranch's Reports*, 120.

And lastly, in the case of *M'Ilvaine* v. *Coxe's lessee*, it was determined,
that a citizen of *New-Jersey*, who had gone over to the enemy during the
revolutionary war, and had, since that time, remained in *England*, enjoying
the privileges of a *British* subject, had not ceased to be a citizen of *New-
Jersey*, and was entitled to claim lands by descent, in that state, because
several laws had been made by its legislature, some before and others after
his emigration, by which emigrants of that description were declared to be
fugitive citizens and *traitors*, punishable as such, but were not considered as
aliens. *Cranch's Reports*, vol. ii. p. 280. vol. iv. p. 209.   T.

livelihood, and why may he not do it by entering into the land or sea service? In the *United Provinces* there is certainly no law to prevent it, and many *Dutchmen*, formerly, as well as within my own recollection, have served other sovereigns by sea as well as by land.

When I speak of *other sovereigns*, I only mean those who are in amity with us; for, it is not lawful to enter into the military service of an enemy, by land or sea, and the states-general have prohibited it by several edicts. It may, indeed, be said, that several of the edicts which prohibit our citizens entering into the service of *any foreign prince or state*, as they speak in general terms, must be understood in the same manner, and not be exclusively applied to the service of an *enemy*. But, if those edicts are attentively examined, it will be found, that they are either occasional statutes, made in time of war, when the states-general were in want of men, or that they are expressly directed against those who then were or might afterwards have gone into the enemy's service, or against deserters from our own army or navy, who had enlisted themselves abroad. Once, a *Dutch* vessel was captured by a *French* privateer, having *eighty* men on board, all of them (except *six Frenchmen*) natives of *Holland* or *Zealand;* the states-general, justly exasperated, issued an edict, on the 28th of *July* 1674, by which it was decreed, that if any of our subjects should enter into the naval service of the enemy, they should be *drowned*. A similar edict was made on the 4th of *April* 1676. But those edicts only relate to such as serve the enemies of our country, and cannot be extended to those who enter into the service of a power in friendship or in alliance with us.

If, therefore, our subjects, whose assistance we do not want in time of war, and who are not prevented by any law from transferring their allegiance, may lawfully hire out their military services to a friendly prince, why may not also that friendly prince enlist soldiers in the territory of a friendly nation? Where it is lawful to let out to hire, it is lawful also to hire, and why should it not be equally so to contract for the hiring of soldiers in the territory of a friend, as to make

† Z

any other contract, and carry on any kind of trade. It will be objected, perhaps, that he who enlists the soldiers, may make use of them against a friend of the sovereign in whose country they have been hired, and perhaps also, against that sovereign himself; but these objections, in my opinion, are not of sufficient force.

As to the first supposition, that the soldiers may be employed to fight against a friend of their own sovereign, it must be observed, that neutrals are bound in war to consider both the belligerents as equally in the right. Such is the doctrine generally admitted as to the purchase and sale of warlike implements, which, indeed, we may not lawfully carry, but we may, in our own country, lawfully sell to either or both the belligerent parties, although we well know, that they intend to make use of them in war against each other.

To the second head of the objection, that the soldiers thus hired may possibly be employed against their own sovereign, I answer, that we are only to attend to the state of our country at the time, and ought not to look so far into futurity. Nor do I see any difference between enlisting men, and purchasing gun-powder, ammunition, arms and warlike stores, which may certainly be done by a friendly sovereign in our country, and which he may also use afterwards against us. I repeat it, the actual relations of our country are alone to be considered; otherwise, there must be an end to amity, friendship, and even alliances between princes.

I am of opinion, therefore, that the same law which obtains as to the purchase of implements of war, must apply in like manner to the enlistment of soldiers in the territory of a friendly nation, unless it should be expressly stipulated otherwise between the two sovereigns. Thus, in the treaty between the *Romans* and *Antiochus* the Great, king of *Syria*, the latter bound himself not to enlist soldiers within the limits of the *Roman* empire.* That treaty was not equal, otherwise he might lawfully have enlisted soldiers in the *Roman* dominions, nor could the senate have prohibited it without doing him an in-

* Liv. l. 38.—Polyb. Excerpt. Legat. c. 35. n. 4.

jury; for, while by the same treaty it was stipulated, on reciprocal terms, that neither of the contracting parties should supply the enemy of the other with provisions, to *Antiochus* alone it was forbidden to do that which otherwise may lawfully be done by every sovereign.

In the *United Provinces*, however, it appears to have been and is still prohibited by law, to enlist soldiers, without the permission of the states-general. There is an ancient edict upon this subject, of the 8th of *January* 1529. A similar edict was made on the 1st of *August* 1612, when the *Danes*, *Swedes* and *Muscovites* had made enlistments on the *Dutch* territory. Those nations were prohibited, by name, from doing the like, without having previously obtained the permission of the states-general in writing, and they were strictly forbidden to seduce the *Dutch* soldiers from the national service, under the penalty of death or some other discretionary punishment. There are a variety of subsequent edicts,* by which it is enacted, " that if any one shall seduce soldiers within the territory or jurisdiction of the *United Netherlands*, without the permission, in writing, of the states-general or their counsellors, the offender shall be liable, not to a discretionary penalty only, but to the punishment of death, without remission or mitigation."† As those edicts agree en-

---

* Edicts of the states-general, of the 16th of *December* 1622—3d of *March* 1627—30th of *March* 1646—21st of *July* 1648—20th of *January* 1652, and 18th of *March* 1658—of the states of *Holland*, of the 27th of *March* 1652, and 16th of *March* 1656.

† By the act of congress of the 5th of *June* 1794, mentioned in one of the preceding notes, page 129, it is provided (§ 2.) " that if any person shall, within the territory or jurisdiction of the *United States*, enlist or enter himself, or hire or retain another person to enlist or enter himself, or to go beyond the limits or jurisdiction of the *United States*, with intent to be enlisted or entered in the service of any foreign prince or state as a soldier, or as a marine or seamen on board of any vessel of war, letter of marque or privateer; every person so offending, shall be deemed guilty of a high misdemeanor, and be fined not exceeding one thousand dollars, and imprisoned not exceeding three years. *Provided*, that this shall not be construed to extend to any subject or citizen of a foreign prince or state, who shall transiently be within the *United States*, and shall, on board of any vessel of war, letter of marque or privateer, which, at the time of its arrival within

tirely with my opinion, I submit them to the reader, without observation or comment.

It may not be improper to notice here, a difference which took place in the year 1666, between the states-general, and the governor-general of the *Spanish Netherlands*. The states complained to him, that the bishop of *Munster*, with whom they were at war, had enlisted soldiers in the *Spanish* territories in the *Low Countries*. The governor answered, that he had not authorised him so to do, but that if he had, there was nothing to prevent him, as *Spain* was neutral in the war, and that the states-general might exercise the same right, if they pleased.* But, whether such a thing is lawful, without the consent of the sovereign, and whether the sovereign may, with propriety, refuse his permission, when applied to for it, is the very subject of our inquiry. Whether or not, the bishop of *Munster* had a right to enlist soldiers in the *Spanish Netherlands*, without the permission of the governor-general, the reader must determine for himself from what has been above stated.

the *United States*, was fitted and equipped as such, enlist or enter himself, or hire or retain another subject or citizen of the same foreign prince or state, who is transiently within the *United States*, to enlist or enter himself to serve such prince or state on board such vessel of war, letter of marque or privateer, if the *United States* shall then be at peace with such prince or state." 3 *Laws U. S.* 88.

* Aitu. l. 40.

CHAPTER XXIII.

Of the right of the several provinces of the United Netherlands *to declare and make war.*

*I*N this chapter our author discusses a constitutional question,
*relating exclusively to his own country, under its former
government. He inquires, " whether the united provinces of
the* Netherlands *had separately the right of declaring and
making war. From the tenor of one of the articles of the* Confederation of Utrecht, *(the* federal constitution *of the* Dutch
union *), it would seem that they had not that power; for, it
is there expressly stipulated,* " that no war shall be made
without the advice and consent of all the provinces;" *but
our author contends and argues at great length, that every
power which by that treaty was not expressly granted, was
retained by the several provinces; that before it was entered
into, they separately had the right of declaring and making
war, and had not explicitly parted with it. That the abovementioned clause in their confederation was only applicable to
national wars, entered into for the redress of national injuries;
but that if a single province should receive an injury from a
foreign state, it might lawfully avenge it by a separate war.*

*As we do not think that this chapter can interest our readers
in any point of view, we have omitted it in this translation,
and believe it sufficient to have given this general outline of its
contents.*   T.

CHAPTER XXIV.

Of Reprisals.

R EPRISALS* were a thing entirely unknown to the ancient *Romans*, and cannot be expressed by an adequate
word in their language. Some writers have used the words
pignoratio, clarigatio, but neither of them renders with precision what we understand by *reprisals*. Nor had the *Romans*
occasion for such a word, who paid the most sacred regard to
the property of their friends, and who would have disdained
to commit hostilities on those for whom they professed friendship, and to subject their good friends to indiscriminate plunder, by sea and land.

As there is no instance of such wickedness in the history
of that magnanimous people, neither do their laws exhibit

* The word *reprisal*, according to its etymology, is synonimous with
recaption or *retaking*, and the thing which is meant by it, is analogous in
name as well as in substance, to the common law process of *withernam;*
with this difference, that the one is a legal retaliation, exercised only
on the goods and chattels of the party who has been guilty of the first
tortious taking; the other is exercised on the property of all the individuals of the same nation. "For," says *Valin*, "it is a principle established
by the universal law of nations, that all the subjects of a state are bound
in solidum, to make reparation for the injuries done to foreigners by the
state itself, or any of its members." *Traité des Prises*, p. 321.

Reprisals are either *general* or *special*.—They are *general*, when a sovereign, who has, or thinks that he has received an injury from another prince,
issues orders to his military officers, and delivers commissions to his subjects to take the persons and property of the subjects of the other nation,
wherever the same may be found. It is, at present, the first step which is
generally taken at the commencement of a public war, and is considered as
equivalent to a declaration of it.

Special reprisals are granted, in time of peace, to individuals who have
suffered an injury from the subjects of another nation, and these alone are
treated of in the present chapter.   *T.*

the least trace of it. How then shall we explain the stipulation which is contained in two different treaties* between *Spain* and the *United Provinces*, " that no letters of marque† or reprisal shall be granted, but with full knowledge of the cause, against those persons only on whom they may lawfully be issued by the *Imperial* laws and constitutions, and conforming to the regulations which those laws prescribe?" For, in the laws of *Justinian*, which are always understood by the general description of *Imperial laws* in countries that are not governed by an *emperor*, there is not a single word about *reprisals*, which, as I have already observed, were entirely unknown to the *Romans*. In order to rescue from the imputation of ignorance, the very learned men who drew up those treaties, I must suppose, that by *Imperial laws*, they meant the *law of nations*, which, as well as the law of *Justinian*, is denominated throughout *Europe*, the *common law*,‡ so that they must have considered the words *common* and *Imperial law*, as convertible terms. I cannot think of any other way of accounting for that mistake.

According to the *law of nations*, then, reprisals are not to be granted but with *a full knowledge of the cause*,§ nor for

---

* Truce of the 9th of *April* 1609, art. 11.—Treaty of *Munster*, of the 23d of *January* 1648, art. 22.

† *Letter of marque and reprisal* is the old technical expression for what we now call a *privateer's commission*. It still preserves, in law, the same signification, although it is common, at present, to apply the denomination *letter of marque*, by way of distinction, to a vessel fitted out for war and merchandize, and armed merely for defence.   *T.*

‡ See note † above, p. 53.   *T.*

§ In order that letters of reprisal may not be granted, without full knowledge of the cause, or without sufficient reasons, various wise precautions were taken by *Louis* XIV. in his *Ordonnance de la Marine*, of *August* 1681. By that ordinance, the party injured, is obliged, as soon as possible after the injury suffered, to cause the facts to be ascertained, and the damage to be estimated by a court of admiralty; after which, and not before, he may petition the crown for letters of reprisal; these are not issued until after a proper and fruitless application to the sovereign of the offending party, nor then, without sufficient security being given by the petitioner; and notwithstanding all that, if at a future day, the statement contained in the petition should be found not to be true, the petitioner is to be condemned to the payment of full damages and interest to the party whose pro-

such causes or against such persons as the law exempts from
them, nor then without conforming to the rules and order of
proceeding which usage has established. The first of these
rules, is, that letters of reprisal are not to be granted, unless
there has been a clear and open denial of justice. Hence, by
the treaties above mentioned,* it was agreed between us and
Spain, " that if any injury should be done not warranted by
the orders of his majesty on the one hand, or of the states-
general on the other, the peace should not be thereby considered as *ipso facto* broken, but that it should be lawful, in
case of *an open denial of justice*, to seek redress according to
custom, by issuing letters of marque and reprisal." Such is
the *common law*, which has long been and still is used among
nations, when justice is denied by the sovereign, and it is conformable to the opinion of all who have written on this subject.
There is never any occasion for reprisals, except in time of
peace, though *Mornac*† is of opinion, that they cannot be
granted, except where there is actual war. But he is certainly
mistaken.

Reprisals, therefore, are a means of redress, to be used
only in case of a denial of justice. They are an authorization,
granted by a sovereign, to take the persons and goods of
the subjects of another prince; in order to obtain satisfaction
for an injury‡ committed upon his own subjects,§ for which

---

perty shall have been seized by virtue of the letters of reprisal, and moreover, to restore four times the amount which he shall have received. For
the sake of greater regularity, letters of reprisal are, in all cases, to
express the sum for which they are given, and to specify a time to which
their exercise is limited, and after the expiration of which, they become
void. *Ord. de la Mar.* l. 3. tit. 10. *Des Représailles.*   *T.*

* Art. 31, of the truce, and 60 of the treaty above mentioned.

† Ad auth. *sed omnino,* cod. *ne uxor pro marito.*

‡ *Valin* is of opinion, that letters of reprisal may be granted not only for
reparation of an *injury* done by means of actual force and violence, but also
for a *debt* justly due by a subject of a foreign power, for which the creditor
has not been able to obtain justice in a regular course of legal proceedings.
Traité des Prises, p. 321.   *T.*

§ Mr. *Valin* is also of opinion, that not only a subject, by birth or
naturalization, may apply for and obtain letters of reprisal, but also a

justice has been denied by the sovereign of the offending party. Thus, an injury committed by force and violence, and not repressed by the competent magistrate, is redressed by the same means and in the same manner.

In order that no one should rashly complain of a denial of justice, special provisions have been made by treaties between different nations. By the 24th article of the treaty of peace between *England* and the states-general of the 5th of *April* 1654, reprisals are not to take place, except *sub modo;* for, it is there stipulated, "that letters of reprisal shall not be granted, unless the prince, whose subject shall conceive himself to have been injured, shall first lay his complaint before the sovereign whose subject is supposed to have committed the tortious act, and unless that sovereign shall not cause justice to be rendered to him within three months after his application. This stipulation was renewed by the 31st article of the treaty of peace between the same nations, of the 31st of *July* 1667.

There are many other instances of treaties between nations, in which this subject has been attended to. In the treaty of commerce between the king of *France* and the states-general, of the 27th of *April* 1669, article 17, after stipulating, that reprisals shall not be resorted to, unless justice shall have been first denied, it is immediately added, " that justice shall not be considered as having been denied, unless the petition by which letters of reprisal are applied for shall have been first communicated to the ambassador of the sovereign whose subjects are complained of, that he may inquire into the truth of the complaint, and if he finds it true, that he may cause justice to be done to the injured party within four months.* Thus, without

---

foreigner, domiciliated in the country (*regnicola;*) the state being bound also to protect him, and to consider the injury done to him as an affront to the majesty of the sovereign. *Ibid.* p. 225.   *T.*

* By the treaty of *Ryswick*, art. 9, and the treaty of *Utrecht*, art. 16, (the latter concluded between *England* and *France* on the 11th of *April* 1713), it is stipulated, " that letters of reprisal shall not thereafter be granted by either of the high contracting parties, to the prejudice or detriment of the subjects of the other, except only in such case wherein justice is denied or delayed; which denial or delay of justice shall not be regarded as verified, unless the petitions of the person who desires the said letters of reprisal

any violation of the existing peace, the sovereign against whose subjects a complaint is made, sits in judgment upon it, and pronounces his own sentence. It is certainly useful to restrict the use of reprisals by similar treaties; for, it would be unjust to take it away altogether between the subjects of independent nations.

It was, however, stipulated, by the 9th article of the treaty between the emperor of *Morocco* and the states-general, of the 24th of *September* 1610, " that neither of the two sovereigns should issue letters of reprisal, but that they should administer justice to each other's subjects." But this is an idle stipulation; for what is to be done, if justice is not administered? The injured sovereign will then have recourse to reprisals, and will say that he is compelled to it by the exigency of the case. If it be agreed between princes, that justice shall be mutually administered to the subjects of each other, that stipulation should be performed with good faith; but still, it is true, that the obligation to render justice to foreigners, exists independent of treaties, and whether there is or not, a special convention to that effect, reprisals are not to be resorted to, unless justice is previously denied.

It might, perhaps, be supposed, that reprisals are entirely taken away by the 16th article of the abovementioned treaty of the 5th of *April* 1654,* because it is there agreed, that if

be communicated to the minister residing there, on the part of the prince against whose subjects they are requested to be granted; that within the space of four months or sooner, if it be possible, he may manifest the contrary, or procure the satisfaction which may be justly due. And if there should not be on the spot, any minister or ambassador from that sovereign, no letters of reprisal shall be issued until after the expiration of the four months, reckoning from the day on which the petition shall have been presented to the prince against whose subjects the letters are applied for, or to his privy council."

The same stipulation is contained in substance, in the 3d article of the treaty of commerce concluded between *Great-Britain* and *France,* on the same day with the treaty of *Utrecht,* and in all the treaties made at *Utrecht* at the same time between the other powers; " and thus," says M. *Valin,* " it has become a part of the *common law of nations." Traité des Prises,* p. 331.—It is also contained (except the last clause) in the treaty of commerce between *France* and *Great-Britain,* of the 26th of *September* 1786, art. 3. *T.*

* Above, p. 185.

any one shall commit an infraction of the peace subsisting between the two powers, the infractor shall be punished, and
judgment shall be given within a certain time, which is limited
by the same article. But such an inference would not be correct, for, what if the criminal should not be punished, or if
what he had forcibly taken away should not be restored? Reprisals, in such a case, would still have to be resorted to; and
that such was the intention of the parties, appears by the 24th
article of the same treaty, in which, as I have already shewn,
there is a mode of proceeding pointed out for the granting of
letters of reprisal. Since reprisals are in use among nations,
these, and war, which follows close at their heels,* are the only
remedies of independent sovereigns, for repelling unjust ag-
gressions, as they cannot submit themselves to the judgment
of a foreign prince, which they would consider as a shameful
prostitution of their own majesty.

It seems that the power of granting letters of reprisal belongs to the sovereign alone; for, it is beyond the authority of
subordinate magistrates. It is so observed every where, even in
France, where formerly letters of reprisal were granted by the
parliaments.† When the towns of the *Netherlands* waged separate wars, they, in like manner, granted letters of reprisal.
There exists an ancient law of the city of *Amsterdam*, by
which it was provided, that if any injury should be done to one
of its citizens out of its territory and jurisdiction, either by
main force and violence, or by an *unjust judgment*, (which
last expression, I beg the reader will particularly observe), the

---

* *Les représailles—sans annoncer précisément la guerre, y conduisent naturellement, & en sont assez souvent le prélude.* Reprisals do not, it is true, precisely
indicate war, but they naturally lead to that state of things, and are often
enough a prelude to it. *Valin, Traité des Prises,* p. 321.   *T.*

† *Cetui droit est de puissance absolue, qui ne se communique ni délègue aux
gouverneurs des provinces, villes & cités, amiraux, vice-amiraux ou autres
magistrats.* The right of granting letters of reprisal, is a right *summi
imperii,* and cannot be communicated nor delegated to the governors of
provinces, cities or towns, nor to the admirals, vice-admirals or other
magistrates. *Le Guidon,* c. 10, art. 10. The parliaments of *France,* however,
exercised it until the year 1485, when *Charles* VIII. by a special ordinance, reserved it exclusively to himself. *Valin, ibid.* p. 329.   *T.*

aggrieved party should prefer his complaint to the **magistrate** of *Amsterdam*, who should write on the subject, to the magistracy of the place where the injury was committed, and if after receiving an answer, he should still think that his fellow-citizen had been injured and was entitled to redress, he should, by his *judicial authority*, indemnify the injured party, by issuing process against the persons or goods of the subjects of the prince whose subjects had done the injury, if they should be found within the territory of *Amsterdam*.*

I have observed, that this law of the city of *Amsterdam*, says, *or by an unjust judgment*. It is not enough that the property of our subjects or citizens be taken by virtue of a judgment, it must be also an *unjust* one. Of this, however, the magistrate of *Amsterdam* alone was to judge; for, such things are seldom trusted to the judgment of others.† The treaties between sovereigns merely say, that letters of reprisal are not to be granted, unless for a denial of justice; but an *unjust sentence* will easily be construed into such a denial, and indeed sovereigns will qualify as **unjust**, every sentence that is not agreeable to them.‡

---

* Those who have obtained letters of reprisal, may, by virtue thereof, seize within their own country, the goods and effects of the subjects of the power, whose subjects have done them the injury; but it must be done *viâ juris*, by some judicial process, and not *manu forti*, by private authority, unless there should be danger of the property being carried out of the country, before application could be made to a competent magistrate. *Valin*, ibid. p. 333.   *T.*

† See above, p. 72.

‡ In the letter of the duke of *New-Castle*, to Mons. *Michell*, on the subject of the celebrated controversy with the king of *Prussia* respecting the *Silesia* loan, are found the sentiments of the *English* jurists upon this subject. "The law of nations," say they, "founded upon justice, equity, convenience and the reason of the thing, and confirmed by long usage, does not allow of reprisals, except in case of violent injuries, directed or supported by the state, and justice absolutely denied *in re minimè dubiâ*, by all the tribunals, and afterwards by the prince.—Where the judges are left free, and give sentence according to their conscience, though it should be erroneous, that would be no ground for reprisals. Upon doubtful questions, different men think and judge differently; and all a friend can desire, is, that justice should be as impartially administered to him, as it is to the subjects of the prince in whose courts the matter is tried." 1 *Magens on Insur.* 491.

These

I have seen many instances in our own country, of letters of reprisal granted by cities and towns. They are vestiges of the ancient liberty of the *Hollanders*, when the several members of the states were more independent than the states themselves; for, the provincial states, ever since the confederation of *Utrecht*, although they are severally independent, cannot issue letters of reprisal generally and in every case. Indeed, it might be said, that they cannot issue them in *any case*, because they are a species of war, and by the 17th article of the said confederation, it is expressly declared to be unlawful for the several provinces to give any cause of war to foreign princes.

☞ *The remainder of this chapter treats only of the right of the several provinces of the* United Netherlands *to issue letters of reprisal; our author thinks that they may do it in their own cause, for an injury done to themselves in their several capacities, but not for an injury done to the union. We have omitted this discussion, as uninteresting to our readers.*

These principles are undoubtedly correct, on the supposition, that law and justice are every where impartially administered, according to the old established rules of the law and usage of nations; but where certain courts (as is at present the case in almost every country of *Europe*) are known to be mere political establishments, and are, properly speaking, *ministerial boards*, obliged to conform to the *decrees* and *orders* of the sovereign, and guided in their decisions by considerations of *state policy*, varying and fluctuating with every change in the aspect of national affairs, such impartiality from them can hardly be presumed, and tribunals so constituted, ought not to be held up as a shield to ward off the responsibility of the sovereign. In the case just cited, the king of *Prussia* was not satisfied with the plausible arguments of the *English* civilians, but demanded and obtained of the *British* court £ 20,000 sterling, as an indemnity for *Prussian* vessels and cargoes illegally condemned. *Examination of the British doctrine, &c.* p. 99. And there have been instances of *commissioners* being appointed, in pursuance of treaties between neutral and belligerent powers, to reform the unjust judgments of *prize tribunals. Treaty between the United States and Great-Britain, of the 19th of November 1794,* art. 7—*between the United States and Spain, of the 27th of October 1795,* art. 21. 2 *Laws U. S.* 473, 534.

T.

CHAPTER XXV.

Miscellaneous Maxims and Observations.

I. *IT is not lawful to take or retain possession of a neutral fortress, for fear the enemy should occupy it.*

In the year 1620, the states-general, who had promised to evacuate the fortress of *Lieroort*, in *East Friesland*, did not do it, but kept possession of it, " lest," said they, " the enemy should occupy it, and make use of it against themselves." They were clearly in the wrong, and acted in this against the opinion of prince *Maurice* of *Orange*, who was no friend to the *Frieslanders*, and was warmly attached to the cause of the states. Their conduct was even blamed by their own counsellors, in 1621, and several times afterwards, as *Aitzema* relates.*

There are men, however, who call themselves lawyers, and who approve of similar injuries, among whom I wish I had not to name the celebrated *Grotius*.† I can tolerate such an opinion in such men as *Zouch*‡ and *Buddæus*;§ the former

* Aitz. l. 2.

† *Hinc colligere est, quomodo ei, qui bellum pium gerit, liceat locum occupare, qui situs sit in solo pacato: nimirùm si non imaginarium, sed certum sit periculum, ne hostis cum locum invadat, & inde irreparabilia damna det.* Hence, it may be inferred, how it is lawful for one who is engaged in a lawful war, to occupy a place situated on neutral territory; particularly if there is a certain and not an imaginary danger of the enemy's occupying it, and from thence doing considerable injury to his adversary. *Grot. De J. B. ac P.* l. 2. c. 2. § 10. *Gronovius*, in a note upon this passage in *Grotius*, considers our author's opinion upon this subject as unreasonable. *Dissentit, absque ratione, amplissimus Bynkershoek.* Whether his dissent was entirely *absque ratione*, the awful events which have taken place in *Europe* within these few years, have surely enabled the reader to decide. *T.*

‡ De Jure Fec. p. 2. § 5.

§ Philosoph. Pract. c. 5. § 6. ¶ ult.

of whom, however, borrows it from *Grotius*. They support it
by adducing instances of similar rapine, as if example, in such
cases, were sufficient; while it is only solving a problem by
another problem, *litem quod lite resolvit*. Nor is what they
say about *embargoes* of ships at all analogous to the present
case; for, ships that are found in the dominions of another
sovereign, are in a manner subject to him, and those embargoes are laid by virtue of a custom universally received
among sovereigns. But, it never has been admitted as a custom,
that the dominions, towns or forts of a friendly nation, may
otherwise than tortiously be invaded or retained.

II. *Conquered countries, like lands purchased, pass* CUM
ONERE.

The king of *Spain* had hypothecated a certain territory for
a sum of money which he had borrowed of one who was in
friendship with him and the states-general. The states conquered that territory in the course of a war. The counsellors of *Holland* were of opinion, that the pledge was extinct.*
But they were mistaken, for the states had only conquered
what belonged to the king of *Spain*, that is to say, the right of
empire and dominion, as he had possessed it. And as he held
it subject to that hypothecation, it could not pass over to the
states in any other manner. If the states, instead of conquer-
ing, had purchased from the king a part of that territory, the
creditor would still have been entitled to his whole pledge.
He would have preserved his rights against the king of *Spain*,
the vendor, who had bound himself for the debt, and against
the states-general, who had purchased the land hypothecated
for its payment, because property, when sold, passes with all
its charges, which remain entire for the benefit of the creditor.
But now the *Dutch* have taken the territory, and consider it
as confiscated to them. And so it is, as far as it belonged to
the king of *Spain*, but that does not include the interest which
the neutral creditor had in it. If the hypothecated debt, indeed, had belonged to an enemy, it might also have been justly
confiscated by the law of war.

---

* Consil. Belg. vol. 3. Consil. 2.

III. *Property captured and afterwards ransomed or given up by the enemy, is not thereby liberated from the claims of the insurer or lender at maritime risk.**

It has been questioned, whether property, particularly ships and merchandize, which after being captured, are ransomed or given up by the enemy, to their former owner, are thereby exonerated from the prior claims of the insurers or of those who had lent money thereon *at maritime risk?* Some lawyers have been of opinion,† that if a ship has been ransomed, or if the captor has given her up to her former owner, she has, as it were, ceased to be entire, and she is to be considered as a new ship, and that a *total loss* has taken place with respect to the insurers and lenders at *maritime risk.*

But this appears to me, neither just nor equitable, because the insurer is only responsible for the damage suffered, and the money lender only liable to a loss on the amount of his loan in proportion to that damage. The one, therefore, is not bound to pay, nor the other to lose more, than the amount of the salvage or ransom. *Philip* the II. in his ordinance upon insurance, of the 20th of *January* 1550,‡ section 27, prohibits the ransoming of vessels from pirates, and therefore permits it from real enemies, with a view, no doubt, to shew, that the insurers are bound for the amount of the salvage, but no farther; otherwise, there was no reason for speaking of *ransom* in an edict which exclusively relates to the subject of *in- surance.* Nay, the last clause of the policies in common use among the merchants sufficiently shews, that when a ship is ransomed, the interest which the insurers have therein, is not less redeemed than the property of the owner himself. I am, therefore, of opinion, that the loss or damage which the in- surers are bound to pay, and which the lenders at maritime risk are obliged to lose, is the precise amount of the money

---

* The civil law denominates *maritime loans* or *loans at maritime risk,* (*fœnus nauticum*), those contracts which at common law are called *bottomry* and *respondentia.*   *T.*

† Consil. Belg. vol. 1. Consil. 52.—vol. 3. Consil. 248.

‡ See note ‡ p. 131. in which this ordinance is mentioned, by mistake, as of the 26th, instead of the 20th of *January.*   *T.*

expended in the salvage or redemption of the property. I grant, however, that if a ship has been captured, carried into port, and there condemned and sold, and afterwards is purchased by her first owners, in that case the loss will be total to the underwriters and money lenders; and the ship thus purchased, will be considered as a new ship in the hands of the first owner. There is an opinion to this effect in the *Consilia Belgica.**

IV. *Orders, in war, are to be strictly obeyed.*

The states-general had ordered, that their troops, who held the citadel of *Reyd*, in the country of *Juliers*, should obey the orders of *Florence van den Boetseler*, who was lord of the place. *Boetseler* exhibited that order to the commandant of the fort, and required him to deliver it up to the *Spaniards*, who were approaching, and the commandant accordingly surrendered it up on the 30th of *August* 1621.† But *Maurice*, prince of *Orange*, was so angry with him on that account, that he punished him with death on the 14th of *September* following, pretending that the order was only applicable to *civil* and not to *military* matters. I doubt whether he did right; for, as the citadel did not belong to the states-general, that order can have meant nothing, but that the rights of the lord of the territory, although he had admitted a garrison within it, were to be kept inviolate, and that the soldiers should not defend the citadel any longer than the lord should think proper, lest he should be involved in the same difficulty with the *Spaniards*, in which the count of *East Friesland* found himself, when the states refused to evacuate fort *Lieroort*, as I have mentioned at the beginning of this chapter.

V. *It is not lawful to repair fortifications during a truce, or pending a capitulation.*

Albericus Gentilis‡ is of opinion, that while a treaty is on foot concerning the surrender of a town or place, it is lawful to finish or repair the fortifications thereof. *Zouch,*§ after him, adopts the same opinion. But *Ferdinand* thought otherwise,

---

* Vol. 1. Consil. 11.——† Aitz. l. 1.
‡ De Jure Belli, l. 2. c. 18.
§ De Jure Fec. p. 2. § 10. Q. 10.

who, after the surrender of. *Reggio*, precipitated the *French* on that very account from the top of the walls;* and when the *Spaniards*, who, in 1622, were besieging *Bergen*, during a truce which had been granted to them to bury their dead, completed their works, and from thence reconnoitered the fortifications of the town, the *Dutch* complained that the truce had been broken, and that the usage of war had been violated.† It was, however, in 1664, agreed at *Bylerschans*, that the truce should not prevent the erecting and perfecting of fortifications on both sides.‡ But it is best, when a truce is made, to suspend every warlike operation, for, such appears to be the intent and meaning of a *truce;* otherwise, it would be very difficult to define it.

VI. *Governments are not bound to repair every loss that is occasioned by the calamities of war.*

When the bishop of *Munster*, in 1665 and 1666, had taken and laid waste certain places in *Over-Yssel*, and the *French*, who had come to the assistance of our countrymen, had not behaved with much more moderation, the people of *Over-Yssel* applied to the states-general to be indemnified for the damage which they had suffered, but the counsellors having been consulted on that subject, gave it as their opinion, that no indemnity ought to be given, except for the deficiency suffered in their taxes and contributions, in proportion to the time during which the places had been occupied by the enemy.§ As to the remainder, it was to be imputed to fate, and was one of those calamities of war which must be supported by those on whom they happen to fall.

Afterwards, however, the same counsellors, having somewhat changed their opinion, thought that an indemnity ought to be allowed to the inhabitants of *Over-Yssel* for other things, and particularly for the money which they had been obliged to raise, to save their towns from threatened conflagration.‖ Agreeably to this latter opinion, the states of *Holland* gave their vote on the 27th of *February* 1667.¶ I think that they

* Gentil. *ubi suprà.*——† Aitz. l. 1.——‡ Aitz. l. 44.——§ Aitz. l. 46.
‖ Aitz. l. 46.——¶ Ibid. l. 47.

were wrong, as far as concerned the monies levied on the inhabitants, to redeem the towns from conflagration; for, although it is certain, that that money actually saved them from being destroyed by fire; still it was not just, that the other confederates should bear the loss, who had not been exposed to the risk of perishing in that manner. For, nobody will venture to say, that a whole fleet ought to contribute, if a single ship is obliged to have recourse to *jettison*, for her own safety.

VII. *Relates solely to the right of the several provinces of the* Dutch *confederation to make peace, as incident to that of making war. It is entirely local, and therefore is omitted in this translation.*

VIII. *One who resides in an enemy's country, under a safe conduct from the sovereign, may sue and be sued.*

It has been questioned, whether, if a safe conduct is granted to an enemy to come into our country, he may be sued here by his creditors. It was so decreed by the court of *Holland*, in 1588, and their judgment was confirmed by the supreme court, on the 18th of *September* 1590. Those decrees, I think, were perfectly just; because, the safe conduct given to an enemy, is only to protect him against hostile acts; he becomes, by virtue of it, as it were, a neutral, and neutrals may be sued and detained for their debts. At the same time, if we permit enemies to be sued, we must not prevent them from prosecuting their demands against us in a course of law,* as I have discussed more at large in a former chapter.†

IX. *A safe conduct to go into or pass through the enemy's country, is no protection out of the enemy's territory.*

A safe conduct, in time of war, is given for no other purpose than that the party may safely come into the enemy's territory, and continue there. Wherefore, I am astonished, that lawyers should have doubted, whether he, who has a safe

---

* In *England*, in a plea of *alien enemy*, the defendant must not only state " that the plaintiff was born in a foreign country, in enmity with *Great-Britain*," but " that *he is not residing in the British dominions under letters of safe conduct from the king.*" *Casseres* v. *Bell*, 8 *Term Rep.* 166.　　T.

† Above, c. 7. p. 55, 56.

conduct to pass through the enemy's territory, may be taken in his own country by the law of war. This question was agitated in the case of the marquis of *Messarano*, who had received a safe conduct from the *Spaniards* to go from his own castle to *Venice*, passing through the *Spanish Milanese* territories; but before he sat out on his journey, the castle was taken by the *Spaniards*, and himself made prisoner. It was asked, whether he was exempted by his safe conduct from paying any ransom? *Bellus*, who himself sat as judge in the cause, did not venture to decide any thing, as he relates himself in his treatise *De Re Militari;*[*] neither does *Zouch*, agreeably to his custom, give any opinion on the point.[†] But *Menochius*[‡] distinguishes, whether the marquis was then ready for his journey, or whether he was not; in the first case, he thinks that the safe conduct would; in the second, that it would not have availed him. The doubts of *Bellus* and *Zouch* appear to me as silly as the decision of *Menochius*. The marquis's castle and territory being invaded by the *Spaniards*, he was himself most lawfully a prisoner; because he had only asked for a protection in the enemy's territory, and not in his own, nor had he stipulated for a peace or a truce, but merely for a passage through the *Milanese* country into the territory of *Venice*. Whatever, therefore, was not within that particular object, was to be decided by the law of war.

X. *It is unjust to compel a sovereign to make war or peace.*

As it is unjust to force a prince to make war against his will, it is so likewise, to compel him to make peace. But, when the states-general, on the one hand, were afraid of the *French*, and the great men of *England*, on the other, were displeased with the extent of the territory of *France*, the kings of *England* and *Sweden* and the states-general, made a treaty on the 23d of *January* 1668, in which, among other things, they stipulated, that the *Spaniards*, who were then at war with the *French*, should be *compelled* to accept of certain conditions,

* P. 9. No. 15, & seq.
† De Jure Fec. p. 2. § 9. Q. 19.
‡ De arbitr. judic. quæst. l. 2. cent. 4. cas. 336. n. 19, & seq.

prescribed by the said treaty; and that after they had accepted them, if the king of *France* should, nevertheless, continue to make war upon *Spain*, the allies should interfere in an hostile manner; *and thus, the French and Spaniards were* COMPELLED *to make peace.*

In another instance, when it was not thought proper for the welfare of *Europe*, that the king of *Sweden* should also possess *Denmark*, the *French*, the *English* and the *states-general*, on the 21st of *May* 1659, *forced* the king of *Sweden* to make peace with the *Danes*,* and thus saved the king of *Denmark* from total ruin, to which he was exposed in consequence of having excited a neighbour more powerful than himself.

These are real injuries, cloaked with the pretence of a wish to make peace; a pretence which has been used to cover injuries of a much greater magnitude, which have been fashionable for some years past; for, princes, in their treaties with each other, have been in the habit of disposing of the dominions and territories of other sovereigns as if they were their own. Such injuries are the offspring of what is called the *reason of state:*

Monstrum horrendum, informe, ingens, cui lumen ademptum.

If governments will yield to that monster, and indulge themselves in following its dictates, and considering the property of other nations as their own, it is idle and useless to investigate any more the law of nations, or discuss its principles.

* Aitz. l. 48.

THE END.

ERRATA.

Page 4, note ‡, line 2, for "first consul," read *emperor.*

Page 21, *dele* note ‡. It was a mere newspaper account, which was not confirmed, and ought not to have had a place in this work.

Page 31, *dele* note *, and in lieu thereof, insert a reference to p. 87.

Page 46, line 10, for "*Paul,*" read *Paulus.*

Page 71, in the note, 3d line from the bottom, after "lord *Hawkesbury,*" read *now earl of Liverpool.*

Page 82, note †, line 7, for "any," read *my.*

Page 91, note ‡. This note is not sufficiently clear, having been written in too much haste. It was enough to have observed, that our author does not seem to have sufficiently attended to the distinction established by the edict to which he refers between neutral vessels, which, after leaving a blockaded port, *go voluntarily* into their own or some other free port, or go into such port on being *chased* and to avoid *pursuit;* in the second case, they are lawfully captured, if met with coming out of such port; and it makes no difference, whether it is the port of their actual destination, another port of their own country, or some other *free* or friendly port. Our author seems to think, that it does make a difference, and this mistake leads him into an unnecessary discussion about *words.*

Page 118, note *, line 4, for "for, of other rights he may judge as if no war existed," read "for, of other rights, *unconnected with the war, or its objects,* he may judge as if no war existed."

Page 120, the note of reference * ought to be placed after the words "commercial intercourse," in the fourth line from the bottom of the text.

Page 131, note ‡, first line, for "26th of *January,*" read 20*th of January.*

Page 148, in the note, line 7, for "3000 rials de vellon, equal to $1500," read 60,000 *rials de vellon, equal to* $3000—and add, that *the amount of that security may be moderated at the discretion of the officers of the admiralty, according to the size of the privateers, and the number of men and guns which they respectively carry.*

Page 183, note §, first line, for "may," read *might.*

Page 186, line 12, in note, for "treaty of *Utrecht,*" read "treaty of *peace* of Utrecht."

Subjoin the mark T to the following notes:

* and † p. 105—† p. 106—§ p. 114—‡ p. 115—‡ p. 125—and in a few copies of this work, to notes, § p. 184—† p. 187, and * p. 188.

A TABLE

Of the Titles contained in the Index.

† 2 C·

INDEX

TEXT AND NOTES.

www.ingramcontent.com/pod-product-compliance
Lightning Source LLC
Chambersburg PA
CBHW031425180326
41458CB00002B/454